SIGNING THE PEACE WITH JAPAN—2 SEPTEMBER 1945

BATTLE STATIONS!

Your Navy in Action

A photographic epic of the naval operations of World War II
told by the great admirals who sailed the fleet from Norfolk to
Normandy and from the Golden Gate
to the Inland Sea

1946

Wm. H. Wise & Co., Inc., New York

ACKNOWLEDGEMENTS

All photographs are official U. S. Navy except as follows:

U. S. MARINE CORPS: 131, 132 (top), 138, 141, 142, 183, 205 (lower), 221, 224 (lower), 226, 232, 269 (top), 270, 275, 276 (lower), 277 (lower), 285, 291, 308 (lower), 310 (top), 322, 324 (lower), 327 (lower), 328, 332, 335 (lower), 336 (top), 337 (lower), 338 (top), 349, 394 (top).

U. S. COAST GUARD: 59, 86 (lower), 132, 161 (lower), 186, 187, 197, 230, 231, 242 (lower), 244, 248 (lower), 249 (lower), 251, 252, 256 (top), 277 (top), 279, 283 (top), 287, 288, 299, 300, 325 (top), 366 (lower).

ACME NEWSPICTURES, INC.: 17, 23, 25 (top), 26 (top), 29 (top), 30, 31 (top), 36, 37, 40 (lower), 68 (lower), 69 (top), 72, 73, 74, 91, 92, 93, 176, 177, 218, 341, 343, 347, 359.

PRESS ASSOCIATION, INC.: 18 (top), 21 (top), 41, 76, 292 (top), 293, 294, 358, 377 (top).

WIDE WORLD PHOTOS, INC.: 18 (lower), 25 (lower), 26 (lower), 28, 29 (lower), 31 (lower), 32 (top), 33, 38 (top), 39, 40 (top), 78, 103, 104, 105, 295, 377 (lower).

INTERNATIONAL NEWS PHOTOS: 21 (lower), 22 (top), 62, 63, 77.

BRITISH COMBINE PHOTOS LTD.: 22 (lower), 38 (lower), 87, 136, 137.

PLANET NEWS LTD.: 27.

BRITISH INFORMATION SERVICE: 346 (lower).

Printed in the United States of America

WELL DONE!

To the 3,500,000 men and women of the U. S. Naval Forces, U.S.N., U.S.N.R., Marine Corps and Coast Guard who manned "Battle Stations" from the Rhine River to Tokyo Bay in World War II

This book is gratefully dedicated.

CONTENTS

QUALIFICATIONS OF
THE NAVAL OFFICER
By John Paul Jones

IT IS by no means enough that an officer of the navy should be a capable mariner. He must be that, of course, but also a great deal more. He should be as well a gentleman of liberal education, refined manners, punctilious courtesy, and the nicest sense of personal honour. . . .

The naval officer should be familiar with the principles of International Law, and the general practice of Admiralty Jurisprudence, because such knowledge may often, when cruising at a distance from home, be necessary to protect his flag from insult or his crew from imposition or injury in foreign ports.

He should also be conversant with the usages of diplomacy, and capable of maintaining, if called upon, a dignified and judicious diplomatic correspondence; because it often happens that sudden emergencies in foreign waters make him the diplomatic as well as the military representative of his country, and in such cases he may have to act without opportunity of consulting his civic or ministerial superiors at home, and such action may easily involve the portentous issue of peace or war between great powers. These are general qualifications, and the nearer the officer approaches the full possession of them the more likely he will be to serve his country well and win fame and honours for himself.

ABOARD SHIP

COMING now to view the naval officer aboard ship and in relation to those under his command, he should be the soul of tact, patience, justice, firmness, and charity. No meritorious act of a subordinate should escape his attention or be left to pass without its reward, even if the reward be only one word of approval. Conversely, he should not be blind to a single fault in any subordinate, though, at the same time, he should be quick and unfailing to distinguish error from malice, thoughtlessness from incompetency, and well-meant shortcoming from heedless or stupid blunder. As he should be universal and impartial in his rewards and approval of merit, so should he be judicial and unbending in his punishment or reproof of misconduct.

In his intercourse with subordinates he should ever maintain the attitude of the Commander, but that need by no means prevent him from the amenities of cordiality or the cultivation of good cheer within proper limits. Every Commanding Officer should hold with his subordinates such relations as will make them constantly anxious to receive invitations to sit at his mess-table, and his bearing towards them should be such as to encourage them to express their feelings to him with freedom and to ask his views without reserve.

It is always for the best interests of the Service that a cordial interchange of sentiments and civilities should subsist between superior and subordinate officers aboard ship. Therefore, it is the worst of policy in superiors to behave towards their subordinates with indiscriminate hauteur, as if the latter were of a lower species. Men of liberal minds, themselves accustomed to command, can ill brook being thus set at naught by others who, from temporary authority, may claim a monopoly of time and sense for the time being. If such men experience rude, ungentle treatment from their superiors, it will create such heartburnings and resentments as are nowise consonant with that cheerful ardour and ambitious spirit that ought ever to be characteristic of officers of all grades. In one word, every Commander should keep constantly before him the great truth, that to be well obeyed he must be perfectly esteemed.

ATTITUDE TOWARD HIS CREW

BUT it is not alone with subordinate officers that a Commander has to deal. Behind them, and the foundation of all, is the crew. To his men, the Commanding Officer should be Prophet, Priest, and King. His authority when off shore being necessarily absolute, the crew should be as one man impressed that the Captain, like the Sovereign, "can do no wrong."

This is the most delicate of all the Commanding Officer's obligations. No rule can be set for meeting it. It must ever be a question of tact and perception of human nature on the spot and to suit the occasion. If an officer fails in this, he cannot make up for such failure by severity, austerity, or cruelty. Use force and apply restraint or punishment as he may, he will always have a sullen crew and an unhappy ship. But force must be used sometimes for the ends of discipline. On such occasions the quality oft he Commander will surely be most sorely tried. . . .

When a Commander has, by tact, patience, justice, and firmness, each exercised in its proper turn, produced such an impression upon those under his orders in a ship of war, he has only to await the appearance of his enemy's topsails upon the horizon. He can never be sure of victory over an equal or somewhat superior force, or honourable defeat by one greatly superior. Or, in rare cases, sometimes justifiable, he may challenge the devotion of his followers to sink with him alongside the more powerful foe, and all go down together with the unstricken flag of their country still waving defiantly over them in their ocean sepulchre.

No such achievements are possible to an unhappy ship with a sullen crew. . . .

FOREWORD

By Admiral of the Fleet Ernest J. King, USN

I CAN best stress the importance of the U. S. Navy to the American people when I state that without sea power on our side the United States would never have become a nation, would not have continued to exist as a nation, and even more specifically would not have won the great World War just so successfully concluded. The destruction of British commerce by our commerce raiders, plus the timely control of the Chesapeake Bay by the French Fleet that made Washington's victory at Yorktown possible, insured our independence. Our similar destruction of British commerce in the War of 1912, plus our naval victories on Lake Erie and Lake Champlain, forced Britain to concede us an equal peace without the great loss of territory which at first seemed inevitable. Our Navy's blockade of the Southern Confederacy and control of the river highways into the heart of the South tore the Confederacy to pieces and preserved the Union. Our naval victories in the Spanish-American War were the greatest factor in winning that war. The combined sea power of the United States and Great Britain in the first World War made possible our tremendous army in Europe which turned the tide of victory for the Allies. And in the recent war the Navy repeated the identical job in Europe and at the same time crushed the Japanese Navy and brought about the surrender of Japan while Army and Air Forces were still largely intact.

Sea power is not the combat Navy alone, but also includes merchant ships, bases, naval air power—all the things that allow a country to gain control of the sea for its own purposes and to deny that use of the sea to the enemy. In its essence you can call it "Our Navy." And the purpose of this history is to tell the story of that Navy.

By its attack on Pearl Harbor Japan attempted to erase the greatest threat to her hoped-for-victory—our Navy. And that attack, demobilizing for a year or more our most powerful warships through bomb and torpedo damage, was a terrible blow. It left Japan with a superior navy in the Pacific, even though we brought all our remaining ships from the Atlantic to help—something we could not do because of our other enemies on the Atlantic side, the Axis Powers of Europe.

THE JOINT CHIEFS OF STAFF

IN THAT trying time our President formed for the first time that unique organization for directing all our military effort—the organization of the Joint Chiefs of Staff.

The Joint Chiefs of Staff was composed of the Chief of Staff of the Army, the Chief of Naval Operations of the Navy, the Commanding General of the Army Air Forces, and the Chief of Staff of the President (Commander-in-Chief of the Army and Navy). Meeting together in Washington, those four men, with the help of their own service staffs, coordinated and directed the whole course of our military operations: the Battle of the Atlantic, the invasion of Africa, Italy, France, and Germany; the vast battle of the Pacific with all its numerous operations—the Coral Sea, Midway, Guam, Saipan, conquest of the Philippines, the Battles of the Philippine Sea and Leyte Gulf that broke the Japanese Fleet—the blockade by air, submarine, and surface ships that strangled Japan—Okinawa, and the final bombing of Japan that shattered the last remnants of Japan's will to resist.

In the Joint Chiefs of Staff each member had an equal voice, and no plan could be made or put into effect without the common consent of all four members. Each man on it was an expert in his own field, and not until his agreement was obtained that a thing could be or should be done was that thing attempted. Frequently proposals were made that did not obtain that unanimous approval—there was not a member who at one time or another did not advocate things that would have been great mistakes. When, as on some few occasions, a dead-lock occurred on a vital matter, the decision was made by the President after hearing the proponents and the opponents. But always decisions were made, and those decisions proved correct.

When once a decision was made, the plan was turned over to be executed by that member whose branch of the service was best fitted to carry it out. If it was primarily an Army job, like the invasion of Europe, it was placed under Army supervision, and the Army commander on the spot, like General Eisenhower, was in complete control not only of the Ground forces but of the Naval forces and the Air forces that were necessary to convoy the troops, crack open the beachhead, land the troops, and then see that they were safeguarded from enemy attack. A similar instance was the invasion of the Philippines where, as it was primarily an Army ground forces job, General MacArthur was in supreme command, and the Navy and Air forces gave their support. Conversely if it was primarily a Naval job, like the operations of Midway, Kwajalein, Guam, Saipan, Iwo Jima, and Okinawa, the Navy's Admiral Nimitz was in overall command, even though Army divisions and Air Force planes supported him in doing that job.

Thus the final victory over the Axis Powers was

not that of any one service alone but that of all the services, cooperating and working together as fellow Americans for the common good.

INTERNATIONAL LIAISON

ANOTHER function of the Joint Chiefs of Staff was coordinating our war effort with those of the other United Nations—chiefly with Great Britain, but also with Russia, China, Canada, Australia and New Zealand, Holland, the South American Republics, etc. Our Joint Chiefs of Staff worked closely with the military leaders of all those other nations and developed the plans for the combined attack of all the United Nations on the Axis enemy.

The part of the U. S. Navy alone in this war was stupendous. And I wish here to acknowledge our debt not only to the men and women of the United States Navy, Marine Corps, Coast Guard, and their several Women's Reserves, but also to all those innumerable civilians who aided the Navy's war effort.

The day after Pearl Harbor our Navy's position in the Pacific was extremely grave. The bulk of our major ships had been put out of commission for a year; only our small Asiatic Fleet under Admiral Hart in the Philippines and portions of the Pacific Fleet that had been absent from Pearl Harbor on the day of the attack were in fighting condition in the Pacific. Even Hawaii might be attacked and overrun at any moment. And in the Atlantic the Axis submarines were destroying a tremendous tonnage of our shipping within sight of our very shores.

THE DECISION

THEN, even at the lowest of the war tide, the decision was made, and correctly: first fight for time, especially in the Pacific—and then assemble the might to conquer first Italy and Germany, and then inevitably Japan must succumb.

It was a difficult decision. Japan swept through Malaya to Singapore, then overran Burma; she battered at the Philippines; she overran the Dutch East Indies, and threatened Australia and New Zealand and even India itself.

Distressful though it was, it was realized immediately that with our Pacific Fleet shattered, and no western Pacific bases left to operate from, we could give no help either to our Army in the Philippines or our Allies in Singapore—we could not even evacuate them. But our little Asiatic Fleet fell back, sacrificing themselves in innumerable battles against overwhelming enemy forces until only the remnants staggered into Australian ports. But they had gained time. And instead of challenging our enfeebled forces in American waters and attacking Hawaii, Alaska, and Panama, or cutting our supply lines in those waters, the Japanese Navy wasted time in serving as a mere adjunct to the Army in its land conquest.

But our shipyards, our ordnance plants, our scientists were working. Radar was perfected, new sonic devices invented, planes and warships built by the thousands, escort carriers and landing craft constructed, and millions of men recruited and trained in all forms of fighting and war effort. The escort carrier, the destroyer, radar and other electronic devices defeated and then smashed the submarine menace. Our Navy transported and safeguarded the invasion forces to Africa and Europe, and then smashed the enemy beachheads to afford them a landing. Our still small forces in the Pacific turned back the threat to our lifeline to Australia at the Coral Sea battle, and then drove the first entering wedge into the Japanese conquered empire at Guadalcanal. At Midway we hurled back the first real Japanese threat at Hawaii, Alaska, and the West Coast. Our ever growing Navy and Marine Corps, and Naval Flying Forces bombed and then seized the stepping stone islands—Tarawa, Kwajalein, Guam, Saipan. We guarded the landings that reconquered the Philippines, our carrier forces seized control of the air everywhere it was needed, and our Fleet broke the back of the Japanese Navy in the great naval battles of the Philippine Sea and of Leyte Gulf. Our submarines destroyed the majority of the Japanese merchant marine, as well as innumerable Japanese naval combat ships. When we seized Okinawa, we seized a point just off Japan from which we could, and did, destroy the remnants of the Japanese Navy and bomb the Japanese homeland into final submission—a submission that would inevitably have come anyway from the strangling blockade we had thrown around Japan. With a greater army and more planes than she had at the time of Pearl Harbor, Japan surrendered—because with the destruction of her Navy and merchant marine she could not obtain from outside those necessities without which Japan could not even live, much less fight.

Nor is the Navy content to rest on its present laurels. Long a leader in invention and research, our Navy is already studying new weapons, new methods—the atomic bomb and guided missiles, for instance. Whatever new weapons, or defenses against new weapons, science can develop, the U. S. Navy intends to incorporate them into itself, to make sure that the Navy shall always be strong enough to perform its historic function of defense of our own country and of offense against enemy countries.

It is to be hoped that every American will exert his effort and influence to see that that goal is achieved—that the U. S. Navy will always remain, as it is today, the world's greatest sea power.

Ernest J. King

A REVIEW OF THE
HISTORY OF THE U. S. NAVY

By Commodore Dudley W. Knox, USN

FROM its inception the U. S. Navy has been a servant of the nation, defending broad national interests no less than our extensive shores. Too weak during the Revolution to cope with Britain's vast armadas, our little Continental Navy strove principally to support our Army with sorely needed supplies by convoying friendly merchantmen or capturing enemy supply ships. However our few naval ships, commanded by such daredevils as John Paul Jones, John Barry, and Lanbert Wickes, aided by reckless American privateers, attacked Britain even in her own homewaters, and their raids on British shipping were a strong force in causing Britain to acknowledge our independence.

Sea power itself, in the shape of the French Navy, did however have a conclusive role in the war by helping Washington's land armies bottle up Cornwallis at Yorktown in what was the decisive battle of the war.

Interference with our rapidly expanding commerce was the main cause of our next three wars—the undeclared war with France beginning in 1798, the war with the Barbary pirates beginning in 1801, and the War of 1812 with Great Britain. In all three wars the U. S. Navy amply justified its existence. Our frigate *Constellation* defeated two French frigates in 1799 and 1800, our Mediteranean squadron under Commodore Preble vanquished Tripoli, and by naval display of force we compelled Tunis to make terms. Against Great Britain our Navy, as during the Revolution, was vastly outnumbered, but our naval ships and privateers again exerted a tremendous effect. Though Washington was captured and burned, a British invasion of New York from Canada was halted by our naval victory under Commodore Macdonough on Lake Champlain, and in similar fashion Commodore Oliver Hazard Perry saved the west by his triumph on Lake Erie. Only our naval successes in this war saved us from harsh terms at the peace table.

THE EARLY 19TH CENTURY

DURING the ensuing fifty years, our Navy's contribution was mainly that of commerce protection, extending our commercial relations abroad, and scientific exploration. The U. S. Navy exterminated piracy in the West Indies, and protected our commerce from the Mediterranean to China and the Philippines. On an official Naval exploration expedition, Commodore Wilkes, USN, discovered the Antarctic Continent and collected much commercial and scientific information. Com-

modore Wilkes's explorations were a forerunner to those of Admiral Robert E. Peary, who discovered the North Pole in 1909, and of Admiral Richard E. Byrd, who flew over both the North and South Poles. Lieutenant Matthew F. Maury, USN, began those scientific studies which originated the present great sciences of oceanography and meteorology. Combining diplomacy and force, Commodore Kearny opened China and Commodore Perry Japan to American trade.

During the Mexican War our Navy was almost entirely responsible for the conquest of California.

The tragic Civil War found many American naval officers "going south" to serve in the Confederate Navy. Their resourcefulness in pioneering new weapons such as the submarine, the ironclad, and the submarine mine was amazing, but the far stronger Federal Navy with its blockade strangled the Confederacy; its ships on inland waters cut the Confederacy into sections, and gave the Federal Armies the naval support necessary for the success of Grant's amphibious operations and other great land campaigns.

In the Spanish-American War our Navy overwhelmed the Spanish fleets in short order. Admiral Sampson's victory at Santiago freed Cuba and gave us Porto Rico; Dewey's victory at Manila made us an Asiatic power with the Philippines in our keeping.

During World War I, the German Navy was so securely "contained" by the British that our naval task was mainly that of convoying our troops to Europe and guarding against enemy U-boat and surface raiders.

WORLD WAR II

THE attack on Pearl Harbor, Dec. 7, 1941, plunged us into World War II which saw our fleets move and support our Armies to help crush the Axis in Europe and, almost singlehanded, crush the Japanese Navy and bring Japan to ultimate surrender. On V-J day Japan's Navy had practically ceased to exist.

The U. S. Navy today is the pre-eminent sea-air power of the world. It is to be hoped that the American people will never permit it to decline from that secure position.

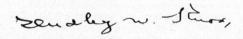

THE FIRST SALUTE! UPPER. The Stars and Stripes flying from the masthead of the U. S. sloop *Ranger*, commanded by the famous John Paul Jones, receives its first national salute from the French naval squadron in Quiberon Bay, France, February 14, 1778. In the *Ranger* John Paul Jones took the first news of Burgoyne's surrender to France—news that brought France into alliance with the Colonies. A year later, on the night of September 23, he laid the old U. S. frigate *Bon Homme Richard* alongside the superior British frigate *Serapis* and finally took her by boarding with his own ship afire and sinking beneath him. It was in this battle that John Paul Jones uttered his famous words: "I have not yet begun to fight!" LOWER. U. S. naval squadron under Commodore Sloat taking possession of Monterey, California, July 7, 1846, during the Mexican War. American ships shown here are the *Cyane*, the *Savannah*, and the *Levant*. Sailors landed from American naval ships made certain our ultimate possession of California,

JAPAN AND THE PHILIPPINES. Our naval policy and our Navy have both affected and been affected by Japan and the Philippines since the 1850's. At that time the Philippines were a Spanish colony almost closed to all foreign trade; Japan was even more isolationist, refusing even to allow foreigners to land, and imprisoning foreign sailors unfortunate enough to be shipwrecked on her coasts.

It was this last that brought the U. S. Navy into the picture, since it was the Navy's job to protect our commerce and seamen anywhere on the globe. Another incentive was the fact that our trade with China was becoming important, and Japan lay on the direct China trade route. Steamships were coming into use, and it was important not only to protect our sailors but also to obtain coaling privileges in Japan for our steamers. Thus it was that Commodore Matthew C. Perry, U S N, was selected as our negotiator. Both by tactful diplomacy and by the eye-opening display of force in the naval squadron that accompanied him, he persuaded the reluctant Japanese to sign the first treaty they had ever made with a foreign power.

From that moment, however, Japan began to progress. By 1894 she had modern industries and a modern navy with which she easily defeated China, thereby acquiring Formosa, and she even looked longingly at the Philippines and other islands to the south. LEFT. She was forestalled there, however, by the victory of Commodore (later Admiral of the Navy) George Dewey, U S N, later honored with the highest naval rank ever conferred by our Congress.

ABOVE. Landing of Commodore Perry, his officers and men, to meet the Japanese Imperial Commissioners at Yokohama, March 8, 1854. The U. S. Naval Squadron, including two of our latest and most powerful steam warships, may be seen at anchor in the harbor. The sight of the powerful ships and guns, as well as the superbly armed and disciplined bluejacket and Marine landing parties, made a very potent impression on the Japanese, who had previously refused to enter into any negotiations with any nation. Perry was both a natural diplomat, as well as a naval officer, however, and he persisted in a combination of presents and sternness until the Japanese signed the treaty.

SEA POWER IN THE CIVIL WAR. In the Civil War the Federal Government retained almost all of the ships of the U. S. Navy, but many crack Southern naval officers joined the Confederacy, where with their inventive skill they tried to perfect new secret weapons. On March 8, 1862, the Confederate ironclad ram *Virginia*, better known as the *Merrimac*, sank two of the finest Union warships at Hampton Road and threatened to destroy others. But next day the North's own version of the ironclad, the famous turreted *Monitor*, appeared and fought the *Merrimac* to a draw. On the Mississippi, fleets of converted river steamboats fought a battle of ramming as well as gunfire; Union victory here destroyed the last Confederate hope of defending the inland rivers. UPPER. The river battle, with the two fleets mixed in a wild melee. LOWER. The *Merrimac* and *Monitor* engaged in the world's first battle between ironclads.

"DONE IN THE SCRAMBLE." In such a way Teddy Roosevelt referred to this Cuban episode in the Spanish-American War. It was the landing of the U. S. Army forces at Siboney, five miles east of Santiago, Cuba. Peculiar to this incident was the army's total dependence upon naval landing force technique at transporting the troops ashore. General Shafter, Commander of the U. S. Army troops, said without naval assistance "he could not have landed in ten days and perhaps not at all." Most of the troop transports, which were minus naval officers, could not be induced to come within reasonable distance of the shore, and the disembarkation could hardly have been accomplished without naval supervision and provision of forty Navy boats and twelve steam launches. Most of the troops were put ashore within two days. Fortunately the landing was entirely unopposed. Naval artillery covered the disembarkation, but, although it was present in subsequent Army operations, it was not needed. LEFT. Troops being ferried ashore in rowboats.

"SPANISH FLEET COMING OUT!" As a result of Spanish atrocities in Cuba, the Spanish American War broke out in April, 1898. An American Army was formed to invade Cuba, and American naval squadrons were sent to blockade the island and to support the troop landings. Spain's best fleet under Admiral Cervera barely slipped into the fortified harbor of Santiago, Cuba, before it was blockaded there by the American naval forces under Admiral Sampson and Commodore Schley. On the morning of July 3 Cervera's fleet tried to escape to the westward. The American battleships and cruisers immediately moved into action, and the running battle lasted for fifty miles along the coast. But within three hours the entire Spanish fleet was destroyed. As the Spanish Asiatic fleet had already been sunk, Spain asked for terms. American sea power had won the war within 100 days. ABOVE. Spanish cruiser *Colon* before running into a wall of shells.

BATTLE OF MANILA BAY, May 1, 1898. On the declaration of war our little fleet in China was ordered immediately to attack the Spanish fleet in the Philippines. Six nights later Commodore Dewey in his flagship *Olympia* slipped into Manila Bay regardless of powerful land forts and underwater mines. At daylight he located the Spanish Fleet off Cavite and before noon had completely destroyed every Spanish vessel. This victory won the Philippines for the United States. UPPER. The USS *Olympia* fighting at one mile range. LOWER. Utility Squadron One, U. S. Navy's oldest aviation unit is shown here in its early days while making an aerial survey of Alaska in 1934.

RED WAR STRIKES THE WORLD! On Sept. 1, 1939, it came—what the world for years had dreaded, evaded, yet feared inevitable. On that day Hitler, despite sacred treaties, despite every promise, hurled the German legions into Poland. It was the end of an era of appeasement during which peace-loving nations had made every effort to placate the Axis Powers. Japan had invaded Manchuria and then China, Italy's Mussolini had overrun Ethiopia, Hitler's storm troopers had swallowed Austria. The League of Nations was powerless. Peaceful America had begged, pleaded. But the Axis was insatiable. Almost on the heels of his brutal ultimatum Hitler marched and began the war that would engulf the world. Desperately the Poles resisted, but within two weeks the German Wehrmacht had swept over the land. Danzig fell; but in the Westerplatte, the Polish fort and munitions dump in Danzig harbor, the little Polish garrison held out heroically. German bombardment by land and sea knocked the fort to rubble; raging fires

swept the ruins. Blood and flesh could do no more—the Nazi swastika flag flew triumphant over the fort. But Poland had not died in vain. Her sufferings, her streams of blood cried aloud to the world.

And even the United States, determined though she was to avoid war, heard, and began to prepare for any eventuality. Keep out of war she would if she could, but with war enflaming the world she must look to her defenses. The first step taken in this line was to strengthen the Navy, always the nation's first line of defense. On September 8 the President declared a limited national emergency and authorized the recall to active duty of the officers, men, and nurses on the retired and reserve lists of the Navy and Marine Corps. By this step the authorized enlisted personnel of the Navy was automatically increased from 131,485 to 191,000. ABOVE. Triumphant German troops raising the swastika flag over the Westerplatte. This is a German Army photograph.

LOOKING WAR IN THE FACE. Unready but unafraid, the British accepted the war, that, by their treaties, was automatically thrust upon them by Hitler's invasion of Poland. Some, even with bags already packed for mobilization, listened solemnly, almost curiously to the war proclamation that applied alike to King and Commoner. Others, more excited, crowded in a milling throng around the front of Number Ten Downing Street, home of Prime Minister Neville Chamberlain. At 11 A.M., Sunday, September 3, 1939, Britain was officially at war with Germany. UPPER. The War Proclamation being read from the steps of the Royal Exchange. LOWER. Crowds in front of Number Ten Downing Street shortly after the Prime Minister's announcement that England was at war.

THE GOLDEN AGE. The war of 1812 consisted of many spectacular encounters between American and British vessels of war. UPPER. The frigate *Essex*, armed with six 12-pound guns instead of the usual 18- or 20-pounders, was the first American man-of-war to round Cape Horn and the Cape of Good Hope. Under Captain David Porter, she took the largest number of prizes in the war, but was defeated by the British ship-of-war *Phoebe* on 28 March 1814 in the engagement shown here. LOWER. The *Enterprise* meets the *Boxer* in an even match, 5 September 1812, with the victory going to the American vessel, although both captains were killed in action.

PROTECTION FOR HARBORS. In peacetime marker buoys, such as are shown above, mark both the channel and the danger spots to guide ships safely in and out of port. But in wartime such safety aids are removed and replaced by deadly mine fields, the location and extent of which are "top secret." A "swept channel" is kept open for the entrance and exit of friendly vessels which can be taken through the mine fields only by specially briefed pilots. Mines were of various types. Magnetic mines were detonated when their magnetic field was disturbed by the passage of a metal ship. The acoustic mine was activated by the noise of a ship's propellers.

SIXIÈME ÉDITION

L'INTRANSIGEANT
le journal de Paris

6ᵉ édition

50¢

LA GUERRE

DEPUIS CE MATIN 11 HEURES

L'ANGLETERRE est en état de guerre avec L'ALLEMAGNE

Comme il avait été prévu, après la dernière démarche de
l'ambassadeur britannique à Berlin, notre représentant a
adressé au Reich la même et ultime injonction dont
LE DELAI EXPIRE A 17 HEURES

WAR'S HEADLINES SCREAM IN FRANCE. The front page of "L'Intransigeant" headlines the news that England has already been at war since eleven o'clock and that France's ultimatum to Germany will expire at five o'clock in the afternoon. But already events were in motion that were to bring the war home to America. On the first day of the war the British liner *Athenia* was suddenly torpedoed by a German U-boat, and 30 Americans were lost. All America was shocked by the news. UPPER. The French newspaper "L'Intransigeant" headlines the British declaration of war and the French ultimatum. LOWER. Survivors of the *Athenia* being brought to Ireland on a tender.

BOUND FOR THE BOTTOM OF THE SEA. The British aircraft carrier *Courageous*, seen here from the deck of the great battle cruiser *Rodney*, had but little time to live after this picture was taken. Putting to sea on the declaration of war, she was sunk by a German submarine in the North Sea on September 17, the submarine in turn being sunk by British warships. So the battle between submarines and surface ships that had been lost by Germany in World War I was resumed still more bitterly in World War II. Again U-boats harried the seas, preying on British, French, and ultimately American shipping in the Atlantic; and again British surface ships set up their strangling blockade on the ports of Germany and German-occupied countries. But warships cannot be built in a day, and Britain had unfortunately permitted her Navy to decline during the long years of peace. The lesson was not wasted on the United States, and American Naval officers strove earnestly to bring the Navy to strength. RIGHT. H.M.S. *Courageous* in the North Sea photographed from the British Battle Cruiser *Rodney*.

STORMING A FRENCH PILLBOX. On land the warring forces faced each other in a stalemate, with Maginot line opposed to the Western Wall. Between the two lines in the no-man's land of field and forest, barbed wire and pillboxes, raiding parties fought with rifle and machine gun, and grenades. Built at a cost of over five hundred million dollars, the French Maginot line proved the futility of trusting to fixed fortifications instead of mobile forces. This German Army photograph shows a Nazi soldier in the act of throwing a hand grenade through the gun port of a French pillbox near the Maginot line. This period of anxious dreary waiting was called the "phony war."

THE ARSENAL OF DEMOCRACY. On November 4, 1939, only two months after the outbreak of the war in Europe, President Roosevelt asked Congress to repeal the Arms Embargo, a provision of our Neutrality Act which prohibited the sale by Americans of arms and munitions to belligerent countries. America's first thought had been to stay out of the European War, and hence the United States, in concert with the other American republics, had in October established a neutral zone around the Americas, excepting belligerent Canada, and the U.S. Navy was already patrolling this neutral zone which extended some 300 miles to sea. In all sorts of weather our destroyers and other patrol craft searched the seas inside the zone, reporting all belligerent vessels found therein. But it was obvious that our fellow democracies in Europe needed all the help they could get to withstand the terrific assault of the Axis armies—and the thing they needed most was arms and ammunition. By repeal of the Arms Embargo Britain and France could buy American arms and munitions and take them home in their ships, whereas Italy and Germany, not having control of the sea, could not. This was the first step taken by the United States to show its sympathy and desire to aid the democracies of Europe and its antagonism to the Axis powers and their ruthless dictators. ABOVE. President Roosevelt, seated at his desk, reads the Repeal Bill, while Vice President Garner, Secretary of State Hull, and other prominent government officials and legislators look on.

THE BURNING OF THE GRAF SPEE. Under the terms to the Treaty of Versailles, Germany's Navy had been limited in numbers and sizes of warships. In an effort of evade the limitations, German Naval engineers had constructed "pocket battleships"—small battleships of great speed, gunpower, and armor. With the outbreak of war Hitler sent these as well as his U-boats to prey on enemy shipping. Most famous of the pocket battleships was the *Admiral Graf Spee,* commanded by Captain Hans Lansdorf. In late 1939 this ship was raiding in the South Atlantic when her presence was reported and three British cruisers under the command of Commodore Harwood were sent to intercept her.

The pursuers finally came up with the German raider off the South American Coast but well inside the Neutrality Zone which the American republics had requested the belligerents to respect. Although armed only with six and eight inch guns against the *Graf Spee's* 11-inch main battery, the British ships resolutely closed for action. While the British cruiser *Exeter* was put out of action, the two remaining cruisers pressed the attack home. In trying to dodge the *Exeter's* torpedoes, the *Graf Spee* took two heavy six-inch broadsides from the *Ajax* and the *Achilles.*

The damaged German turned and ran full speed for the safety of the territorial waters of Uruguay and dropped anchor in the harbor of Montevideo. Under the rules of International Law the *Graf Spee* could not remain long in neutral waters, nor make battle repairs there, and she was thousands of miles away from any assistance from a German base.

The pocket battleship remained in Montevideo harbor for the three days allowed under International Law, but then was forced by the Uruguayan government to put to sea. Rather than fight again, the German captain stopped in the Rio de la Plata, opened the sea-cocks, and set the ship afire. The destruction of the *Graf Spee* brought home to Hitler what American naval officers have always known —the value of far-spread naval bases from which ships can operate and to which they can return for repairs and renewing stores. And it also brought home to Hitler the fact that even the strongest army in the world cannot take the place of a Navy. The picture shows the scuttled and flaming raider in her death throes. She was described by the British commander as " . . . . ablaze from end to end, flames reaching almost as high as the top of the control tower, a magnificent and most cheerful sight."

NORWAY FIGHTS BACK. Advances of the Germans in Norway were met by continued resistance. British planes and warships sped to the battle where, in the harbor of Narvik, they, together with other Allied sea forces, inflicted a severe defeat on the Germans by destroying seven destroyers and practically clearing the harbor of German craft. From the newly acquired bases in Norway, German bombing planes raided the Scapa Flow area where they attacked three cruisers and the battleship Rodney upon which they scored a bomb hit. The Germans in southern Norway, after consolidating their gains, began dividing the region into isolated pockets by a series of panzer movements as they had done in Poland. UPPER. German sea planes float calmly on a mirror-like lake at Stavanger before being attacked by British Royal Air Force bombers from which the picture was taken. The German planes had been used to ferry troops by way of Denmark. LOWER. German and Norwegian officers salute the mast as the Norwegian flag is lowered on a Nazi-captured vessel in this photograph from German sources.

THE WORTH OF GERMAN PROMISES. From the start of the war Germany, in floods of propaganda, had proclaimed brotherhood with her Northern neighbors. UPPER. How much this meant to the Scandinavian countries can be seen in this picture where four Danish submarines lie next to their mother ship ready for action in any emergency. The emergency finally struck April 9, 1940. Germany, still proclaiming "benevolent protection" of the Northern countries against the designs of the Allies, sent hordes of her troops pouring into Norway and Denmark by air, sea, and, LOWER, by land. Norway reciprocated Germany's "spirit of fraternity" by sinking the German cruiser *Bluecher* laden with troops and 800 Gestapo men and the cruiser *Karlsruhe.*

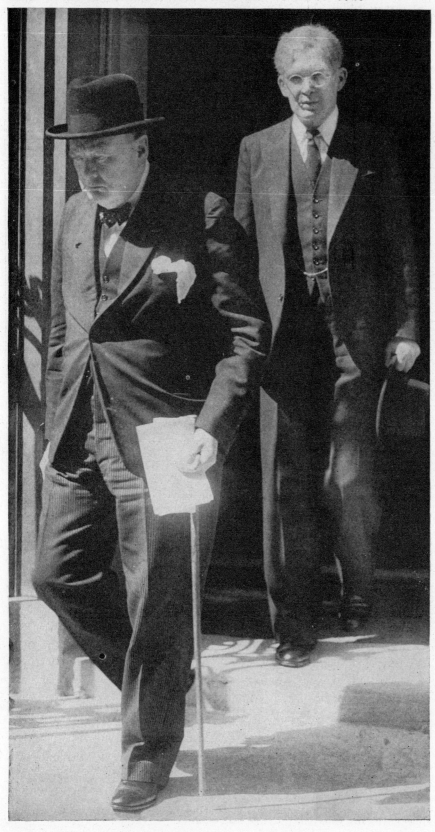

CHURCHILL IS PRIME MINISTER. On May 10, 1940, Neville Chamberlain was forced to resign as Prime Minister of Great Britain and was succeeded by Winston Churchill. He was to lead the English people through the most terrible time in their history and was to go down as one of England's greatest war leaders. Here he is shown leaving Number Ten Downing Street to make his statement to the House of Commons on the capitulation of France. This was one of Churchill's speeches in which he represented the indomitable spirit of the British. A month later he spoke again to Commons after Dunkirk, when England was in danger of invasion—this time his immortal " . . . . We shall fight them on the landing grounds, we shall fight them in the fields and in the streets . . . . We shall never surrender . . . ."

GERMAN PARATROOPERS OVER NORWAY. With this war came many new methods of warfare including the use of parachute troops and air-borne supplies to strike swift, stunning blows and capture objectives far beyond the enemy lines. This German photograph shows how the Nazis, fighting in the Narvik area, from which the British were evacuated, were kept supplied with ammunition and food. Planes flew from the southern part of the Norwegian peninsula in all types of weather to drop men and supplies by parachute. The Germans later used this type of war in the invasions of Crete and Greece. The supplies shown here are being dropped on the Narvik area. The plane is a Junkers JU-52, a tri-motored personnel, cargo plane with a large load capacity.

HOLLAND AND BELGIUM INVADED. Six days before the invasion of Poland, Germany pledged to respect the Low Countries, Holland and Belgium, in return for their absolute neutrality. However, on May 10, 1940, after falsely accusing these countries of being unneutral, the Nazis bombed The Hague and the Nazi war machine rolled again. In two weeks the two countries had surrendered. UPPER. Trenches along the Harbor of Schemingue, Holland, dug as that peaceful country got ready for the event of war. LOWER. A Nazi soldier examines the litter of abandoned ration boxes and uniforms alongside a truck in territory retaken by the Germans.

THE "STAB IN THE BACK!" On 10 June, 1940, while France was at the last gasp of organized resistance against the Nazis, Italy declared war. After stabbing her in the back, Italy confined herself to air bombing of Malta, Alexandria, and Gibraltar. She invaded the southern part of France around the Alps just in time to join in the hurrah and the spoils. Il Duce's troops which had beaten down the primitive Ethiopians were soon to make a sorry showing against Greece. Italy attempted to gain supremacy of the sea in the Mediterranean, but met with no degree of success. The British fleet tried to seek the Italians out and engage them in battle, but the Italian fleet remained in hiding and finally surrendered when Italy capitulated. Here Benito Mussolini is shown reading the Declaration of War against France to a throng of Italian Fascists in Rome.

BEATEN FRANCE BEGS FOR TERMS. UPPER. The wheel of history took a full and tragic turn for France on 23 June, 1940, when representatives of a beaten France were compelled to come to terms with German military chieftains. To stress the reversed situation the armistice was signed in the same railroad car where the Armistice of 1918 was signed. General Charles Huntzinger, member of the French Deputation, is second from the left. LOWER. Weisbaden, Germany. The Armistice Commission that arranged the carrying out by France of the German terms is shown here in their first session. The humiliation of France was complete.

LONDON BLITZ BEGINS. UPPER. Bombs are no respecter of property. Amid the ruins of a peer's 17th century mansion, Londoners curiously browse in the library whose roof has been demolished in the course of a Luftwaffe bombing raid. Accounts of damage and destruction in London slowly impressed Americans with the potential horrors of metropolitan air raids and made them determined that enemy planes should never be given the opportunity to wreak similar destruction on our own cities. LOWER. A good many Americans, however, did not appreciate the extent of the suffering and destruction borne by Londoners with typical British fortitude. It was difficult for New Yorkers or San Franscians or Texans to visualize how an enemy's bombs could disrupt the familiar organization of any city's life. Pictures like this one gave us an idea of what we might suddenly have to face some night. If a bomb missed your house, as in this picture (see crater at left), its concussion could still kill you or at least make you homeless. And there was little humor in finding a double-decker bus in your living-room. But the British people carried on, undaunted.

THERE WILL ALWAYS BE AN ENGLAND! While London reeled under the impact of Luftwaffe block-busters, President Roosevelt and Prime Minister Churchill went ahead with joint conferences of mutual interest to their two countries. One of the most decisive acts resulted from such interest in March of 1941, when the vital "Lend-Lease" provision was signed. Yet Londoners still had to run for their underground bomb shelters when the air raids came, and dig out the explosion rubble in the morning. UPPER RIGHT. Here is a typical morning scene where crews have already cleared the obstructions to transportation. LOWER. Often the most sacred temples of British institutions were indiscriminately hit in the blitz raids. The very heart of English legal tradition, the Middle Temple, is shown here mercilessly damaged by an attack that also struck the Cathederal of St. Paul and the Parliament Buildings. Museums, libraries, and priceless collections of legal records were destroyed. Such wanton demolition was a vivid warning to Americans who knew the services to civilization performed by national institutions.

NAVAL BASES FOR DESTROYERS. At the beginning of the war Great Britain had suffered severely from the attrition of operations at sea, particularly in destroyers. Faced with this situation, Great Britain entered into an agreement with the United States under the terms of which 50 of our older destroyers were exchanged for the right to establish naval bases on British territory in the Atlantic. In addition we were granted long leases for bases in Newfoundland and Bermuda. UPPER. This map shows the Atlantic bases leased from Great Britain by the United States. LOWER. Winston Churchill signing the agreement, watched by Mr. Winant, left, the American Ambassador, and Mr. Vincent Massey, the Canadian High Commissioner, right.

A GOOD BARGAIN FOR BOTH COUNTRIES. The acquisition of bases operated to advance our sea frontier several hundred miles in the direction of our potential enemies in the Atlantic and gave us added security not only for the present, but for many years in the future. The bases thus leased by the United States were, briefly; Antigua, B.W.I., Naval Air Station; British Guiana, S.A., Naval Air Station; Jamaica, B.W.I., Naval Air Station; St. Lucia, B.W.I., Naval Air Station; Bermuda, B.W.I., Naval Air Station; Great Exuma, Bahamas, Naval Air Station; Newfoundland, Naval Operating Base and Naval Air Station; and Trinidad, Naval Operating Base and Naval Air Station combined with a Lighter-than-Air Base radio station. ABOVE. American sailors acquainting their British comrades with the depth charge mechanism on one of the fifty over-age destroyers which were transferred.

ADVANCE BASE UNITS.

Early in the war the Navy undertook a great expansion of its system of advance bases, many of which represented the consolidation of gains made by combat units. Depending on the circumstances, whether they were gained as a result of a raid or as a result of an advance, the permanency of their construction was varied to meet the situation. In the south and central Pacific the entire campaign was a battle for advance bases where we could establish supply ports, ship repair facilities, and landing fields to act as a backstop for continuing offensives. Advance bases range in size from small units for the maintenance and repair of PT boats, manned by a handful of officers and men, to major bases comprising floating drydocks, pattern ships, foundries, fully equipped machine shops, and electrical shops, staffed by thousands of specialists. Some of these bases are general purpose bases, others are established for a special purpose. UPPER LEFT. The airbase at Bermuda, looking southwest. LOWER LEFT. Pearl Harbor Navy Yard. UPPER RIGHT. A radioman stands duty in the control tower at the U.S. Naval Air Station, Argentia, Newfoundland clearing planes for take-offs and landings. LOWER RIGHT. Construction Battalion (Seabee) advance base, Iceland.

LEND LEASE BEGINS. With the flow of lend-lease materials from U.S. factories and farms, the Navy extended and intensified its neutrality patrol. Western Hemisphere lines were set as far east as Iceland, and the United States declared all waters to the westward to be neutral. The United States was the only nation in the Western Hemisphere able to patrol this vast area. Germany, although not at war with this nation, boldly entered these waters to torpedo the U.S. destroyers *Kearny* and *Reuben James*. It was during this period that the Navy brought occupation troops to Iceland, that the Coast Guard helped patrol Greenland, long eyed by the Nazis as a weather observation post. Attacks by Germany on the warships and on merchant ships flying the U.S. flag led Congress to authorize the arming of merchant ships. The first guns on merchant ships were mounted just a few months before Pearl Harbor. UPPER. English docks piled high with Lend-Lease materials from the United States. LOWER. Reverse Lend-Lease: English goods for New York loading at a British Port under the watchful eyes of the Home Guard.

RAGING RIVERS TO CROSS. In early April, 1941, mighty Germany invaded tiny Yugoslavia and in three weeks occupied the country. It was while Germany was over-running such helpless countries as Yugoslavia that the Congress authorized, in a series of legislative efforts, the increase of our Navy from a two-ocean Navy to a five-ocean Navy, and U. S. Naval strategists foresaw the day when Germany would have to be defeated at sea in order to defeat her on the land. Thus began the planning which eventually won the Battle of the Atlantic. Here, in a German Army photograph, radioed to the United States, are shown Nazi troops in rubber boats fording the Drava River in the drive on Zagreb, capital of Croatia, in northern Yugoslavia.

THE INVASION OF GREECE, APRIL 30, 1941. Quickly completing the Yugoslav campaign, the Nazis moved into Greece to save the face of partner Mussolini. British surface vessels entered the Grecian campaign depending upon support from shore based aircraft, which was inadequate. This failure on the part of shore based aircraft when oper- ating with surface units gave impetus to the United States carrier construction program and proved the theory which was to give our Navy the great mobile, carrier task forces. UPPER. German heavy artillery in action during the drive through Greece. LOWER. Retreating, but undiscouraged, smiling British troops board ship as they left Greece.

ON TO MOSCOW! Flushed with easy victories over Poland, France, and the Low Countries, and the Balkans, Hitler suddenly turned treacherously on Russia whom he thought he had deceived with one of his false peace pacts. On June 22, 1941 he began an all out attack on the greatest scale ever yet conceived by man. With between 150 and 180 divisions in the surprise attack, the Germans counted on a quick capture of Moscow and the Caucasus. UPPER. German grenadiers waving a swastika flag to show Stuka pilots their positions so they would not bomb their own lines. LOWER. German tanks and half-tracks advancing on a Soviet position in a thrust on the Orel-Belgorod sector. Both pictures are German Army photographs.

THE NAVY TRAINS FOR WAR

By Vice-Admiral Louis L. Denfeld, U. S. N.

SEA POWER means more than fleets of ships and swarms of planes. It means men—trained to fight the ships and planes; repair, supply, maintain them; plan strategy and tactics, outwit the enemy and detect the enemy's plans, and search along the frontiers of scientific research for new combat devices and new techniques.

Trained manpower is the most scarce and most valuable element in the formula of naval power—and the most difficult to obtain readily in sufficient quantities. Even in the future of scientific miracles when perhaps a push-button Navy might become possible, a multitude of men still would be required to maintain, repair and supply the delicate instruments which would control the new-fangled missiles and ghost ships. And at least some men would be needed to push the many-colored buttons!

A modern Navy in war or peace is a vast and complex organization of warships, auxiliaries, planes, ports, harbors—from hulking aircraft carriers manned by thousands of tiny PT boats, from teeming Navy yards deafening with the roar of industry to the lonely quiet of island outposts sending out an electronic pulse beat to guide some ship or plane to safety.

For such a sprawling, intricate machine is required a multitude of skills and crafts, brains and brawn: machinists, metalsmiths, radarmen, signalmen, boatswain's mates, and just ordinary seamen to perform the many jobs required to keep the machine operating effectively.

Also needed are qualified officers to lead the men, supervise their activities and training, and administer the Navy's operations. And these leaders must have the personal qualities of character and executive ability, general knowledge and understanding to be able to handle men under the cramped and trying living conditions on fighting ships.

In peacetime, training men for the Navy can afford a leisurely, careful, thoroughgoing process with time available for theory, minute details and niceties of naval customs and traditions.

But in the headlong rush of wartime, training must be telescoped, concentrated, packed hard and delivered fast, taking advantage of every shortcut, cutting away every peacetime frill.

PREPARATION FOR WAR

IN THE recent war, the Navy training program had to be accelerated and expanded simultaneously to supply almost overnight the men needed to man the ships, planes and other Naval weapons. At one time eleven ships were coming from the yards daily—ready for action. Supply depots, repair bases, and advanced bases were mushrooming in a globe-wide expansion of the United States Navy.

The Navy's training mission was to draw more than three million Americans from their civilian occupations and transform them rapidly into seamen, gunner's mates, air gunners, combat air crewmen, firemen, armed guardsmen, signalmen, Seabees, bomb disposal experts, radarmen, amphibians, chemical warfare experts, ship repairmen, photograph interpreters, ordnance men, sonarmen, and damage control experts, and 500 other specialties.

Aviation training presented such a tremendous undertaking that a separate program was created to fulfill the Navy's mission to become absolute masters of the air. To accomplish this task, the Navy trained 60,000 pilots, 360,000 air technicians, 3,000 air navigators, and 45,000 combat aircrewmen.

To service carrier based and land based planes, over 150 units, such as overhaul units and carrier service units were staffed, trained and sent to forward combat areas.

It was a comparatively simple move to take trained or skilled men and assign them tasks closely related to their civilian jobs. Stenographers became yeomen after brief training. Carpenters became Seabees after learning how to defend what they were building.

But for the mass of men who had to be taught entirely new skills the training job became a monumental program, the success of which was attested to by the defeat of the Axis powers.

THE TRAINING PROGRAM

TRAINING men for the Navy is a three-ply program:
1. Introducing them to Navy life, customs, traditions, discipline, and teamwork.
2. Educating them in a specialty, craft, or professional skill.
3. Training them in advanced courses.

Newcomers to the Navy are first introduced to military life. Enlisted men are taught to live, work, and fight together. This basic education is known as recruit training—an intensive period of drills and lectures lasting from 8 to 12 weeks. For officers, this basic course is provided by Naval Reserve, Midshipmen, and indoctrination schools.

After this basic training, officers and men usually are sent to sea or to specialty schools where they are instructed in definite skills or the fundamentals of the naval profession.

Enlisted trade schools are operated on the highest educational standards. The finest of equipment, textbooks, training aids, and skilled guidance are supplied.

Advanced officers' schools train Naval officers in special skills or technical knowledge, such as radar, gunnery, and communications. They are trained as administrators of high technical ability who must learn how to integrate the tasks of many technicians operating in many different fields.

Beyond this advanced training, officers and men are sent to Fleet Operational Training Commands where they are organized into tactical units for more extensive instruction. From this course they board their ships for combat operations.

As many as a quarter of a million officers and men at one time have undergone basic training during the war. About 80 per cent of these went to the Fleet training commands, and the other 20 per cent direct to the Fleet.

The training program derives its original strength from the mature and experienced petty officers and chiefs, and from professional Navy officers usually trained in the Naval Academy.

With this nucleus of enlisted men and officers carefully schooled during peacetime, the Navy's training program shifts to a wartime basis by rapid pyramiding.

The educational program is directed from the Training Activity of the Bureau of Naval Personnel. Policies, standards, curricula, and textbooks stem from this central source.

With the coming of war, training courses were streamlined, abbreviated, slimmed down to bare essentials. Experienced educators were brought in from the nation's leading universities and schools to help formulate the program and engage in the actual instruction.

Classroom facilities were established at a double-quick rate—in traditional halls of learning, in hastily built structures, in drafty piers, in seaport warehouses, and on every ship. Classes were held formally in the usual schoolroom manner or informally in mess rooms, on decks, around a 20mm gun, anywhere possible. There was nothing cut or dried about this training. It was given whenever it could be arranged, sandwiched in between periods of combat and ship maintenance. And even during combat, the learning process continued, often most effectively.

TRAINING DEVICES

EVERY educational device, either long tried or in the experimental stage, was employed to train the men faster and better. Visual aids were used, such as moving pictures and slides, simply written and cartoon illustrated books, mock-up models of ship and instruments, actual models, blackboard talks, bull sessions, special teaching devices like the attack teacher for anti-submarine warfare, miniature layouts of navigational aids, etc.

Basically, Navy men learned by doing, by repeating the same motions and mental processes until they became almost reflex actions. Under the stress of battle, what was imperative was the prompt decision, the quick execution of previously well-rehearsed maneuvers.

The Navy's training program during the recent war period has revealed significantly that American men from all walks of life can be welded rapidly into a fighting team, that they can absorb unfamiliar knowledge and skills under high pressure and intensive instruction, and that they can employ the newest technical knowledge in effective operation of the latest weapons to win a war.

THE MAKING OF A SAILOR! This war highlighted the historic anomaly that is America—a peace-loving giant who can turn overnight into the world's most fearsome warrior. Men from all walks of life, from the farms and factories, from the schools and shops, all answered the call for men to man the ships and planes of an expanding "first line of defense," a Navy which all too soon was to be called upon to protect the country from the enemy. Into the Training Centers at Great Lakes, Illinois; San Diego, California; and Sampson, New York came these men, many of whom had never seen the ocean before, to learn seamanship, communications, gunnery, and maintainence, to learn to work together and fight together as part of a team.

They were trained in the Arts of War by the most modern and complete system of training aids, special devices that helped them learn to distinguish between friendly and enemy aircraft, to save their lives if they should be marooned at sea, to do their jobs in the Fighting Fleet. In a matter of weeks the farmer, the machinist, the student, and the storekeeper had been forged into a fighting body of men, disciplined, well trained, and ready to carry out their share of the fighting.

In coastal shipyards the race to produce more, faster, better armed and armored ships became hotter and hotter. Battleships, which normally took 38 months to build, were ready to fight in 30 to 32 months. Carriers, the mainstay of our war time fleet, were built in 16 months, less than half of the time required during peacetime years. Submarines and destroyers slid down the ways in "impossible" time. The giant that is America was awakened to the dangers that surrounded her, prepared to meet any and all aggressors.

ABOVE. A graduation review at Great Lakes Naval Training Center, Great Lakes, Ill. This review marks the end of "boot" training for the recruit. He is now ready to join the Fleet or to be sent to a service school to learn a specialized trade. At this point in his Naval career he has learned all that can be learned ashore. The next phase of his training, at sea, gives him a chance to put into practice the things he has learned. RIGHT. Abandon Ship Drill at an East Coast port. Drills and practices are held constantly to keep the lessons learned in training camps fresh in mind.

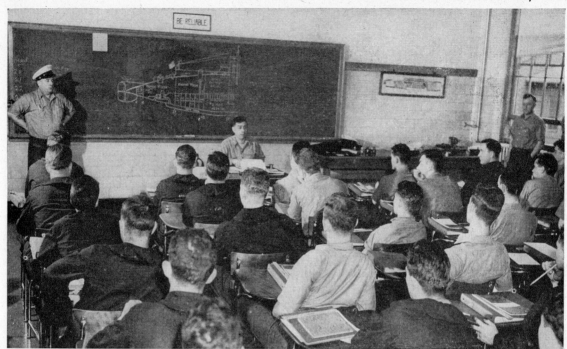

THE NAVY MUST ALWAYS BE READY! The first blows of war invariably are directed at the Navy, the great bulwark behind which the other forces can begin to organize. So the Navy trains ahead of time. At the U.S. Naval Submarine Training School in New London, Conn., eager young recruits for the submarine service learn what makes a submarine go. Skipper or messboy, every man was expected to qualify at cruising, diving, fighting, or repairs. How they learned this deadliest and most dangerous of all fighting trades the Japanese were fated to find out all too well. UPPER. Classroom instructor teaching the theory and nomenclature of submarines. LOWER. Learning how to operate and repair the diesel engines that drive a submarine.

SUBMARINE TRAINING—ESCAPE TANK. As a part of the training which makes American submarines the world's best, recruits learn to use the Escape Tank. After a course of instruction in the use of the Momsen "lung," an artificial breathing device, the men are taken to escape chambers at various levels below the surface of the tank. From these chambers the men ascend to the surface, using the "lung." The picture above shows the inside of an escape chamber. Before the hatch leading to the main tank is opened the chamber is flooded and all apparatus tested. This type of practical work characterizes the Navy system of instruction and training for any eventuality.

"CLAY PIGEONS" FOR NAVY'S ANTI-AIRCRAFT GUNNERS. As a part of the Navy's extensive training aids program, radio controlled "drones" or pilotless aircraft were used to train anti-aircraft gunners. These "aerial robots" can be made to simulate suicide, dive bomber, and torpedo plane attacks, TDD's—Naval designation for one type of drone—frequently were used while the fleet was on its way to and returning from attacks against the enemy. These controlled robots developed greater accuracy and were far more popular with the men than the towed target sleeve, the gunnery device which they replaced. ABOVE. A radio controlled target drone (TDD-2) takes off from a ship's catapult under a reduced charge. It is then flown over the task force to give all the anti-aircraft gunners of the fleet a warm up for impending battles and to keep their skill at a high level.

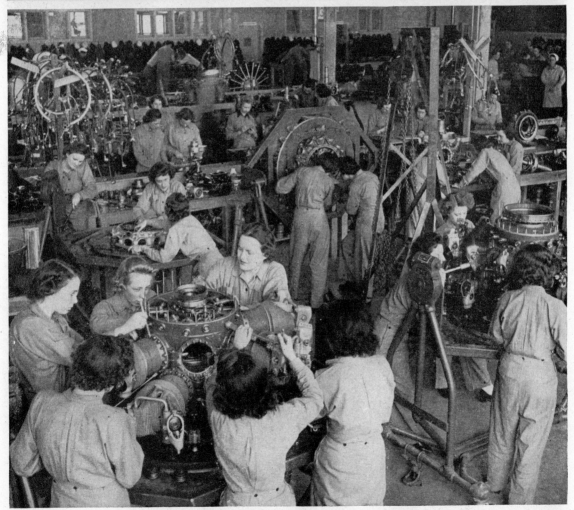

ANNAPOLIS—SCHOOL FOR FUTURE ADMIRALS. UPPER. Into the busy classrooms and laboratories of the Naval Academy at Annapolis, Md. pour unending streams of young Americans to dedicate themselves to the arts of war—to preserve the peace. Here they strive to master the military and nautical sciences, and to master themselves, through unending discipline. Wearing their working uni- forms, Academy midshipmen tackle an examination. LOW- ER. Being trained to release men from shore jobs to sea duty, Waves tackle the job of becoming Aviation Machinist's mates and Aviation Metalsmiths. These Waves receive a concentrated four months practical course in all phases of engine operation and maintenance which fits them for work on shore based aircraft.

WINNING THEIR WINGS. UPPER LEFT. Thanks to ingenious devices conceived and developed at the Navy Bureau of Aeronautics Special Devices Division in Washington, D. C., under the command of Rear Admiral Luis de Florez, Navy pilots now go into combat with a confidence engendered by the thought that they have done this before. These devices enable fledgling fliers to shoot down enemy planes, bomb objectives, engage in blind flying and many other activities—all without leaving the ground. Shown above is a star recognition trainer. This device enables the instructor to demonstrate the relationship of the heavenly bodies to one another. CENTER. A view of the Naval Aviation Training Center, Corpus Christi, Texas, one of the world's largest aviation training bases. One section in formation is preparing to land, while another is taxiing into position for a takeoff. LOWER LEFT. Gathered around the schedule board a group of students listens to a last minute briefing by their instructor.

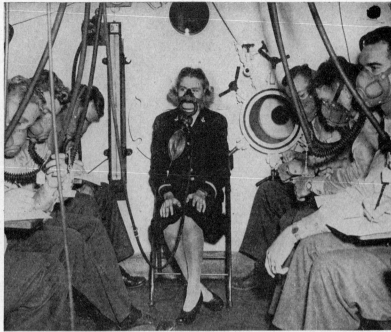

THE BEST TRAINED PILOTS IN THE WORLD. UPPER RIGHT. As part of the complex program that makes the United States Naval Aviator the best trained pilot in the world, aviation cadets are given instruction in the use of oxygen and high-altitude flying equipment. Cadets spend many hours in low pressure, low temperature tanks getting used to the sensations of high altitude work. Shown is the Oxygen Indoctrination Unit at the Naval Air Training Center, Pensacola, Florida. LOWER. A student officer reloads the twin .30 caliber machine guns in the rear gun position of a Helldiver dive bombing plane. Rearming and conditioning of all aerial gunnery equipment is an important phase of aviation training. The student pilot must learn not only to fly the plane, but also to do all of the work on it normally done by the air crewman. This work includes engines, structures, ordnance and overall maintenance, and gives the pilot a thorough knowledge of every phase of his work and the ability to check on his crewmen.

THE MAKING OF A SAILOR. During the war years the Navy trained for its fighting fleets more than 3,000,000 officers and men at naval and air training stations, midshipman schools, and NROTC colleges. Picked enlisted men were sent to special service schools which turned out everything from machinist's mates to cooks and bakers. Regulars, both officers and enlisted personnel, trained the new reserves, and then these in turn trained other reserves. Experts, with fresh combat experience, came back to train new replacements in all the latest tactics and weapons of war. The picture above shows recruits getting a lesson in lowering away a lifeboat at the Great Lakes Training Station.

THE FLEET PREPARES. As part of its program to release sufficient men for fighting, the women's reserves were set up to handle many shore-based jobs. UPPER. Wave mechanics cross the field at the naval air station where they are stationed. Before long there were few jobs in the maintenance and repair of planes that were not being performed by women. LOWER. With the tremendous need for ships to supply the seven-ocean fleet, the United States shipyards performed a masterful job of building and repairing. This 1942 view of the Newport News Shipyard shows carriers and cruisers being built and outfitted to take their places with the Fleet.

A TANKER BURNS AT SEA. While most of the merchant ships lost in the Atlantic during the dark days of 1942 and 1943 were lost as a result of enemy action, some were the victims of accident and shipwreck. Sailing in convoy, blacked out, was difficult to say the least. ABOVE. The oil tanker *Montana* burns at sea after colliding with the freighter *John Morgan*, 1 June 1943, about twenty miles off Cape Henry, Virginia. The fire was put out and the tanker returned to port for repairs. When casualties occurred further from shore the results were not always so fortuitous.

BY THESE GUNS THE JAPS KNEW US. In order to maintain its consistently high standard of accuracy in the specialized field of naval ordnance, the Navy has hundreds of thousands of acres set aside in the United States for use as Naval proving grounds to test new devices, guns, rockets, and guided missiles. UPPER. At Dahlgren, Virginia, one of the Navy's largest proving grounds, a 16-inch naval gun fires a projectile through rings to determine its velocity. LOWER. Smaller caliber guns are proved in salvoes to speed up the tempo of wartime production.

BRITISH GUNS BUT AN AMERICAN PRESIDENT! In mid-August, 1941, the world was amazed to learn that President Roosevelt had secretly met Prime Minister Churchill of Great Britain, and the two leaders had agreed on the provisions of the memorable "Atlantic Charter." The Charter stated the conditions required for world peace, and indicted dictators and aggression. The picture shows Presiden Roosevelt being greeted by the captain of H.M.S. *Prince o Wales* as he stepped aboard from the U.S.S. *Augusta* at Placentia Bay, Newfoundland.

THE "V FOR VICTORY" SIGN. During a conversation with Prime Minister Churchill during their momentous Atlantic Charter meeting on August 10, 1941, President Roosevelt makes the British victory sign. The Charter was part of America's answer to the Tripartite Pact signed by Germany, Italy, and Japan in September, 1940, which threatened combined Axis action against any neutral which should interfere with Axis aggressions.

The United States had already challenged that threat by its Lend-Lease aid, its occupation of Iceland to forestall possible German invasion, and its naval patrol of northern hemispheric waters east to Greenland. The Axis dictators should have recognized the importance of the Charter Meeting. ABOVE. In addition to the President and the British Premier, the meeting included Admiral Ernest J. King, General George C. Marshall, and British General Sir John Dill,

BOUND TO DELIVER THE GOODS! With the Lend-Lease Act the United States had bound itself to provide materials for the defense of the European democracies against the Axis aggressors. But with Nazi U-boats sinking neutral ships even in the Western Atlantic, what was the use of making and shipping goods only to be sunk? The answer was President Roosevelt's announcement of July, 1941, that our Navy would convoy lend-lease goods as far as Iceland. It was cold, arduous work in the foggy, freezing, iceberg menaced waters around Greenland and Iceland. UPPER. A U. S. Navy blimp hovering over a brood of merchantmen as it scans the water for U-boats. LOWER. Freighter taking aboard a tank landing craft manufactured in the United States for use overseas.

THE COAST GUARD LENDS A HAND. On November 1, 1941, President Roosevelt transferred the Coast Guard to the Navy, and on November 11 announced that henceforth American naval vessels would "shoot on sight" upon encountering any Axis raiders within American defensive areas. The Coast Guard cutters proved adept at "sub-hunting," as shown by the pictures of the cutter *Spenser* in her victorious attack on a U-boat. UPPER. The *Spenser's* crew watch the exploding of a depth-charge aimed at a U-boat submerged between her and the convoy in the background. The depth-charge blew the U-boat to the surface where she was quickly finished off by the cutter. LOWER. The stricken U-boat plunges bottomward, with one German in the water, swimming toward rescue.

THE SHIP THAT DIDN'T SINK. Enemy torpedoes were not the only things to be feared in the convoy runs across the North Atlantic. In the foggy, rainy, or blizzardy weather of the northern latitudes ships in convoy formation had to beware of running each other down.

Equally dangerous were collisions with giant icebergs drifting down from the mighty glaciers of Greenland. On the convoy ships sharp-eyed lookouts forward and on the bridge squinted anxiously into the fog and night, and down below grimy engineers stood ready instantly to stop or back.

ABOVE. This merchant ship was not lucky enough to detect the icy menace and rammed an iceflow head-on. With gaping holes in her bow and tons of ocean inside her, the ship managed to limp into port, however, where U. S. shipyards did a superhuman job during the war in repairing damaged ships like this. These "ships that didn't sink" were of incalculable value in helping move overseas the tremendous numbers of men and tons of stores called for.

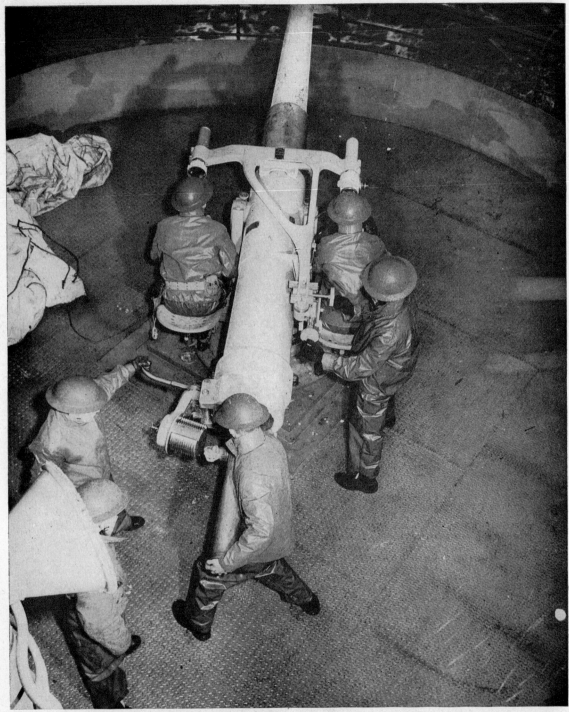

MAKING IT TOUGH FOR U-BOATS. Two days after the Neutrality Law was amended in November, 1941, the Navy was ready to place trained gun crews aboard merchant ships. This prompt action was the result of a foresighted training program initiated by the Navy eight months previously.

Gun crews consisted of from ten to twenty men, and they manned 3-inch to 5-inch guns, as well as heavy caliber machine guns. These Navy gun crews effectively transformed merchantmen from sitting duck targets into disagreeable wasps that could sting back. In order to train the men who manned the guns of our 1375 merchant ships, Armed Guard schools were established by the Navy. Basic courses were taught in regular, anti-aircraft, and rapid fire guns.

Operating pools for the personnel were established in Brooklyn and San Francisco, where crews were quartered and equipped between their long periods aboard ships away from any central Navy facility. ABOVE. An armed guard crew mans and loads a 3-inch gun on a rain-swept deck in preparation for any U-boat ahead.

THE NAVY TRAINS SHIPBUILDERS. The outbreak of World War II was the signal for the Navy to launch into a greatly accelerated shipbuilding program. Though the pace increased tremendously after Pearl Harbor, the program was well underway at the time the picture at the left was taken in the summer of 1941.

Here we see an 800-pound ladle pouring metal for Naval anti-aircraft gun bases. In the face of the nation's greatest emergency Americans went to work to build ships—more ships and better ships—with the help of the professional shipbuilders and civilian experts comprising the Navy's industrial training division. Too realistic to rely on patriotism alone, the Navy offered many industrial incentive awards. Men and women of all ages, laboring on arduous day and night shifts, achieved results that won the world's admiration. Every branch of American industry felt the effects.

The Navy's program went deeper than the mere speeding up of shipyard production. In order to meet the requirements of a two-ocean Navy, the program had to bring about a huge expansion in general industry —enlargement first of plants producing basic raw materials, then of plants manufacturing the countless component parts of modern men-of-war—from jewel bearings to mammoth turbines. Manufacturers let out their contracts to sub-contractors and thus brought all factories into the war effort, even those working with non-essential materials. For example, an automobile manufacturer began to produce an extremely intricate gyroscopic compass. A stone finishing concern found itself manufacturing towing machines and deck winches.

The program operated at a dizzy pace. Owing to a crisis in the production of turbo-electric propulsion machinery, it was necessary to build an enormous new plant in a 50-acre cornfield. Construction of the plant was not begun until May, 1942. Within seven months the first machine had been produced, completed, and shipped. A comparison of the time required to build Naval vessels before and after Pearl Harbor speaks for itself. Before: battleship, 38 to 40 months; aircraft carrier, 32 to 34 months; submarine, 14 to 15 months; destroyer, 13 to 14 months. After: battleship, 32 months; carrier, 15 months; submarine, 7 months; destroyer, 5 months. Through such progress we soon shifted from the defensive to the offensive.

PEARL HARBOR

Rear Admiral William R. Furlong, USN

TO THE American people "Pearl Harbor" is more than a name; it is a day of History, of Decision, of a great upsurge of patriotism and national unity.

On Sunday morning, December 7, 1941, even while Japan's "peace" commissioners were waiting in our Secretary of State's anteroom presumably to settle the differences between the two countries, 350 Japanese planes from six carriers struck at Pearl Harbor and the Pacific Fleet, the attack beginning at 7:55 A.M. While Japanese fighters and bombers were demolishing the U. S. Army and Navy airfields and shore-based planes, bombers and torpedoes came in low to attack the ships. Even two-man Japanese submarines infiltrated into the harbor in a sneak attack. Despite the crews' bravery, within the matter of minutes five battleships, three cruisers, three destroyers, a minelayer, a target ship, and a floating drydock were sunk or badly damaged, out of a total of 93 naval vessels in the harbor. But to Americans, the most serious loss was the 3,077 naval personnel killed and missing.

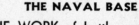

Even while bombs still burst and ships flamed, the Navy began its colossal salvage and fitting-out operations, one of the greatest salvage feats in all history. The bomb hits had done comparatively little damage; it was the torpedo hits, blasting the battleships' sides, that had wrought the greatest havoc.

SALVAGE BEGINS

ALL OF the lightly damaged ships were back in the service within weeks. Giant cripples like the *Nevada*, *California*, and *West Virginia* were raised and repaired. Technical experts, both naval and civilian, were flown from the West Coast; other workers went by ship to join the regular Navy Yard force at Pearl Harbor. They composed a tremendous organization of men, materials, divers, burners, pumpers, electricians, laborers, and mechanics, who did much of their work in diving suits underwater. To prepare the sunken ships for reflotation alone required 28,336 hours of diving.

From ships damaged beyond repair all usable armament and equipment was removed for use elsewhere—the 14-inch rifles from the sunken *Oklahoma* eventually went into the turrets of the veteran *Pennsylvania* when later on the main batteries of that ship were worn out in bombarding the Japanese. Ammunition from stricken ships was reprocessed and reissued to be fired in subsequent battles. Great rotary pumps sucked out tons of water, a battery of powerful winches on the land righted the capsized ships, and the ships rose and were nursed tenderly into drydock. This was the work of Naval officers, Navy Yard workmen and enlisted men, and of the civilian workers. Ultimately all of the battleships sunk at Pearl Harbor, except the *Arizona* and *Oklahoma,* went back to their places in the fleet—and they went out in better fighting condition than before they were hit.

THE NAVAL BASE

THE WORK of battle repairs for other ships damaged during the four years of war was as phenomenal as the great salvage job. During the war the Navy Yard multiplied its facilities and personnel sixfold. As many as 27,000 civilians and 3,000 enlisted men were at work in the Navy Yard. These workers repaired or installed new equipment in 7,000 ships, there being as many as 100 ships constantly under repair during the last year of the war. The motto of the workers was "We Keep Them Fit To Fight!"

From its bombed wreckage Pearl Harbor rose to be one of the greatest naval bases in the world. Huge warehouses were built for the oceans of supplies flowing in and out; giant tanks provided millions of gallons of oil and gasoline for ships and planes; the Naval Supply Depot became the heart of the Pacific naval supply activity, pumping vital resources to the fleet. Thousands of tons of projectiles, bombs, torpedoes, mines, rockets, and powder went out to our fighting men from the underground and surface storage of the Naval Ammunition Depot. At the Submarine Base as many as 24 submarines at a time were refitting after cruises, to go out and cruise against the enemy again. From the huge Sea Bee (Naval Construction Battalion) Base at Pearl Harbor, containing as many as 20,000 men, the Sea Bees poured out to do their phenomenal construction work in the Pacific islands. The Naval Air Station on Ford Island repaired and serviced planes for use throughout the Pacific. Hospitals increased to a point where they had a total bed capacity of 10,000.

William R. Furlong.

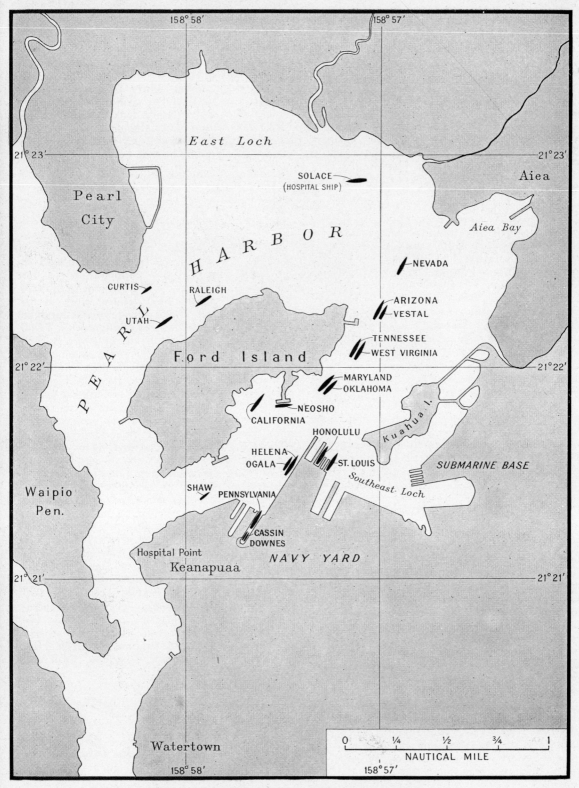

**Map showing the disposition of the fleet at Pearl
Harbor on 7 December 1941.**

PLAN FOR TREACHERY. This captured Japanese map which was used by a Japanese naval aviator on the morning of December 7th shows the relative positions of American fleet units on that fateful morning. This crude chart, evidently prepared on the carrier from the last minute reports of spies operating in the Pearl Harbor area, is in itself ample testimony of the very effective spy system that existed in Hawaii prior to Pearl Harbor. The Japanese master stroke was certainly well planned and the results of the attack prove that the Jap fliers who executed the stroke were not inexperienced. They demonstrated considerable resourcefulness and military prowess throughout the attack. Along the north shore of Ford Island, situated in the center of the chart, are the Japanese representations of battleship row. The writing in the upper left reads "Report for location of warships;" that in the lower right "Pearl Harbor."

BATTLESHIP ROW. This Japanese propaganda photograph, circulated to neutral countries, carried the caption, "Our Sea Eagles' determined attack had already opened, and a column of water from a direct torpedo hit on a *Maryland* class is rising. On the surface of the water concentric waves are traced by the direct torpedo hits, while murky oil flows out. The three bright white streaks between the waves are the torpedo tracks. In the distance the conflagration at the Hickam Field hangars is seen." At Pearl Harbor the Japanese were clever in that they destroyed our planes and bombed the airfields before their heavy assault upon our major fleet units.

UNDER ATTACK. The upper photograph is one captured from the Japanese. It was taken by a Jap aviator almost directly overhead during the early part of the attack on Pearl Harbor. The white splashes alongside the ships are made by the dropping bombs. Ford Island appears in the lower right hand corner. The three outboard ships from left to right are the *Vestal*, the *West Virginia*, and the *Oklahoma*. Inboard from left to right are the *Nevada*, the *Arizona*, the *Tennessee*, and the *Maryland*. LOWER. The *Nevada*, sustaining minor damage, gets up steam and pulls away from the other burning ships. The *Nevada* was the only battleship to get under way during the attack.

SUNDAY MORNING. UPPER. Undergoing routine availability in Dry Dock Number One, Navy Yard, Pearl Harbor, the USS. *Pennsylvania*, 33,100 ton flagship of the Pacific Fleet, rests on keel blocks in company with the 1,500 ton destroyers, USS. *Downes* and USS. *Cassin* (lying on her side). Preparations were being made to hold mass on the battleship's quarterdeck. Suddenly and with complete surprise, Japanese dive-bombers and torpedo planes came roaring down out of the high overcast. Repeated attempts to torpedo the caisson of the drydock failed. The enemy strafed ships and surrounding dock areas severely. A medium bomb struck the starboard side of the "Pensy's" boatdeck, bursting inside casement nine, and wiping out the crew of the 5"/51. The destroyers took hits and were seriously damaged, the intensity of the fires in the *Downes* exploding her fuel tanks. On deck at least two warheads of her armed torpedoes went off with a mighty roar, capsizing the *Cassin* and showering that section of the harbor with metal fragments. A portion of a torpedo tube weighing nearly a thousand pounds settled on the *Pennsylvania's* forecastle.

LOWER. The *West Virginia*, moored outboard of the *Tennessee* at Ford Island, bore the brunt of the attack which swept down from Merry's Point. Two bombs and six torpedoes left her main deck awash. The *Tennessee* shot down five attacking Japanese bombers. But she herself received hits in two turrets. The steel decks grew white hot from the oil blazing on the water; and the *Tennessee* restricted in movement, churned the water with her props to keep the flames away.

THROUGH THE SMOKE AND FLAME. UPPER. Through fire, through choking black smoke and flaming water, we catch another glimpse of the *West Virginia* and the *Tennessee*. At the extreme left, forward of the capsized *Oklahoma*, the motor launch which rescued survivors makes its way to comparative safety. **LOWER.** The *Nevada* was the only capital ship able to get under way during the attack on Pearl Harbor. In spite of hits, she moved under her own power to Hospital Point, where she was beached so as to avoid the possibility of blocking the harbor channel. In the foreground the crew of the Naval tug man their battle stations, watching for the next would-be assailant.

DEEP IN THE MUD. The task of refloating the battleship *Oklahoma* was the most difficult salvage operation undertaken by the Navy's repair crews. Hit on her port side by four Japanese torpedoes during the raid, she began immediately to list badly and soon capsized. Most of the crew below were trapped. When the tappings were heard later along her exposed hull, workmen and sailors began frantic efforts to rescue trapped survivors still alive. LEFT. Cutting a hole through the steel bottom plates, out of which 32 crew members were taken alive. The *Maryland* is alongside. The *Oklahoma* remained in her capsized position for months while Navy engineers devised many ingenious ways for righting and refloating her. Navy divers worked long hours in the murky waters to place temporary seals over the holes ripped along a third of her 538-foot length. The *Oklahoma*, sister ship of the *Nevada*, was originally built in 1912.

AN INGENIOUS SYSTEM OF CABLES. As part of the gigantic task of righting the *Oklahoma*, a system of cables was stretched over wooden "A" frames, rigged on her exposed starboard side. These were stretched to a multiple system of electric motors set up ashore on Ford Island where several acres of land were cleared to provide space for equipment. Very slowly the perfectly coordinated network drew the 29,000 ton capsized hulk over. RIGHT. This aerial view shows the hulk of the giant cripple more than half turned. Ford Island, with the cable and electric motor equipment, appears in the background. At this stage of the salvage, loose gear and part of the superstructure were cut away from the hull. The ship had become encrusted with barnacles and marine life after lying so long in the water. As the *Oklahoma's* hull lacked all buoyancy, a great patch had to be built around the damaged areas before it could be pumped out.

TRIUMPH. At the left, the shattered hull of of the *Oklahoma*, a triumph of the Navy's salvage technique, finally rests in drydock. Visible is part of the crumpled 13-inch armor plate which extended around the belt of the ship. Special warheads used by the Japanese in their aerial torpedoes caused this terrific destruction. The *Oklahoma* was so extensively damaged that naval officials decided to abandon repair efforts. Instead, the personnel who would have worked on her spent their efforts repairing the newer battleships. All battleships sunk or damaged at Pearl Harbor, with the exceptions of the *Arizona* and *Oklahoma*, lived to see the day when their guns again pounded the Japs. Some of the 14-inch guns salvaged from the *Oklahoma* were used to rearm the less damaged *Pennsylvania*. A tremendous organization employing 3,000 Navy enlisted men and 27,000 civilians was built up to accomplish these feats of salvage.

REPAIR JOB. During the early phase of the Japanese attack on Pearl Harbor, the enemy torpedo planes launched their fish at the ships tied up in Battleship Row. Among those hit was the *West Virginia*. She sustained heavy damage and slowly settled in her berth. To put the *West Virginia* back in the fighting line involved a major salvage job. The repair parties worked night and day to float the *West Virginia* and return her to the fighting line. It was discovered that during the attack six to eight torpedos hit her port side, and subsequently, it was decided that to float the ship would require a wooden side or blister placed over the holes made by the warheads of the Japanese torpedoes. **RIGHT.** The caissons on the *West Virginia's* port side six months after she was hit.

SETTING BROKEN BONES. LEFT. Another photograph showing the port side of the *West Virginia*. To repair the damage the ship was fitted with a wooden side extending ⅔ the length of the hull and covering all the torpedo holes. This "blister" consisted of two sections, of which the forward part covered one torpedo hit and the after part the middle portion of the ship's side, where she had suffered two hits on the armor, one above the armor, and possibly three below the armor. A hit in the stern took off her rudder. Each rectangular metal frame along the bottom of the blister held 4 tons of lead for sinking the section into place. Each section of the blister was 12 feet wide. It was by such indefatigable work as this giant repair job that our Navy finally got even with the Japs.

PORT SIDE LOOKING AFT. After sections were built on the dock a large floating crane lowered them on to the ship's side which rested in the mud. Since this work was done entirely under water, it called for considerable courage and ingenuity on the part of the divers and repair crew. **RIGHT.** This photo shows the middle section after the forward patch had been removed. Most of the after patch has been cut away except for the forward and after sections and the lower part which is located near the turn of the bilge. This is filled with cement and refuses to come away. Finally, after months of effort, the job was completed, and the *West Virginia* sailed from Pearl Harbor to bring her power to bear against her arch enemy, the Imperial Japanese Navy, the culmination of months of work.

HITLER SIGNS HIS OWN DEATH WARRANT. With the triumphant reports of the Japanese after Pearl Harbor still ringing in his ears, Chancellor Hitler stood in the Reichstag and launched the German state into the war with the United States that was to cost the Nazis all that they had already won. Although sure of victory he bombastically announced that he would give his life, if necessary, for the German cause, and that in that case Marshal Herman Goering (seated directly above him) would be his successor. ABOVE. The scene in the Reichstag as Hitler announced to the German nation that Germany was at war with the United States.

AT WAR WITH GERMANY AND ITALY. On December 11, 1941, thinking that their Japanese Allies had destroyed United States sea power in their treacherous Pearl Harbor attack, Germany and Italy also declared war on the United States. On that same day Congress unanimously recognized the state of war thrust upon us. Just as unanimously did the people of the United States take up the challenge. Volunteers swarmed to recruiting offices, training stations expanded a hundred fold; shipyards, munitions plants, airplane factories grew overnight. ABOVE. The picture shows President Roosevelt at his desk in the White House signing the war resolution of Congress.

THE JAPANESE DRIVE FOR MANILA. Almost immediately after Pearl Harbor, the Japanese bombed our bases in the Philippines and by December 10 had landed invasion troops. Our little Asiatic Fleet fought a desperate delaying action until the remnants reached Australia. Our remaining ships and planes hung on, knowing that no possible help could come. Slow patrol planes of Navy Patrol Wing Ten tackled new Japanese fighters; Lieut. Bulkeley's little squadron of PT boats attacked everything from Japanese troop carriers to cruisers. Our submarines fought their way out when nothing was left to fight with. Our remaining naval forces and Marines joined the Army as a naval brigade and fought as land soldiers through the whole campaign to Bataan and Corregidor.

ABOVE. This picture, one of the first brought out of the Philippines after the war began, shows barges in the U. S. Navy Yard at Cavite burning fiercely after the Japanese bombing of Dec. 12, 1941.

A HOPELESS FIGHT. Within 24 hours of Pearl Harbor, Guam, two-thirds of the way from Hawaii to the Philippines, was bombed, and the next morning the Japanese poured ashore to overwhelm the small American garrison. RIGHT. This photograph was taken from a Japanese propaganda booklet "Victory on the March" published in December, 1942. The photograph was captioned "The Naval Ensign being hoisted over the former American base."

GALLANT DEFENSE. Four hours after Pearl Harbor the Japanese attacked Wake Island. For two weeks the brave defenders fought, shooting down planes, repulsing attacks, and even sinking Japanese destroyers and cruisers. With the final enemy thrust on December 22, the Marines transmitted their last signal: "Urgent! Enemy on island. The issue is in doubt!" Then silence. ABOVE. The picture shows the Wake airstrip under later attack by our planes. In the foreground lie wrecks of Japanese ships, mementos of the heroic American defense.

HEROES OF WAKE. Stripped to the waist, men of the U. S. Marine Corps on Wake Island are filling gasoline drums from the island's storage tank. This was one of the last photos sent out from Wake before war flamed in the Pacific. UPPER. Shortly after this picture was made these men were matching bullets with the vastly outnumbering Japanese forces. LOWER. This picture reproduced from a Japanese propaganda magazine printed in Shanghai identifies the naval officer in blue as Commander Cunningham, U.S.N., garrison chief at Wake, and the others as part of the prisoners taken at Wake. The Americans were enroute to a prison camp at Zentsuji when the picture was taken. By their smiles the Americans seem confident of eventual victory.

HONGKONG FALLS. Aerial view of the island of Hong-kong. Known to seamen, merchants, and tourists the world over, Hongkong with its polyglot Oriental and British population had been a British Crown Colony for exactly a century when it succumbed to the Japanese juggernaut less

than three weeks after Pearl Harbor. Great Britain took possession of the island in 1841 after the "Opium War." Owing to Hongkong's position as one of the chief centers of
European and American trade in the Far East, the Allies
keenly felt its loss.

AN ALLY IN TROUBLE. The above photograph appeared in a Japanese propaganda booklet over the caption: "A Dutch destroyer in the Banda Sea in its last moments as it is subjected to a concentrated bombing attack." Dutch destroyers frequently helped convoy troops and supplies to Singapore before the city fell to the Japanese. The Netherlands government declared war on Japan a few hours after the assault on Pearl Harbor, without waiting for an attack on Dutch territory. Prophetically the Dutch had greatly extended their East Indies naval air patrol on December 6 to include more outlying islands. Dutch naval strength in the East Indies included two light cruisers, seven destroyers, a large flotilla leader, and more than a dozen submarines. The rest of the Netherlands fleet was operating with Allied units in the European Theatre. In both theatres the Dutch played gallant roles.

THE SMOKE OF BATTLE CLEARS. This photograph was copied from a Japanese propaganda booklet "Victory on the March" published in 1942. The caption read "An impressive wreckage of American planes which were bombed from the air." These planes, Navy F4F "Wildcat" fighters, were destroyed on the ground.

In the early Japanese aerial attacks many of our planes were caught on the ground and destroyed before they got into the air. Notable examples of planes destroyed before they took to the air were at Clark and Hickam fields in the Philippines and Hawaii. In the surprise Japanese raids on the 7th and 8th of December almost all of the American Air Force in the Pacific was destroyed or damaged. The American planes, drawn up in neat, orderly, peacetime rows, were easy bombing targets for the Nipponese fliers.

While the Japanese do not identify the locale of the picture, it is believed to have been taken at Midway Island, where, with less than a dozen planes, the American forces stood off the onslaught of ten to twelve times that number of Japanese planes.

BATTLE OF THE ATLANTIC

By Admiral Jonas H. Ingram, USN

MORE than two years before the formal entry of the United States into World War II, the Atlantic Fleet began to support the British Fleet. This was done by the Neutrality Patrol, established in September 1939.

Fifteen months before the Japanese attack on Pearl Harbor, fifty Atlantic Fleet destroyers were turned over to Great Britain in exchange for base rights, and the rapid development of theee outposts during 1941 permitted the Atlantic Fleet to prepare a series of valuable stepping stones for wartime operations. Another vital extension of our defenses occurred in May 1941 when Brazil authorized the Atlantic Fleet to build and use advanced bases for planes and surface craft at Recife, Bahia, and Natal.

Aggressively committed to the task of maintaining the war-making capacity of the British Isles, the United States could not afford to let German submarines sink lend-lease supplies en route, and the Atlantic Fleet joined British and Canadian naval forces during the summer of 1941, with orders to "shoot on sight" at any ships, planes or submarines which threatened this steady flow of war materials through the Western Atlantic.

By the time the attack on Pearl Harbor occurred, the Atlantic Fleet had already completed and had begun to use a destroyer base in Londonderry, Ireland. In the far-flung struggle to maintain convoy lanes which soon stretched from the United Kingdom to Halifax, New York, Trinidad, Aruba, Recife, and Rio de Janeiro, Admiral Doenitz's ruthless offensive maintained a decided edge. But in May 1943, Allied team-work with long-range planes, surface ships and baby flat tops succeeded in sinking 43 U-boats, and this stunning defeat was the climax of the Battle of the Atlantic. Thereafter, the initiative in that phase of the conflict passed to the Allies and was never again lost.

SUPPORTING THE EUROPEAN LANDINGS

CLOSELY interlocked with the submarine war were the overseas movements of great armadas to launch those major amphibious operations which led to the final defeat of the Axis: the landings in North Africa, the Sicilian and Italian campaigns, and the invasions of Normandy and Southern France. To assist the British and Canadians in all of these difficult tasks, the Amphibious Force of the Atlantic Fleet provided extensive training to our Army troops. The important part played by Atlantic Fleet ships in transporting these specially trained troops, in landing them successfully on hostile shores, and in supporting their initial assaults, won the grudging praise of an enemy who had never understood the importance or true function of sea power.

All of these landings required preliminary build-up of supplies and subsequent feeding of additional materials and troops from the United States—responsibilities which continued to be taken by units of the Atlantic Fleet. Shipments for the initial invasion of Normandy alone piled up more than 16,000,000 tons of supplies in Britain during one year before D-day.

Another important aspect of the Battle of the Atlantic was the Allied campaign against blockade runners which shuttled high priority minerals and rubber from Japan to Germany, high grade steel and precision instruments from Germany to Japan. During 1941 and 1942, the enemy sent out 49 blockade-running freighters or tankers from Europe, and 40 of them made the round trip successfully. An Allied "barrier" of ships and planes across the narrows of the South Atlantic (greatly strengthened by our Army-Navy air base on Ascension) was gradually developed to maximum efficiency toward the end of 1943 and the beginning of 1944. Climax of this "barrier" strategy was achieved during the first week of 1944, when planes and surface craft of the Atlantic Fleet's South Atlantic Force pulled off a triple play and sank three blockade runners in three consecutive days. Forced to abandon such costly and fruitless endeavors, the enemy resorted to using his largest supply-submarines, and again suffered heavy losses. The only Japanese submarine sunk in the Atlantic was one of these supply-submarines, loaded with raw rubber, which was nailed by coordinated attacks of an Atlantic Fleet killer group built around a baby flat top and operating south of the Azores.

Final tabulations revealed that 126 enemy submarines were sunk by Atlantic Fleet units. On the defensive side of the ledger, Atlantic Fleet ships escorted 17,707 ships in convoy, of which only 17 were sunk and 14 damaged by enemy action. As the Battle of the Atlantic drew to successful conclusion, more than 800 ships, trained in the Atlantic Fleet, passed through the Panama Canal to join forces in the Pacific between 1 January and 16 May 1945.

JH Ingram

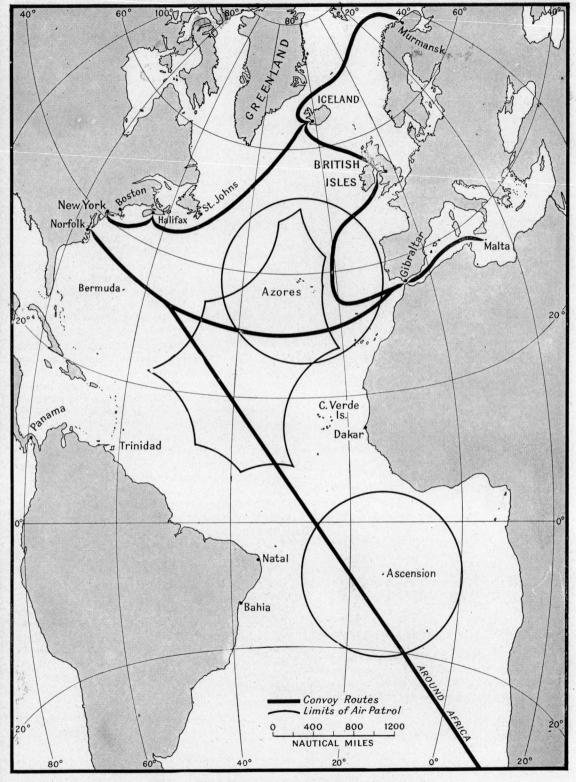

Chart of the Atlantic showing convoy lanes and
protective air patrols.

HEADQUARTERS OF THE U-BOAT HUNTERS. To combat German submarine activities in the Atlantic a huge headquarters was set up in New York City, as a nerve center of operation. Here, behind guarded and locked doors, at Eastern Sea Frontier headquarters scattered reports on Nazi undersea raiders, listings of convoys, and other sea and air intelligence data becomes an ever changing battle plan on the main situation board. UPPER. The control platform faces the main situation board. Here officer experts assemble and translate reports on ship and aircraft movement along the Atlantic coast. LOWER. "Pips" or plastic symbols indicate ships, convoys, and subs; "hamburgers" or cloth covered strips give data; colored lights show weather. These two photographs give just a hint of the infinite detail,

A WINDJAMMER ON PATROL. When the battle for the Atlantic began, the United States Coast Guard recruited large numbers of pleasure and fishing craft to supplement its own ships. These vessels patrolled for submarines and lent valuable aid to the regular fleet. Many civilians in the Auxiliary Coast Guard donated one day or so a week to do patrol duty in their own boats. Many of the Auxiliary boats met U-boats in action. ABOVE. Here a Navy gun crew aboard a U. S. aircraft carrier stand at battle stations as an Auxiliary schooner passes.

UNDERWATER NETWORK. Guarding our harbors and the ships within them in wartime is a small Navy within a Navy, the men and tenders who handle the anti-submarine and anti-torpedo nets, and anti-motor boat booms, which spread across the mouth of a port making it a safe haven.

The "Net Navy" has a highly specialized job. Nets may be more than two miles long, extending from the surface of the water to the bottom. Storms and overly strong currents may tear holes in the nets, necessitating instant repairs. Tenders notable for their two-horned prow, over which winch wires pass to raise and lower the heavy net equipment, must follow the advances of the war fleet. They spin out their webwork even while their big sisters are still blazing away in the battle for an enemy port. And, despite their size, tenders can fight—one of them opened the war for the "Net Navy" by shooting down a Japanese Zero at Pearl Harbor.

UPPER. One of these net tenders may be seen at a harbor entrance. A gate can be opened to let friendly vessels through; it is operated under the watchful supervision of the ship standing guard.

LOWER. Friend or foe, the Coast Guard rescued all possible survivors. Coast Guard planes scouted the oceans looking for submarines and survivors. Here, alongside a United States Coast Guard rescue plane, four oil-smeared U-boat survivors of the crew of a destroyed submarine wait to be helped aboard. The life raft had previously been dropped by a patrol blimp.

SOFTENED UP. While Japanese forces, in a kind of jungle blitzkrieg, were rapidly moving down the Malay peninsula by forced marches, infiltration, and bypassing British strong points, Singapore rocked under a severe aerial siege of more than a month. Thirty to ninety Japanese bombers raided the city and naval base from once to three times daily.

Prepared for assault from the sea, but vulnerable to attack from the air or from the jungles in the rear. Singapore's fate really was sealed when the battleship *Prince of Wales* (of Atlantic Charter fame) and the battle cruiser *Repulse* were trapped off the Malay coast without air cover by Japanese torpedo planes and sunk, December 10, 1941. Under cover of an intense artillery bombardment Japanese land forces crossed the river-like Strait of Johore the night of February

8-9. They then succeeded in isolating the naval base and reservoirs, after which Singapore had no choice but to surrender unconditionally February 15.

The fall of Singapore was described by Prime Minister Churchill as "the greatest disaster to British arms which history records." Not only did Japan secure the most powerful naval base in the Orient, outside of her own borders, but she also captured some 70,000 Imperial troops. Worst of all, the way lay wide open now for Japanese conquest of Burma and India, and the Allied forces in Southeast Asia were forced to fall back on the Netherlands East Indies, and, eventually, Australia.

ABOVE. Typical of the destruction wrought in Singapore by raiding Japanese bombers is this wrecked tower in the heart of the city.

THE FORTRESS FALLS! On the night of February 8, 1942, after fighting their way through the Malaysian jungles, the Japanese opened their all-out assault on Singapore Island. In rubber boats and over pontoon causeways, the Japanese troops swarmed ashore. With its reservoir captured, the great British fortress surrendered after seven days' fighting.

UPPER. This picture, from a Japanese propaganda booklet "Victory on the March" shows Japanese troops advancing over a bridge repaired by their engineers. LOWER. Also from a Japanese propaganda source—the "scorched earth" policy carried out by the British. Oil tanks are left in ruins to prevent the Japs making use of the oil.

FIGHT, AND RETIRE, AND FIGHT AGAIN! Just before the Japanese struck Manila, the small U.S. Asiatic Fleet had gone south and west to team up with Dutch and British ships based on Java. American destroyers made a brilliant repulse of Japanese advance units in Macassar Strait, but a joint American and Dutch force, including the American cruisers *Houston* and *Marblehead* headed for the Java Sea, only to come under a terrific bombing attack by Japanese planes during which both the *Houston* and *Marblehead* were badly damaged. At last on February 27 the weakened American-British-Dutch force, now under the command of the Dutch Admiral, Doorman, engaged in a last desperate attempt to halt the Japanese movement south. Under combined torpedo attack and gunfire from heavier gunned Japanese ships, two Dutch cruisers were sunk, and the *Houston* and other ships badly damaged. The two following nights the damaged allied ships attempted to escape through Soenda Strait. Heavy gunfire was heard from shore, but the allied ships never reached port. Later it was learned how the *Houston,* surrounded by Japanese cruisers, had gone down after a terrific night battle. It was practically the end of the old U. S. Asiatic Fleet. Only the *Marblehead* and a few destroyers escaped from the solid month of fighting.

ABOVE. This Jap aerial photograph shows the death throes of the gallant British heavy cruiser *Exeter,* one of Admiral Doorman's fleet, in the Battle of the Java Sea.

NAVAL OPPONENTS IN JAVA. The gallant campaign of the Java Sea which we fought with an inferiority of numbers in men and materiel ended on February 28 when the Japanese, in spite of the damages they suffered, landed on the north coast of Java. UPPER. The *Marblehead*, badly crippled after action in the Java Sea, ties up in a Java port for temporary repairs and cares for her wounded.

The seriously wounded crew members went by the hospital train on the left to safer terrain in the mountains. LOWER. Still another photograph from the Japanese propaganda booklet, "Victory on the March." This one bears the caption "Men of the undersea fleet sending off comrades leaving for action at sea to wreak havoc on enemy warships and shipping."

THE LAST MEN OUT OF CORREGIDOR. UPPER. The U.S. Naval Base at Olongapo, on the west coast of Luzon, one of the strategic positions which fell to the Japanese during the retreat. Before its evacuation, the Dewey floating drydock at the right was destroyed by U.S. forces. **LOWER.** Corregidor was the last ditch. Bataan had fallen on the 8th of April, and American forces put Cebu to the torch. In the last hours there was nothing for the naval men to do but scuttle their remaining vessels. A few men managed to escape in a PBY, and others, as shown in this photograph, navigated to Australia in a 36-foot launch. They flew a flag made from a red petticoat, a blue shirt, and white cloth.

THE FIGHTING RETREAT. It was a bitter time. Over-powered both in numbers and equipment, lacking in medical supplies and care, the American and Filipino forces were obliged to withdraw into the jungles of Bataan and resort to a delaying warfare. With little support, and employing troops but recently mobilized and organized into regimental groups, our forces executed an orderly retreat. American-Filipino troops struck back and slowed the advance of the numerically superior Japanese army with subterfuge and skillful rear guard action. Installations which might have been of use to the Japanese during their ad-vance or after their capture of the Philippines were destroyed. ABOVE. This picture shows Filipino soldiers preparing a bridge for demolition. The soldier in the foreground is distributing stocks of dynamite, and others in the picture are securing the dynamite to the bridge and wiring it. After the American-Filipino forces had established themselves on the peninsula the enemy drew his forces together quickly and launched severe attacks against the American garrison on Bataan. Our forces contested every river, slope, and valley, and the exploits of American fighting men on Bataan against terrific odds are history.

DEATH ON THE MARCH. The calculated Japanese campaign of brutality commenced as soon as the battle-spent American and Filipino soldiers surrendered. The "March of Death" began at daylight on April 10th, 1942 after thousands of prisoners had been herded together at Mariveles Air Field on Bataan.

The Japanese soldiers took all personal belongings from them and beheaded those who had Japanese tokens or money. In groups of from 500 to 1,000 men, the prisoners were marched off Bataan toward San Fernando, in Pampanga Province. The Japanese slapped and beat the prisoners with stocks, and throughout that scorchingly hot day gave them neither food nor water. Men recently killed

were lying along the roadside. At night the prisoners were crowded into enclosures too narrow to allow the men to lie down. During the first few days the stronger were not permitted to help the weaker, and those prisoners who fell met violent death.

On the 12th the Japanese introduced the prisoners to a form of torture which came to be known as the sun treatment. Prisoners were made to sit in the sun all day without cover. Some of the groups covered the 85 miles without so much as a spoonful of rice. Hundreds died along the way.

ABOVE. This photo, captured from the Japanese, shows American prisoners on the "March of Death" using improvised litters to carry those who were unable to walk.

THE JAP ADVANCES. UPPER. This photograph was taken from the Japanese propaganda booklet. "Victory on the March." The caption of the photo reads "Thrusting into enemy positions in the mountain fastness of Samat in Bataan, our stalwarts charge on." LOWER. This photograph, taken from the same source, appeared with the caption, "A wreckage of enemy armored cars left along the roadside of retreat." Despite the bitterness of the retreat, the American soldiers on Bataan retained their sense of humor. During the march, monkeys stirring in the trees were sometimes mistaken for Jap snipers. The Americans accordingly adopted a steadfast rule: "Only shoot the ones wearing glasses." It is this attitude which carried the Americans through to victory.

THE YELLOW TIDE. American forces left Manila without opposing the overwhelming numbers of the Japanese Army which swept toward the Philippine capital. Hourly the Japanese troops drew nearer to the city. From landings on the northwest and eastern coasts of Luzon others joined them. The First of January, 1942 was a dismal New Year's day in Manila. The civilian population awaited what they knew would soon arrive, and the fires from military installations which had been destroyed before the American withdrawal were symbolic of the people's hopelessness. This photograph from a Japanese propaganda booklet shows the march on Manila.

JAPS OCCUPY MANILA. Manila changed almost beyond recognition in the first days of her occupation by the Japanese. The streets at night became empty. American stores, pillaged of their goods, stood silent with windows nailed shut. Japanese civilians who days before had set off flares and other signals to guide Jap forces to radio stations and air fields were rewarded for their treachery by being granted sole access to marketing privileges and wholesale houses.

It was not long before the Japs were prospering—making up to 500 percent profit on goods resold to the very people from whom the goods had been looted. Steady streams of Jap trucks drove northward from Manila carting precious loot to ships in Lingayen Gulf, which then carried it back to Japan. The city lay quiet and frightened, still smoldering from fires begun by the incessant bombings of Jap squadron after squadron. The once beautiful and proud Cathedral of Santo Domingo lay a heap of ash and rubble.

Three thousand Americans were barbarously herded into a concentration camp set up on what was once the campus of Santo Tomas University, a seat of civilized learning. Jap sentries tossed them their meals like dogs, and shot any friendly Filipino caught attempting to smuggle food to them. Thousands of homeless Filipinos fled to the city's outskirts. Women, children, and aged men lived in the open air, preferring Bataan's bombings to life under the Nipponese new order.

That new order was symbolized by arrogant Jap officers with long curved swords at their sides strutting along Escota Street, pictured here, and by sentries with sharp bayonets standing guard in Manila's streets. In the jungle these refugees clustered about field kitchens where bakeries turned out the Army's supply of bread. For meat they slaughtered Caraboa, the Philippine beasts of burden. This Japanese photograph was captioned, "Escota Street, Manila's shopping center, returns to normal." Note the platoon of troops and the military trucks.

DESPERATE DAYS IN THE BAY OF BENGAL. The months following Pearl Harbor were critical times for the British in the Bay of Bengal. With Singapore, Java, and Sumatra lost to the Japanese, the British Navy was alerted to guard Ceylon, the next strongpoint the Japanese were expected to strike. British Naval resources in Indian waters were acutely limited. But Admiral Somerville, Commander of the British Far Eastern Fleet, assigned what hard pressed units he could spare to protect the island.

Late in March these units scouted to the southeast of Ceylon. But they made no contact with the Japanese, and had to return to Columbo and Trincomalee to refuel. The force had scarcely been dispersed when a Japanese force was sighted southeast of Ceylon, steaming for the island. Somerville immediately ordered his two cruisers HMS *Dorsetshire* and HMS *Cornwall* to clear harbor and rendezvous at sea with other forces.

Daybreak, April 5, the air attack on Columbo came. The harbor was clear of ships, and the Japanese planes were driven off without inflicting much damage. Later in the day another force of Japanese planes spotted the *Dorsetshire* and *Cornwall* at sea. The planes attacked and sank both ships within a few minutes. Four days later, on April 9, Jap planes struck at Trincomalee, and sank the old carrier HMS *Hermes* in the harbor. These were devastating blows to the small British forces, and Ceylon was laid open to invasion by the Japanese.

ABOVE. This photograph from Japanese sources is reputed to be the *Hermes* in her last tragic moments in the Bay of Bengal.

EARLY RETRIBUTION. It was March, 1942. After rolling through most of the gigantic British-Dutch-Australian island of New Guinea, the Japanese were now setting up naval bases in the northern ports. "Concentration of enemy naval units at Lae and Salamaua," came our intelligence report. On March 10 more than 100 planes took off from the carriers *Lexington* and *Yorktown.* Up from the south they sped to the attack—through wild, razor-backed ridges of the Owen Stanley Range, over 13,000-foot peaks, above savage lands uncharted and unexplored. Brown-skinned jungle tribesmen, some of them still head-hunters, looked up in wonder.

No warning reached the Japs until the planes were eight minutes away. Roaring from behind the high ridges, the *Lexington's* group swooped down on Salamaua, and the *Yorktown's* on Lae. First a torpedo squadron struck an enemy cruiser and three transports under way off Salamaua. Then six bombers sank the cruiser with a direct hit and five near misses. A division from the same squadron crippled a Jap transport.

At Lae a scouting squadron went after the harbor, sinking two large transports and setting a third afire. An enemy cruiser strove desperately to get out of the harbor, but two American planes pulled out of their dives and dropped their bombs. A 500-pound bomb struck the cruiser squarely abaft the second stack. She crawled toward the beach burning fiercely. Again and again the planes returned. A minesweeper burst into flames. Another destroyer was hit! Then a cruiser! Two other cruisers took three direct hits from dive-bombers!

ABOVE. All the while fighter planes strafed ships and ground installations, and accomplished the amazing feat of severely damaging, probably even sinking, an enemy destroyer by machine gun fire. The Japs were reeling. Two auxiliaries beached and burning! Another sinking fast! The seaplane tender *Kamoi* dead in the water after a torpedo plane attack! This was not what the Japs had planned at all, not at all! The Japs shook their fists as our carrier groups flew in formation back to their mother ships. Only one plane was missing.

AWAITING ORDERS. Order in hand, Captain Marc A. Mitscher, USN chats with Lt. Col. James H. Doolittle, USAAF before addressing the Doolittle raiders and giving them final tips about taking off from a heaving, salt sprayed air strip which was known only as "Shangri-la." The man who later made Task Force 58 appear as a new constellation in the Japanese heavens had little to say except "Good luck and good hunting."

This first attempt to launch medium bombers from a carrier sparked the confidence of the lads who Tokyo Rose was saying would "never fly over our house-tops." America's stalwarts stood ready to seek revenge for Pearl Harbor. People at home thirsted for a victory. "If only we could strike her cities they would burn like tinder." But how? "The Flying Fort hasn't the range." "A round trip to China via Japan?"—no bases in China big enough "What about Russia?"—Russia was busy.

It was April 18, 1942. Admiral Halsey was in command. The weather was overcast with frequent squalls and high winds—just the way the Admiral liked it. The original plan called for a dusk rendezvous 400 miles off Tokyo, a night strike at Japan and a landing on Chinese airfields early the next morning. But in dodging enemy gun-boats the task force ran into a Japanese patrol vessel. Dive-bombers sank her immediately. Had she warned Tokyo before going down? Col. Doolittle offered to let any man withdraw if he wished. Nobody accepted the offer. "Launch all bombers" blinked the signal bridge, ten hours early. Propellers whirred. Within a very few hours Americans were over the house-tops of Tokyo.

TOKYO BOUND. A crisp wind whips the sea. The bow leaps like a porpoise and plunges down again as the stern yaws and the deck wanders uneasily underfoot. Flight deck screws stand by, plane handlers ready to pull chocks. Plane captains manning fire bottles, give the all clear signal, "thumbs up." The landing signal officer concentrates on the ship's pitch—every plane must leave the deck as the bow nears the peak of its upswing.

Inside the Mitchell bombers, the flyers check their instruments and flight gear. The pilot is briefing the crew on "ditching" procedure to be used if they fail to make the China coast. As the landing signal officer waves him off in the photograph above, the pilot releases his brakes, steadies his controls and starts to sweat it out. One by one the sixteen North American B-25's roar up the flight deck of the USS *Hornet*. Bridge personnel flinch as each right wing-tip with four feet of grace whisks past the island structure. Spectactors along the gallery deck tense every muscle and hold their breath as the pilot strains forward in his seat, as if trying by his very will to coax the plane into the air.

At 0920 the first plane leaves the deck, Jimmy Doolittle at the controls. At 2120 he will bail out over China, but not before his squadron has made history. Tokyo, Yokohama, Osaka, Kobe . . . sixteen tons of bombs! The winged raiders from "Shangri-la" vanish as quickly as they came. The cost: eleven men killed or captured, five interned in Russia, sixty-four smuggled through by the Chinese underground. All planes lost. The hopes of free men, everywhere burn brighter, and the Jap begins to wonder.

JOURNEY INTO FEAR. Corregidor was doomed. But in those last weeks a job remained to be done—that of transporting the negotiable wealth of the Philippines to a location out of the reach of the Japanese. The task of assembling the vast amount of gold, silver and securities began in December. Americans and Filipinos collected the shipments and took them at night to the docks in Manila, and from there to the island fortress of Corregidor. Finally all the valuables lay in the vault at Corregidor, and there was nothing left to do but await the arrival of the submarine.

Then on February 3rd, under cover of darkness, the USS *Trout* poked her prow into Manila Bay, slipped past the Japanese guns and tied up alongside a pier at Fort Mills. There she unloaded anti-aircraft shells for the Army batteries and took aboard the cargo. Ton upon ton of gold and silver was placed aboard that night Army and Navy personnel, Treasury Department men, officials of the Philippine

Commonwealth, and Filipino stevedores helped carry the valuable metals to the dock and stow it away in the submarine. Loading operations ceased shortly before 4 a.m. The submarine cast off and went out three miles where she submerged and lay on the bottom throughout the daylight hours of the 4th. That night the sub rendezvoused with an auxiliary vessel in Manila Bay and took aboard the remainder of the consignment for the United States.

Then the submarine turned and headed for the Pacific base where she was to meet the cruiser chosen to carry the shipment on the final leg of its journey to the United States. This picture shows the transfer of the gold and silver from the USS *Trout* to the cruiser. It was a job well done. The strongly fortified enemy positions located near Corregidor constituted an ever-present threat to the submarine's safety. But with calm deliberation she performed her task and kept her rendezvous.

CORREGIDOR BEFORE THE FALL. The "unsinkable battleship" Corregidor, commonly believed to have been the most heavily fortified point in the world, was the pivotal point in Philippine defenses. A rocky mountainous island, four miles long and one mile wide, set squarely in the mouth of Manila Bay, it constituted the most readily defensible part of the whole Philippine archipelago. Corregidor held access to the rugged Bataan peninsula and barred the Japanese Navy from Manila Bay. Hollowed out of the hill, beneath the island surface, stood a hospital and caches for ammunition, spare parts, fuel, and food. A subterranean railway connected it with Caballo Island, a small rocky bluff standing about a mile out in the bay. In order to take these armored islands whose main defenses of six to twelve-inch guns rested on mountain crests and bluffs, Japan would have to use vastly superior manpower and a large measure of her air power diverted from other areas. ABOVE. Three officers of the garrison which defended the island against months of Japanese air and shore attacks make an inspection of defense positions during a lull in enemy attacks. Left to right: Lieut. Colonel John P. Adams, USMC, recipient of the Navy Cross; Colonel Samuel L. Howard, USMC, commander of the island's 1500 Marine defenders; and Major General George F. Moore, USA.

THEY WERE EXPENDABLE. Bataan had fallen on the 9th of April, and the epic resistance which had lasted for four months ended. Those of the American-Filipino forces who had not been killed or captured escaped to the island of Corregidor, where they continued to hold out. It was another great stand. The Japanese batteries on the mainland subjected Corregidor to intense artillery fire at point-blank range. This, together with heavy aerial bombardment, inflicted heavy casualties on the defenders and destroyed many of the island's military installations. Then came the 5th of May. After a particularly severe bombardment which swept away the beach defenses, Japanese troops crossed the narrow channel that separates Corregidor from the mainland and assaulted the island. Although outnumbered six to one, the defending forces succeeded in inflicting 60,000 casualties on the enemy. It was only after the defenders were physically exhausted by days and nights of continuous fighting that they finally gave up. ABOVE. This Japanese photograph shows the end of their stand before one of the underground shelters.

CORREGIDOR, FALLEN. This Japanese photograph reached the United States by way of Brazil. According to the Japs, this picture shows the desolation on the island fortress, the lines of prisoners, and the bomb-blasted terrain. The mangled palm trees, their blackened leaves hanging in shreds, gave no shade as the Philippine sun blazed down on the weary American captives trudging over the lacerated, debris-strewn earth. What the Japanese did not mention was the stomach-turning horror which the prisoners were to experience in the days and months ahead. For these heroic men the Japanese had designed a deliberate campaign of brutality. An American Army officer who was captured, but who later escaped, stated, "Though beaten, hungry and tired from the terrible last days of combat, though further resistance was hopeless, our American soldiers and their Filipino comrades in arms would not have surrendered had they known the fate in store for them." Japanese Generals Homma and Yamashita, who were responsible for the atrocities in the Philippines, have both faced juries and been found guilty of crimes against mankind. Homma was sentenced to be shot, Yamashita hanged. Replying to critics who questioned the justice of the Japanese Generals' fate, General MacArthur made the following statement: "A soldier, be he friend or foe, is charged with the protection of the weak and unarmed. It is the very essence and reason for his being. When he violates this sacred trust he not only profanes his entire cult but threatens the very fabric of international society."

THE BATTLE OF
THE CORAL SEA

By Vice-Admiral Aubrey W. Fitch, USN

THE face behind the mask of Japan had been dramatically revealed on December 7, and during the next four months her quick strides to the Southeast left the world wondering if Australia was soon to fall within her orbit of conquered territory. Control of the Coral Sea was a prerequisite for cutting the line of supply to Australia, and the Japanese Navy bade fair to achieve that control in the spring of 1942.

The task of stopping this Japanese drive to the South rested with a force of ships consisting of two carriers, eight cruisers, and eleven destroyers of our own Navy, and two Australian cruisers. On the morning of May 7th our ships were headed westward in search of an enemy force reported moving southward. At 0845 one of our scout planes reported sighting the enemy about 160 miles away. At 1130 a Jap carrier, the *Shoho*, became the target of dive bombers and torpedo planes from our carriers, the *Lexington* and the *Yorktown*. The fliers from the *Lexington* arrived on the scene first and scored several hits. As the *Lexington* air group withdrew, the fliers from the *Yorktown* launched their attack. In a matter of minutes, Lieutenant Commander Bob Dixon was able to make his famous report—"Scratch one flattop." The phrase later became standard for reporting the sinking of a carrier. So great was the destruction on the carrier that the last bomber pulled away and released his bomb at a light cruiser. He made a direct hit on the stern, and the ship sank rapidly.

THE SECOND DAY

THE climax of the battle was reached the following day. Early on the morning of the 8th another enemy force, including two carriers, was sighted by our scout planes. The *Yorktown* and *Lexington* again launched their planes. On the way to the target the fliers met the Japanese air group on its way to attack our task force. Unlike the previous day our pilots met strong fighter opposition as they approached the target. One of the *Yorktown* fighters, Lt. John F. Powers, had sworn that he would get a hit at any cost and made good his promise by diving to within several hundred feet of the enemy carrier's flight deck. When our air groups rendezvoused to return to their ships, a Japanese carrier, the *Shokaku*, had been seriously damaged.

At almost the identical moment that our pilots were launching their attack, we were being subjected to heavy attack by 105 Jap planes. Both of our carriers were hit. The *Yorktown* suffered considerable damage but was still capable of a maximum speed of 30 knots. The *Lexington* was less fortunate. Hit with bombs and torpedoes she was still able to maintain a speed of 24 knots, and returning pilots thought she had escaped attack. In the afternoon internal explosions, probably caused by gasoline fumes, rocked the ship, and fires were started which were soon beyond control. We found it necessary to give orders to abandon ship. The *Lexington* did not die easily and she sank only after a spread of torpedoes from one of our own destroyers was fired into her. Ninety-two percent of her crew was saved.

A TEMPERED VICTORY

THE acts of heroism are too numerous to mention. The tenacity and courage of the men was symbolized in the dogged devotion to duty of a group of sailors found manning a gun by Captain Sherman as he made a final inspection before leaving the ship. They had refused to abandon ship until ordered to do so.

As we saw the historic old *Lexington* sink, many of our men wept unashamedly. However there was reason to rejoice even at this dark moment for the Japanese had lost one carrier and one cruiser, and another of their carriers had been seriously damaged. More than sixty enemy planes had gone into the ocean. The Japanese drive toward Australia and New Zealand had been brought to a sharp halt, and by the time they were ready to renew the attack, our own forces had seized the offensive first at Midway and later at Guadalcanal.

Not until the excitement of battle had died away did we realize that this was the first major engagement in history in which the issue was decided without surface ships having exchanged a shot.

Aubrey W. Fitch

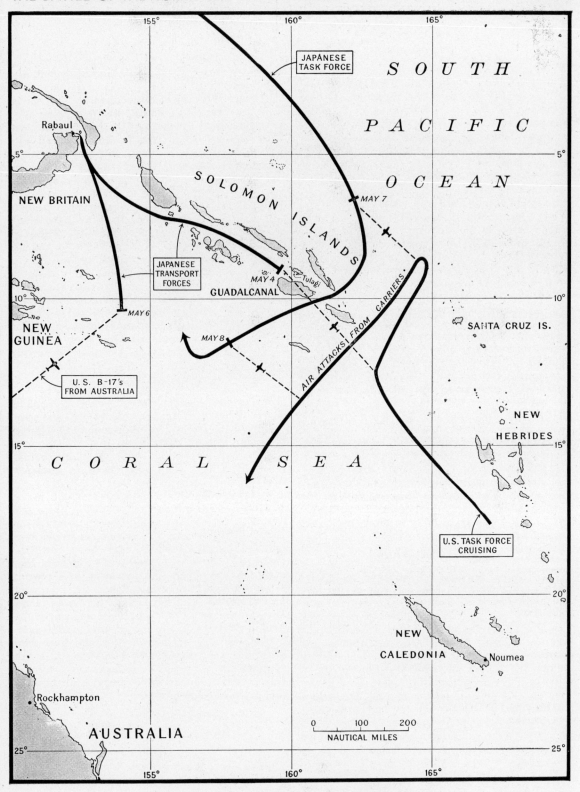

Chart showing the tracks of Japanese and American
forces in the Battle of the Coral Sea.

TURNING OF THE TIDE. The Battle of the Coral Sea was the first major engagement in naval history in which the issue was decided without surface ships having exchanged a shot. It was purely an air action, that is, aircraft against ships, with each side seeking to gain the upper hand by depriving the other of naval air support. By a strange coincidence both Japanese and American forces sought to accomplish the same thing at almost the same time by the same means. The resultant overlapping found our carrier groups striking the enemy carriers at almost the same instant that Japanese carrier-based planes were attacking the *Lexington* and *Yorktown*.

The Battle of the Coral Sea was really the highwater mark of Nippon's southward expansion to cut the American-Australian lifeline. Our air raids on Lae and Salamaua, in March 1942, hindered but did not stop the yellow tide of conquest, and by mid-April the Japs had footholds in New Guinea, New Britain, and the Solomon Islands that put them in a position to threaten all Melanesia and Australia itself.

The battle really began when intelligence reports indicated that the Japs had begun to occupy Florida Island, in the Solomons, going ashore from transports in Tulagi harbor. Rear Admiral Frank J. Fletcher, commander of our forces, immediately ordered planes from the *Yorktown* to attack, which they did (May 4), sinking seven enemy ships, damaging two others, and losing only three planes.

The second phase of the battle came on May 7, when the oiler *Neosho* and destroyer *Sims* were sunk by Japanese bombers. Rear Admiral Fletcher meanwhile joined forces with the task group commanded by Rear Admiral Aubrey W. Fitch, who later was to assume command of the combined task group. Intelligence reports again told of a large enemy fleet moving southward from New Guinea. It was not known whether the enemy objective was Port Moresby, or some point in the Solomons or beyond.

In the third phase of the battle, May 7, our planes spotted a Jap task force 20 miles northeast of Misima, sinking two ships, one of them the Jap carrier *Shoho,* with most of her personnel and planes. The climax of the four-day battle came, however, on May 8, when both the enemy and ourselves released large numbers of planes and headed for each other's carriers. This day's fighting, the heaviest, resulted in the loss of the *Lexington,* and damage to the *Yorktown* and to the Jap carrier *Shokaku.*

Despite the loss of one of four carriers in the Pacific, the battle was a U. S. Navy victory. The Japs, who lost more planes and men, withdrew northward.

LEXINGTON'S LAST FIGHT. No part of the Battle of the Coral Sea was as dramatic as the fight put up by the 33,000-ton aircraft carrier *Lexington,* first against attacking Japanese planes, and then against terrific internal explosions which several times were brought under control and then broke out again. When, reluctantly, it was realized that, even with the assistance of several destroyers to fight the fires, the situation was beyond control, Admiral Fitch directed Captain Sherman to abandon ship.

The stout old carrier, however, refused to sink, despite continuous explosions that showered the sea with flaming debris. So the destroyer *Phelps* was detailed to execute the coup de grace. Five torpedos were fired and the *Lexington* went down suddenly at 7:32 p.m.

UPPER LEFT. The crew of the *Lexington* slide down lines into the water when the order came to "abandon ship." The destroyer alongside, almost hidden in smoke, assisted in fire fighting efforts and took off many of the *Lexington's* wounded. A whaleboat and gig rescued scores from the water, and towed life rafts to the cruisers *Minneapolis* and *New Orleans,* standing by.

CENTER. A furious explosion seals the fate of the Lexington. The war heads of spare torpedoes, or the ready bomb storage on the hangar deck, probably went off in this blast. The small boat (left) is about to pick up Captain F. C. Sherman, commanding officer, who, true to the traditions of the sea, was last man to leave his stricken ship. Note the plane, blasted from the deck by the force of the explosion. The destroyers *Anderson, Hammann,* and *Morris* picked up many survivors, risking damage or destruction, because no one knew at what moment the fires aboard the *Lexington* might reach her main magazines.

ABOVE. Death throes of the mighty *Lex* as the fires reach the great gasoline supply tanks. In the attack that crippled the *Lexington* two Japanese torpedo bombers made hits, one torpedo exploding just forward of the port gun gallery, and the second further aft. Jap dive bombers, meanwhile, dropped a 1,000 pound bomb near the forward gun gallery, a 500-pound bomb on the port side, and a small bomb down the stack.

Fires were soon brought under control, and the *Lex* was steaming along at 25 knots when the explosion occurred that doomed the ship. At first believed a "sleeper bomb" it was finally decided that the blast was caused by an accumulation of gasoline vapors resulting from gasoline lines broken earlier in the day by the concussion of the bomb and torpedo hits. Ninety percent of the personnel was rescued.

JAP CARRIERS HIT. While Japanese planes were attacking the American carriers *Lexington* and *Yorktown* during the Battle of the Coral Sea, May 8, U. S. Navy planes from these ships were scoring hits on the home carriers of the enemy fliers. The task forces were about 170 miles apart at the time. The two Jap carriers, *Ryukaku* and *Shokako*, had as escorts a battleship or very large cruiser, three heavy cruisers, and four destroyers. Our planes made repeated hits with both bombs and torpedoes, but subsequent developments showed that neither carrier had gone down. The *Shokaku*, however, was seriously damaged and might have been sunk if it had not been lost in the heavy overcast.

UPPER. The *Shoho* takes a torpedo hit from a U. S. Navy plane. In the action of May 7 this Japanese carrier was at first mistaken for the *Ryukaku*. Bomber and torpedo planes from both the *Lexington* and the *Yorktown* scored many times on the *Shoho*, approaching the ship closely through the smoke resulting from the first attack. Within a few minutes the enemy carrier slid under the surface.

LOWER. Twisting and turning in a giant "S" maneuver, the Japanese carrier *Shokako* attempts to avoid torpedoes dropped by U. S. Navy planes. Spray from the near-misses of Navy bombs showers her flight deck.

BOMBER GOES ABOARD. From the huge 35,000 ton carriers, to the fast, compact escort carriers the Navy's floating airports played an exceedingly important part in the winning of the war. Flying from these floating fields U. S. Naval pilots protected convoys, sank submarines, and routed both the Japanese carrier and land-based planes in the Western Pacific. UPPER. Here is a Grumman Avenger being swung aboard a U. S. carrier. After it is brought aboard, it is stored below on the hangar deck. At a signal these planes are carried to the flight deck by elevators. LOWER. In about thirty minutes, including warm up and take off time, the planes can be in the air from the hangar deck.

CARRIER LIFE. UPPER LEFT. Here in the radar plot room aboard on *Essex* class aircraft carrier, Naval experts plot death and destruction for Japan. This photograph illustrates the tension and cold calculation of men who work with information provided by radar's "extra-sensory" perceptions. Radar was first developed by two scientists at the Naval Research Laboratory in the summer of 1922. Since then it has undergone amazingly rapid growth. First used to detect nearby surface objects in poor visibility, radar was soon insuring long-range detection of airborne objects, fire control accuracy, safety in navigation, and long-distance identification of planes and ships. LOWER LEFT. While their buddies in the radar plot room lay plans for the destruction of the enemy, these sailors turn to on the lowly but essential work of the ship's laundry. Clean clothes aboard ship provide excellent insurance against poor health and poor morale. Complete laundries similar to this one on the *Saratoga* operate aboard all larger ships, and whenever possible furnish service also to smaller craft such as destroyers, minesweepers, and landing craft.

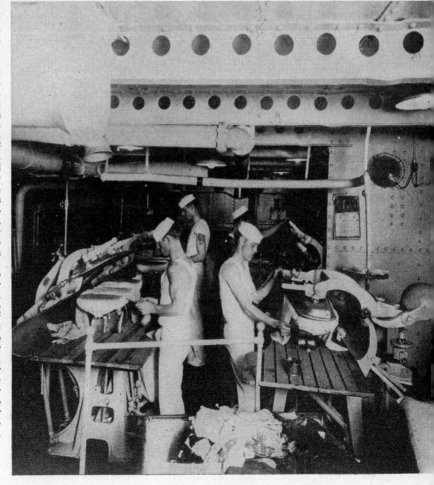

CARRIER LIFE. UPPER CENTER. The huge flight deck of aircraft carriers offers an opportunity for the men aboard to enjoy more extensive athletics than on other types of ships. When not in battle zones the men play touch football, baseball, and other competitive sports. Boxing and wrestling rings are often set up, giving an opportunity to participate and also watch these sports. From such competitive sports the U.S. Navy has produced several World's Champions. Here bluejackets go through their daily morning calisthenics. UPPER RIGHT. Garbed in asbestos suits, "hot papas," as firefighters are known aboard carriers, await the landing of planes aloft on a mission. These suits are equipped with their own oxygen breathing devices enabling the men to walk into all but the hottest flames to get right at the source of the fire. LOWER RIGHT. A close-up view of the radio-radar antenna installation atop the aircraft carrier *Lexington*. Following is the key to identifying numbers on the photograph: 1-9, radio communications; 10, air-search and height finder radar; 11, radio communications; 12, radar test equipment; 13, surface search radar; 14, radio communication; 15, homing beacon (radar); 16-20, radio communications; 21, air-search radar; 22, radio homing beacon; 23, air search radar; 24-25, radio communications; 26, identification radar; 27-28, radio communications.

THE BATTLE OF
MIDWAY

By Vice-Admiral Frank J. Fletcher, USN

THROUGHOUT the first half of 1942 our position in the Pacific was extremely precarious. Our damage and losses at Pearl Harbor had not yet been replaced by newly constructed ships. What remained of our Pacific Fleet and our little Asiatic Fleet had to perform miracles to prevent the vastly superior Japanese fleets from surging over the whole Pacific.

Our small Asiatic Fleet performed a first miracle of delaying actions in the Philippines and Dutch East Indies, even at the cost of almost all its ships. Our small carrier and cruiser force at Coral Sea performed a second miracle in turning back the Japanese threat at Australia and New Zealand. The third miracle occurred at Midway, in June, 1942.

Up until then the Japanese Navy, instead of pressing an aggressive offensive against Hawaii and even Panama or the West Coast, had allowed itself to be pressed into the service of the Japanese Army in its sweep of territorial conquest through The Philippines, Malaysia, the Dutch East Indies, Burma, and the Solomons. Now our Naval Intelligence learned that the Japanese Navy, counting on our losses and dispersed forces in the Southwest Pacific, planned a bold stroke at gaining control of the northern and central, and even eastern Pacific—perhaps a stroke at Hawaii, and Alaska itself.

Practically our whole remaining force in the Pacific was hurriedly assembled at Pearl Harbor, including even the damaged Yorktown, hurriedly recalled from the Coral Sea. Our total forces were formed into two task forces, these consisting of the carriers Enterprise, Yorktown, and Hornet, plus 7 heavy cruisers, 1 light cruiser, 14 destroyers, and about 20 submarines. Scouting and patrol lines were assembled westward of Midway Island, our small island outpost west and north of Hawaii. Also available were a Marine Corps air group at Midway, and Army bombers from Hawaii.

THE ENEMY IS SIGHTED

ON JUNE 3 a large enemy attack force was sighted several hundred miles southwest of Midway and later in the same afternoon were bombed by Army B-17's. On the following morning the main enemy attack force including carriers, battleships, cruisers, destroyers, and transports, was sighted and attacked immediately by Army, Navy, and Marine Corps planes from Midway which severely damaged one carrier. Our carriers north of Midway also launched first torpedo planes, and then dive bombers against the enemy. Torpedo Squadron Eight from the Hornet was shot down to the last plane, but only after making several hits on four enemy carriers. The other torpedo squadrons and dive bombers made further hits, as a result of which two enemy carriers were set on fire and put out of commission, and a third badly damaged. This third carrier was sunk the next day by our submarine Nautilus.

Meanwhile enemy planes had attacked Midway, but suffered heavy losses from our own planes and anti-aircraft fire. Planes from the remaining Japanese aircraft attacked the Yorktown and were annihilated, but only after making three bomb hits. Enemy torpedo planes shortly afterward made two torpedo hits on the damaged Yorktown which left her in a sinking condition. The only un-damaged Japanese carrier was found and attacked by carrier planes from the Yorktown and Hornet, and left in a mass of flames. By now two Japanese battleships and two cruisers had also been hit and damaged by our dive bombers, and the whole Japanese force turned in full retirement.

THE JAPS ARE DEFEATED

ON the two following days planes from the Hornet and the Enterprise located the fleeing enemy and further damaged four cruisers and a destroyer. Due to poor visibility and the dispersal of the fleeing Japanese ships, we were unable to come up with them again, and the battle was at an end.

This battle, fought almost entirely by air and during which the opposing surface ships never even sighted each other, was the first decisive defeat suffered by the Japanese Navy in 350 years. But, more important, it ended the period of Japanese offensive activity in the Pacific, removed the threat to Hawaii and the West Coast, and paved the way for our assumption of the offensive in the Pacific—an offensive that through successive stages saw us reconquer the Solomon Islands, Guam, and the Philippines, capture Tarawa, Saipan, Iwo Jima, and Okinawa, break the back of the Japanese Fleet in the Battle of the Philippine Sea and the Battle of Leyte Gulf, and eventually blockade and bomb Japan into submission from her own home waters.

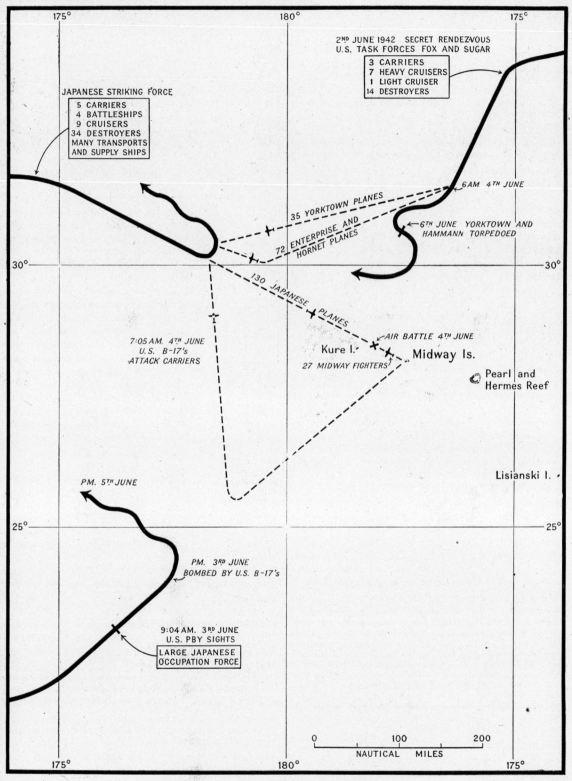

2ND JUNE 1942 SECRET RENDEZVOUS
U.S. TASK FORCES FOX AND SUGAR

> 3 CARRIERS
> 7 HEAVY CRUISERS
> 1 LIGHT CRUISER
> 14 DESTROYERS

JAPANESE STRIKING FORCE

> 5 CARRIERS
> 4 BATTLESHIPS
> 9 CRUISERS
> 34 DESTROYERS
> MANY TRANSPORTS
> AND SUPPLY SHIPS

6AM 4TH JUNE

35 YORKTOWN PLANES

6TH JUNE YORKTOWN AND
HAMMANN TORPEDOED

72 ENTERPRISE AND
HORNET PLANES

130 JAPANESE PLANES

7:05 A.M. 4TH JUNE
U.S. B-17's
ATTACK CARRIERS

AIR BATTLE 4TH JUNE

Kure I.   Midway Is.

27 MIDWAY FIGHTERS

Pearl and
Hermes Reef

Lisianski I.

P.M. 5TH JUNE

P.M. 3RD JUNE
BOMBED BY U.S. B-17's

9:04 A.M. 3RD JUNE
U.S. PBY SIGHTS

> LARGE JAPANESE
> OCCUPATION FORCE

0   100   200
NAUTICAL   MILES

Chart showing the tracks of the Japanese and
American forces in the Battle of Midway.

PAYING BACK FOR PEARL HARBOR. Within a month after the Battle of the Coral Sea U. S. Navy air-power again demonstrated the vital part it was to play in the war. On June 3, under cover of a Japanese feint attack at Dutch Harbor in Alaska, two powerful Japanese fleets, including everything from carriers and battleships, struck at Midway Island on the path to Hawaii. To intercept it we had rushed all our available forces in the Pacific, even including the carrier *Yorktown,* barely repaired after her Coral Sea damage, but even so the Japanese forces far outnumbered ours.

For three days an homeric struggle ensued between the two opponents, never in sight of each other, but hurling their fighter, torpedo, and bomber planes at each other through the air. We lost the *Yorktown* and a destroyer but

the Japanese lost two heavy cruisers, three destroyers, and four of the carriers that had taken part in the Pearl Harbor raid, besides numerous other ships damaged. It was almost entirely a victory of U. S. Navy carrier and Marine Corps land-based dive-bombers, fighters, and torpedo planes.

ABOVE. The picture, an enlargement from a 16mm original, shows Navy "Dauntless" dive bombers making a bombing run on the burning Japanese ship at right center. This first major Japanese defeat in 350 years cost the Japanese 4800 personnel killed and ship losses far exceeding even the German losses in the great Battle of Jutland. From that moment Japanese forward progress ceased and the United States Navy assumed the offensive never to be checked short of total victory.

HOT SPOT OF BATTLE. Tiny Midway knew what it was to be the center of a battlefield those June days in 1942 when fierce fighting raged over it and around it for hundreds of miles. From its runways American planes took off to hurl themselves through Japanese flak and fighter screens to get at the ships beyond. And down at the runways and oil tanks and other installations Japanese planes came diving from above with bombs and incendiaries in return. UPPER. A general view of the damage done on Midway Island by the Japanese air attack. LOWER. A view of the oil storage tanks hit and burning after the Japanese attack on the island. The gooney birds in the foreground seem undisturbed.

SWAN SONG — AMERICAN AND JAPANESE. UPPER. Smoke billowing from her island, the *Yorktown* lists heavily after withstanding an attack by Japanese aircraft during the Battle of Midway. Two days later, while under tow, she was hit again. This time it was two torpedoes from the same Japanese submarine which sank the *Yorktown's* escort destroyer, the *Hammann*. In spite of valiant efforts to keep the 19,900-ton ship afloat she went down with colors flying on June 7, 1942. LOWER. The Japanese heavy cruiser *Mikuma*, an 8500 ton ship of the *Mogami* class. These cruisers were fitted shortly before the war to carry 8" guns, in unabashed violation of the Washington Treaty. The *Mikuma*, bombed almost beyond recognition by U.S. Navy planes, found little use for guns.

FIREFIGHTING ABOARD A CARRIER. The most modern scientific equipment, and men specially trained in the Navy's fire-fighter schools are ready for crash landings aboard a carrier. UPPER. An F4U flames wildly after crash landing aboard an *Essex*-class carrier. Shot up by enemy action, the plane landed out of control and was cut in two just aft of the cockpit. Within seconds fire-fighters are on the scene, the crew has been rescued, and foamite is sprayed on the fire. LOWER. The fire is brought under control. Various agents are used to extinguish fires depending on the material involved. Foamite smothers burning gasoline very rapidly.

FROM THE BLUE OF ICE TO THE BLUE OF OCEAN. UPPER. A Catalina flying boat patrols its lonesome way over the frozen wastes of the North. LOWER. A seaplane tender "mothers" PT boats as well as seaplanes. A Catalina is tied up astern and three PT boats are moored alongside. The tender has provisions for refueling, replenishing, and minor repairs, as well as an opportunity for the crews to relax in more spacious quarters.

THE FLEET'S EYES SCOUR THE OCEANS. Slower, less glamorous sisters of the fighter planes, the Navy's patrol bombers played a role in the war at sea. But the story of these fleet air units is a mixture of gallantry and boredom. For each brief, heroic moment, there were interminable hours of uneventful patrols over the vast oceans. From Casablanca to the Philippines Navy patrol bombers swept thousands of miles of ocean, keeping watch for the enemy. They covered column after column of convoys in the sea-planes. They spotted and rescued countless survivors of sinkings and forced landings.

A patrol bombing squadron, the famous Pat Wing 10, was the sole Naval air unit in the Philippines when the Japs overran the islands in the fateful December days of 1941. Starting out with forty patrol bombers, the heroic men of this squadron fought a gallant withdrawing action, and ended ninety days later with only two planes. The Navy fliers, carefully trained in identification of surface craft, gave accurate warning of the approaching enemy units. Had sufficient forces been available to act on these reports, the outcome of the Philippine campaign would have been different.

Development of patrol bombers as seaplanes has been exclusively a Naval task. A Navy patrol bomber, the NC-4, made the first Atlantic air crossing in 1919. ABOVE. A PBM, the Martin Mariner, a post-Pearl Harbor version of a patrol bomber, is shown being hauled from the water onto a ramp. Powered with two 1,700 horsepower engines, it can develop a speed of around 200 miles per hour and has a range of over 3000 miles.

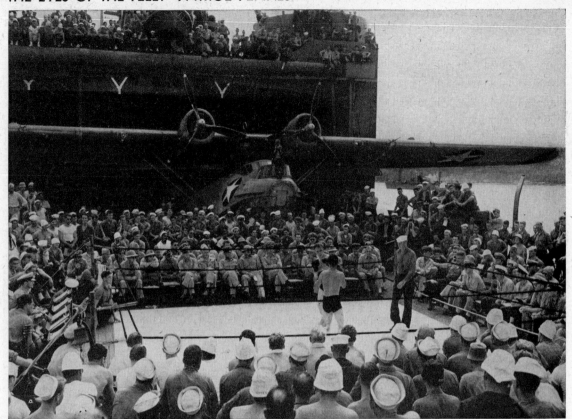

FOG, STORM, MORE FOG...BUT THE "CATS" STALK THE ENEMY. In the fogbound, stormridden wastes of the Aleutian Islands the Navy's patrol bombers, the famous PBY's or Catalinas, passed their most gruelling tests. In weather so continuously bad that "even the seagulls were walking," the Navy's "Cats" hunted down the enemy.

In the summer of 1942, amid utmost secrecy, two airports were constructed in the eastern islands to defend the important and vulnerable base at Dutch Harbor. The attack, though long anticipated, came as a momentary surprise. Under cover of the never-lifting fogs, the Japanese assault fleet crept in. Just before dawn on June 3, coincident with the strike at Midway, Jap carrier-based planes swept in to bomb and strafe Dutch Harbor. Several ships, including the Catalinas' own tender, lay in port. Blasting away at the attackers they weighed anchor, got under way, and took evading action. After the first wave of Jap planes had withdrawn, Catalinas from the Patrol Wing sped off to search for the attacking force. One of them had just spotted a lurking enemy carrier to the south when the murk closed in again and prevented an attack.

UPPER LEFT. A Catalina returning from patrol in the Aleutians ready to be hauled alongside her tender. Tenders make advance operations possible when no shore facilities are available. They supply oil and gasoline, serve as repair shops, and provide facilities for berthing and messing the plane crews. LOWER LEFT. A Catalina fueling preparatory to a patrol. UPPER RIGHT. Officers and men enjoy a boxing bout aboard the tender. LOWER RIGHT. A member of the PBY's crew prepares to "chow down" in flight.

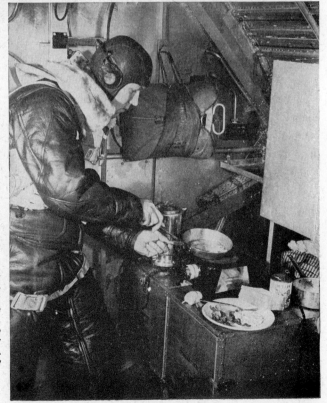

JAPANESE SNEAK RAID ON DUTCH HARBOR. It was the day after the first attack on Dutch Harbor, June 4, 1942. Out of the arctic summer skies, Jap Navy Zeros suddenly swung in from their carriers to deliver another blow ar Dutch Harbor. Abandoning the idea of seizing the base, the Japs were now intent on destroying it. Shore ack-ack opened up on the attacking planes. The enemy did not relent. High level bombers loomed up through the clouds and let go their heavy explosives and incendiaries. Fires blazed in several buildings. The old station ship *Northwestern*, above, used as a workers' barracks, was hit, and burned on the beach.

Slowly the Jap bombers circled for another try. They anticipated little air opposition. But then out of the west, more planes suddenly appeared. They were army fighters: Warhawks, new Lightnings, Marauder medium bombers. They plunged into the Jap attackers, their machine guns biting away. One enemy observation plane went down under their attack. Another, wounded, limped away. The Jap flyers were stunned. They turned and fled westward, wondering where all our planes had come from. The two airfields secretly built in March paid their dividends. In their fleeing haste, some Japs actually flew over the secret airfield on Unmak, the island to the west of Dutch Harbor. P-40s

immediately jumped on them, destroying three Jap dive-bombers and a Zero.

In the meantime, offshore, Navy Catalinas and Army planes were ferreting out the assault fleet. They landed a few attacks, but they were battling two forces: the Japs and the weather. Several PBY's and Army fortresses failed to return. When the weather permitted, the Catalinas found that the assault forces had fled westward. As second choice the Japs had contented themselves by occupying Kiska and Attu at the extreme western end of the Aleutians.

Additional Navy "Cats" were rounded up from their base at San Diego, California. A short four days after leaving their home base, they were in the midst of the fog and fighting. During the first hectic days, the crew of the Catalinas' tender worked 36 hours without sleep. One pilot flew nineteen hours out of twenty-four. Attacks against the Japs in Kiska harbor began immediately. Lumbering Catalinas, together with the Army Fortresses and Liberators, bombed the Jap force on June 10 and 11, undeterred by the heavy anti-aircraft fire. One Liberator, dropping below the clouds at 2000 feet, took a hit. The others were forced to 18,000 feet to drop their bombs, but nevertheless scored a hit on a Jap cruiser. As consistently as the weather allowed our planes kept up attacks from Dutch Harbor.

NIPPONESE NEW ORDER. Strict military rule prevailed throughout the Jap-occupied Philippines. Japanese meted out punishments of torture or death for deeds of "misbehavior" such as walking behind a Japanese sentry or touching ropes that marked off forbidden zones. The numerous prohibitory signs were difficult to understand because they were written in Japanese. In addition to individual looting, the Japanese carried out a well-calculated, systematic denuding of Philippine resources. Their propaganda booklets proudly carried pictures like the ones shown here. UPPER. "Shipping copper to Japan from Lapulapu in the Philippines." LOWER. "Teak wood up in a Manila lumber yard and soon to be transformed into ships and what have you." The Japs knew how to exploit their victims.

NON-STOP LIFELINE. During the war the U. S. Navy had many so-called "secret weapons." Some were devices, some simply "know how," and some were a combination of both. Refueling while under way at sea was such a combination, and photographs of the rig used were withheld until almost the end of the war. But refueling is more than rig. Good seamanship is involved to avoid collisions, and specially-trained crews must know exactly how to handle lines, hose, tackle, etc.

Long before Pearl Harbor, the Navy, aware of the vastness of the Pacific and the distances between its far scattered bases, perfected the technique for fueling at sea so that, in the event of war, ships might not be limited to short operational raids from shore bases. Soon refueling at sea was a routine exercise. When war came, and most of our Pacific fleet was incapacitated in Pearl Harbor, the fast carrier task force became our only means of taking the offensive, even briefly. Repeatedly they steamed deep into enemy-held waters on strikes of longer range than had ever been known, because they could rendezvous with our oilers and keep going for weeks at a time.

Puzzled Japs must have thought we had more ships in the area than their intelligence reports indicated! Calling for the smartest kind of seamanship, fueling at sea would be hazardous even on calm days were it not for skilfully trained crews. In heavy seas there is always real danger, for ships must be kept close alongside each other for the duration of the fueling. Both vessels must keep headway, too, because ships refueling at sea are "sitting ducks" for enemy submarines.

LEFT. The USS *Housatonic*, oiler, refuels the USS *Ranger*, carrier, at sea. After towing cables and breast lines are rigged, the heavy fuel hose is passed over. Fitted in a saddle, which is suspended from a boom on the tanker, the hose rides along a messenger line. As the ships glide together slack is taken up, to prevent the hose from dragging in the water; if the gap widens, the hose is eased away.

UP AND AWAY. The come-back of lighter-than-air ships after the stigma of the disasters in the 1930's was a direct result of the war. Patrol blimps, operated exclusively by the Navy, covered thousands of miles of convoy lanes from our east and west coasts. Made of rubberized cotton and inflated with non-inflammable helium gas, they are relatively cheap and easy to build. A characteristic of the blimps is their ability to maneuver at slow speeds, which made them particularly suitable for spotting enemy submarines lurking off our coasts.

Balloon training provides valuable experience for lighter-than-air pilot trainees. It instructs them in the idiosyncrasies of air currents, and gives them the "feel" of the powered blimps which they must learn to fly. ABOVE. At the Navy's balloon school at Moffett Field, Calif., a free balloon strains at the ropes.

SUB BUSTER IN ACTION. Patrol blimps, carrying crews of eight or more men, have a cruising radius of 1500 miles. It is tedious work to remain on the lookout for submarines hour after hour above the vast stretches of ocean. Observers alternate every two hours, and spend off-time relaxing or sleeping on bunks slung in the blimp's gondola. Equipment includes a few depth bombs and machine guns. The blimp's greatest value is in its reconnaissance. UPPER. An echelon of blimps glides through maneuvers near Moffett Field, California. LOWER. A blimp guides a nearby Coast Guard cutter to the scene of a suspected enemy submarine. The cutter has just dropped a pattern of depth charges.

THE NAVY NURSE CORPS

By Sue S. Dauser, Captain (NC) USN

ESTABLISHED in 1907, the Navy Nurse Corps began to expand in 1939 from a total membership of 442 to over 11,000 by July, 1945. The Navy Nurse served in the Caribbean, in Central and South American Republics, and in the British Isles, North Africa and Sicily. She went with the Navy's many fleets and task forces over all the oceans, aboard twelve hospital ships and many ambulance planes.

The Navy Nurse cared for the wounded and sick in prison camps as in hospitals; she taught Corpsmen, Cadet Nurses, and Waves the skills of

nursing; she assisted the medical and surgeons; she flew with the wounded from target areas to base hospitals; she set up schools and trained native nurses on the islands of the Pacific, as well as Brazilian flight nurses in Rio de Janeiro. She served wherever she was needed—at 364 stations at home and overseas.

In recognition of their service Navy Nurses received many military awards during World War II, among them one Distinguished Service Medal, one Legion of Merit, 14 Bronze Star Medals, and 11 Gold Stars in lieu of second Bronze Star Medals.

Sue S Dauser

THE WOMEN'S RESERVE, UNITED STATES NAVAL RESERVE
WAVES

By Captain Jean T. Palmer, USNR(W)

THE Women's Reserve of the United States Naval Reserve was established on July 30, 1942 by an Act of Congress, thus permitting Waves (Women Accepted for Volunteer Emergency Service) to fill shore billets and release men for combat duty. The first Wave, and Director of the Women's Reserve until February 1946 was Captain Mildred McAfee Horton, under whose leadership the organization advanced to a peak strength of 86,000 in August 1945.

Training for Waves included a recruit school in New York City and a school for midshipmen in Northampton, Massachusetts. Advanced courses at more than 40 naval activities equipped enlisted Waves for such specialized duties as link trainer

instructor, pharmacist's mate, radioman, storekeeper, yeoman, and gunnery instructor. Forty different ratings are open to enlisted women. At advanced schools officers were prepared for duties in aerology, technical and administrative radar, air combat information, Japanese language, communications, supply, and link celestial navigation instruction as well as actual navigation officers.

At the time of the Japanese surrender there were 4,000 on duty in Hawaii. On V-J Day Waves were on duty at 900 shore stations in the United States and Hawaii. Nearly 20,000 Waves were serving in the Washington, D. C. area, and in the Navy Department 55 percent of its military personnel were Waves.

Jean T. Palmer

SPARS' WARTIME SERVICE

By Captain Dorothy C. Stratton, USCGR(W)

ORGANIZED November 23, 1942 the Spars numbered nearly 10,000 at the peak of their strength. Spars served as commissioned officers and in 30 different ratings, including radarman, aerographer, printer, musician, radioman, carpenter's mate, parachute rigger, photographer's mate, ship's cook, yeoman, storekeeper, barker, tailor, and all the seamen ratings up to and including chief boatswain's mate. Officers filled nearly every type of shore establishment billet, but were particularly active in communications and pay and supply work.

Releasing men for sea duty, Spars took over jobs at district offices, repair bases, air stations, radio stations, captain of the port offices, and other shore stations throughout the country. The greatest concentration was at Coast Guard Headquarters where over 1,000 Spars were on duty. More than 450 were assigned to jobs in Hawaii and Alaska.

The Spars were an integral part of the Coast Guard subject to the same regulations, entitled to the same privileges as the men of the service, and receiving similar ratings and pay.

Dorothy C. Stratton

THE U. S. MARINE CORPS WOMEN'S RESERVE

By Colonel Ruth Cheney Streeter, USMCR

THEY will not be an auxiliary organization. They will not be a separate command. They will be Marines, an integral part of the Corps." Those were the policies established by the U. S. Marine Corps when on 13 February 1943, it activated the Women's Reserve.

If women Marines had not been present at all major posts and stations in the continental United States and Hawaii, carrying much of the burden of administration, training, repair, and supply services, it would have been necessary to hold men Marines back from the fighting for such purposes. And in order that they might realize their role as supporting members of a combat team, it was part of their indoctrination in the Corps to study the organization of a rifle platoon and see demonstrated all weapons used by the fighting Marines.

Office work was only one of their innumerable duties. They worked on airplane engines, they drove trucks, they were control tower operators, they were photographers—indeed, there was hardly a section of any of the major Marine Corps bases which did not have its share of women Marines hard at work. Although the old-time marines were sceptical at first, they soon accepted the women.

Wherever they served, the members of the Women's Reserve never forgot their proud title, "We are Marines."

Ruth Cheney Streeter

NO POWDER PUFF JOB. Not all Waves and Women Marines worked in offices on the Navy's home front. Nearly every naval activity in the continental United States had its quota of women reservists. From pharmacist's mates to aviation machinist's mates, the Navy's requirements found as great a variety of talents in the Women's Reserve as in the Men's. Almost one fourth of the Women's Reserve are attached to Naval air activities. They overhaul engines, they run Link trainers, they teach blind flying to future aviators. Because of the excellence of their work the Navy had no hesitation in assigning members of the Women's Reserve to man Navy shore establishments so that thousands of men who would not otherwise have seen combat could help fight the Navy's battles. UPPER. Members of the Marine Corps Women's Reserve taking a course at the Station Ordnance School at Quantico, Va., position a depth charge as they prepare to load and arm it in the bay of a plane. LEFT. Here at the Jacksonville Naval Air Station, three aviation machinist's mates work on an SNJ training plane. All are graduates of the Naval Air Technical Training Center, at Norman, Oklahoma where they spent four months learning to repair and overhaul airplane engines. These girls scored high in mechanical aptitude.

EIGHTY-SIX THOUSAND WAVES CELEBRATE THIRD ANNIVERSARY. At the inception of the Wave program, Mildred McAfee, President of Wellesley College, was commissioned Lieutenant Commander and head of the Women's Reserve. Under her guidance and under the pressure of the need for manpower, the organization swelled from its original 10,000 to 86,000 on its third birthday, July 30, 1945. Waves at this time composed 18 percent of the total naval personnel assigned to shore bases. They filled 38 enlisted ratings and a wide variety of both line and staff officer assignments. They have done their work so thoroughly that the Navy's new plan for a large reserve includes women as an essential element. UPPER. Captain McAfee is greeted upon her arrival in Hawaii by Waves stationed at a naval air base on the island. Despite their masculine jobs, these girls maintained their feminine appearance in smartly designed, stylish uniforms. RIGHT. Mysteries of airplane motors hold no terror for these girls, both of them aviation machinist's mates. They have proved that they can do as good a job as men in what used to be considered strictly a man's field. The war showed that women's sensitive fingers and delicate touch were better than men's for many kinds of detailed work.

NAVY WAVES TAKE TO THE AIR. The Navy has classified eighty Wave officers as Naval Air Navigators. Proudly displaying navigator's wings on their uniforms, they are the first women in the U.S. military organization entitled to perform duties as part of a military crew. While these Waves were trained primarily to replace male navigators assigned to sea duty, they have already proved their versatility in every phase of air navigation, and are serving at present as instructors. They may in addition be assigned trans-ocean duty in some areas. During their training period at schools in Hollywood, Fla., and Shawnee, Okla., the Waves studied in the same classes as Navy men. They received the navigation training, flew the same cross country check flights, and graduated in the same classes. ABOVE A Wave navigator walks to her plane at the U.S. Naval Air Station at Alameda, Calif.

AN ENEMY TOE-HOLD. The Jap occupation of Kiska in June 1942 was a strategic move. It prevented us from using this westernmost Aleutian island as a harbor and air base, and it placed us on the defensive in an area where we had expected to take the offensive. The Japs began immediately to build a base. Our air attacks continued incessantly for several weeks following our first raid on June 10. Several hits on enemy vessels were claimed during this time, but the only accredited sinking is that of one trans-port on June 18. ABOVE. The transport, burning badly, lists after being hit. In July air raids were supplemented by daring submarine attacks. On August 7, a Navy surface force poked through the fog to within a few miles of Kiska. Undetected, our ships opened up with their batteries and pounded enemy installations for twenty minutes. The surprised Japanese put up no effective opposition, and our accurate fire sank several of their ships. But the real strike against the Aleutians was to come later.

DIEPPE—FORETASTE OF INVASION. One of the largest combined operations carried out between the retreat from France and the invasion of the Continent in June of 1944, was the "reconnaissance in force" made by Canadian Commandos at Dieppe, France, August 19, 1942. The objects of this raid were: (1) to test the defenses of what was known to be strongly fortified section of enemy coast; (2) to destroy German heavy gun batteries and a radio-location station in the area; (3) to capture prisoners for interrogation. UPPER. LCP's (landing craft, personnel) head toward the beach with demolition equipment. LOWER. Peering over the bow of an LCT (landing craft, tank), Canadian troops remain quiet and relaxed as the ship noses in toward shore.

DIEPPE—FORETASTE OF IN-VASION. Escorted by units of the British fleet, the Dieppe land-ing force plowed through the enemy minefields in the area and landed according to schedule, at 0450, on the six selected beaches. At Varengeville, 4½ miles west of Dieppe, a Commando force succeeded in smashing a 6″ howit-zer battery, but at Berneval, 4 miles east of Dieppe, a chance encounter with enemy E-boats and a "flak" ship delayed the landings and brought heavy enemy opposition to that sector. Although some landings occurred here, the heavy batteries in this area were never completely si-lenced, a fact which hindered the operations on the central beaches. Newly developed LCTs (landing craft, tank) put tanks ashore in the Pourville-Puys sector, where heavy tanks and anti-tank battles soon raged. These tanks formed the rear guard and covered the with-drawal. They fought an action which one admiring correspondent declared "Canada could well write into her military history." UPPER. Unloading the landing craft on English beaches after the raid. LOWER. A British de-stroyer rescues soldiers from a landing craft sunk during the landings.

VICTORY AT GUADALCANAL

By General Alexander A. Vandegrift, USMC

ON AUGUST 7, 1942, this nation launched its first major offensive in World War II when the First Marine Division made the beachhead at Guadalcanal. It was there in the British Solomon Islands that our land, sea, and air forces broke the crest of the enemy invasion tide and decisively began the bitter, arduous task of rolling it back to its source—the homeland of Japan.

Before final victory was achieved in the Pacific, we fought a seemingly endless series of battles. Some were briefer and bloodier than Guadalcanal, others were longer, yet less costly. All the subsequent campaigns were enhanced by virtue of greater experience, longer planning, and the increasing flow of men, weapons, and matériel to the Pacific.

The four-month-long battle for Guadalcanal made its unique niche in history because it was the first true test by fire—the crucible in which everything our nation pinned its hopes upon for final victory was gambled—and it was a gamble, a deadly one. The grim questions then were: could we, with what little we had, make a successful invasion of a lunging, powerful enemy's own territory? Could we save New Zealand and Australia? Could we do it immediately with what we had and not what we expected to get? Could we invade with a bare minimum of aerial reconnaissance and hurried planning? Could we make that first major ship-to-shore landing without wholesale air support and softening up by the fleet? Could we take Henderson Field and hold it against relentless opposition without benefit of coast artillery or even air cover during those first weeks ashore? Could our Marines fight day and night on iron rations, fishheads, and rice in a malarial jungle hell without once envisioning defeat? Could they stand up under the stunning night broadsides by heavy warships and the relentless heckling by enemy bombers? Could our meager sea and air support break through the enemy ring of steel at sea and in the air to keep us going? Could we forge our varied components by teamwork of the first order into ultimate amphibious mastery? Could we turn Guadalcanal into a death-trap for crack units of the Japanese army and for hundreds of their highly prized warships, transports, planes, and pilots? Could we win decisively at Guadalcanal and then use the amphibious doctrine which we tested, developed, and proved there to push the enemy back across the entire Pacific to Japan and final defeat?

We could and, by the grace of God, superior skill, courage, and equipment, we did.

"In area covered and numbers engaged, the Battle of Guadalcanal is small compared with the titanic struggles in Russia or even in North Africa. But in the history of the Pacific war it will assume the symbolic import that Verdun did in the last war, and Stalingrad in this war." Thus was the victory at Guadalcanal appraised in the editorial columns of the *New York Times*.

However kindly our victory in that first major American offensive may be evaluated, it will never be forgotten by those who fought there . . . and survived. For them it will always have a special significance. They came through four difficult months that were hell-laden with heat, sweat, dirt, loneliness, disease and death. But they did far more than that. They destroyed the myth of Japanese invincibility in that laboratory of jungle warfare and set the pattern and the spirit for the victory to come. Our nation could have asked little more of any men.

As a personal tribute to all those who fought so ably there, may I take the liberty of recounting in part my letter to them. It was written on that island, preparatory to our leaving, and dated 7 December 1942.

"To the soldiers and marines who have faced the enemy in the fierceness of night combat; to the pilots, Army, Navy, and Marine, whose unbelievable achievements have made the name 'Guadalcanal' a synonym for death and disaster in the language of our enemy; to those who have labored and sweated within the lines at all manner of prodigious and vital tasks; to the men of the torpedo boat command slashing at the enemy in night sortie; to our small band of devoted allies who have contributed so vastly in proportion to their numbers; to the surface forces of the Navy associated with us in signal triumphs of their own, I say that at all times you have faced without flinching the worst that the enemy could do to us and have thrown back the best that he could send against us."

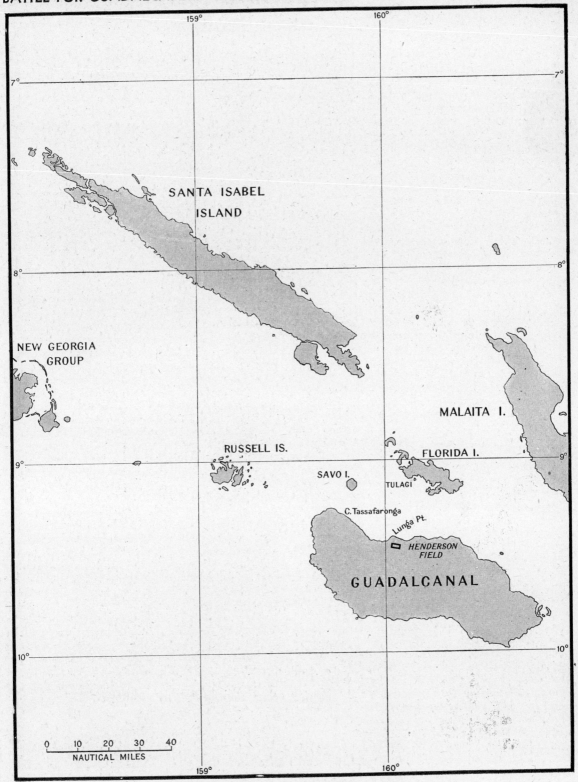

Chart of Guadalcanal Island and surrounding Islands, showing the location of Henderson Field.

THE MARINES LAND. UPPER. Standing off Tanamboga Island in the Solomons, U. S. men-of-war shell enemy installations prior to ship-to-shore operations by Marines. The Marines landed on August 7, 1942 and found the Japanese seaplane base and planes and a tender in the harbor burning. Prelanding barrages by guns of the Navy set the pattern for softening up island strongholds from the Solomons to Okinawa. Carrier-based planes also joined in the bombardment. LOWER. An Amphibious operation by Marines off Florida Island in the Solomons as seen from the air. The troop laden landing barges zigzag to minimize damage from aerial attack and shore batteries.

WEST MEETS EAST. UPPER. This pagoda was converted into a headquarters for U. S. Marine and Navy fliers at Henderson Field, Guadalcanal Island, after the tide of battle had swept the tenacious Japs from the area. However, the foe fought dozens of last ditch stands in the dense tropical jungles and persistently contested our control of the air. LOWER. S-shaped trenches like this one provided protection from Jap bombers for U. S. Marines on Guadalcanal. They were constructed to give cover against strafing attacks from any direction. They were also good positions for ground defense. But when the tropical rains came, the mosquitos made foxholes and trenches almost unbearable.

FOREVER ALERT. Constant vigilance, day and night, was a necessary Marine habit on Guadalcanal. Although the wily Jap specialized in surprise attacks at night, the dense tropical jungle of this island offered excellent concealment for daylight sniping. Moreover, the tactics of the enemy called for continual harassment of the invading forces. Hence, night-long activity to keep the Marines awake. Here as battle-weary, mud-caked Americans take a dip in a turgid stream, they never cease to be aware of the possibility of a sudden enemy attack. The machine gunner on guard not only watches the shoreline, but he scans the water too, in case a Jap might try to place a demolition charge under the foot bridge. The guard is ready to nail the first Jap who shows his head. The Guadalcanal operation stopped the Japanese advance in the direction of Australia and New Zealand.

COCONUT PALM COMMUNICATIONS. Wherever the U. S. Marines went in the vastness of the Pacific, they brought with them technical know-how in adapting methods of running a war to their immediate surroundings. As an example of this, here are two linemen making good use of palm trees on Guadalcanal. Not long after the initial land-ing on this Jap-held island, American forces had networked the portion they held with a dependable telephone com-munications system. This accomplishment, among others, greatly assisted in coordinating defense and attack, and permitted the Marines to put operational plans into effect without delay.

NIGHT OF DISASTER.

The Battle of Savo Island ranks next to Pearl Harbor in the list of America's World War II naval catastrophes. In a Japanese attack lasting only thirty minutes our Navy lost three heavy cruisers—the *Astoria* (pictured at left camouflaged for Pacific duty), the *Quincy*, and the *Vincennes*. Australian allies lost the cruiser *Canberra*.

Date, August 9, 1942. Place, the Solomon Islands. Our Guadalcanal campaign was well under way. Our carriers had withdrawn from the immediate area in order to take on fuel and also to avoid possible enemy air and submarine attack. A screening force of Allied cruisers and destroyers remained to protect the landing operations.

Assuming night disposition, the *Astoria*, the *Vincennes*, and the *Quincy*, with the destroyers *Helm* and *Wilson*, took up their stations in the channel on both sides of tiny Savo Island. The USS. *Chicago* with the Australian cruiser *Canberra*, screened by the destroyers *Patterson* and *Bagley*, protected the area between Guadalcanal and Florida Island. The destroyers *Blue* and *Ralph Talbot* operated not far away. About 0145 an ominous flare suddenly appeared in the night sky. That could only mean one thing—enemy planes overhead! Before the Allied ships could take action, gunfire and torpedoes burst out of the northwest.

It was some time before we realized that an enemy force of cruisers and destroyers had slipped into the area undetected. Their fire was tragically effective, and we were unable to offer adequate opposition. At 0215 the Japs ceased fire and sped off to the northeast. They left four Allied cruisers sinking, and another cruiser and destroyer seriously damaged.

But the Allies took grim consolation in the fact that the Japs failed to attack the scores of transports unloading men and supplies on the beaches of Guadalcanal. Evidently the Japs did not know how much damage they had inflicted. Had they known it seems likely that they would have forced a fleet battle in order to take advantage of their superior power.

BATTLE OF THE EASTERN SOLOMONS. After the Battle of Savo Island and the ensuing lull in naval activity, the American naval commanders had concentrated two task forces southeast of the island of Guadalcanal. These were built around the carriers *Wasp, Saratoga,* and *Enterprise,* and included the battleship *North Carolina,* the cruisers *Minneapolis, Portland, New Orleans* and *Atlanta,* and 11 destroyers.

On the morning of August 23, 1942, a reconnaissance plane sighted a Jap transport group, loaded with reinforcements for the Solomon Islands area. During the night our combined force moved north and contact was made the next morning. In the afternoon of the 24th, planes from the *Saratoga* and *Wasp* bombed an aircraft carrier and in addition damaged a cruiser and a destroyer.

While these attacks were in progress, a flight of about 75 Japanese planes attacked the *Enterprise* and her escort ships and inflicted some damage on the *Enterprise.* That night, Marine air attack groups from Guadalcanal attacked and damaged two more enemy destroyers and the next morning destroyed a transport. In addition to these attacks, Army planes scored hits on a cruiser, planes from the *Saratoga* reported hits on a battleship and two cruisers, and Marine pilots damaged another cruiser.

As a result of this action, the Japanese were all but stripped of carrier support in this area and broke off the fight although their powerful surface forces were still largely intact. ABOVE. Planes being spotted on the deck of the *Wasp* prior to taking off to attack Japanese forces. Two other flights, already in the air, appear at the center of the picture.

THE DEATH THROES OF THE WASP. Listing badly, smoke pouring from her sides, the USS. *Wasp* prepares to take the final plunge. The *Wasp* a 14,700 ton carrier, took three submarine torpedo hits while escorting a convoy to the Solomon Islands. Game to the last, the *Wasp* stayed afloat long enough to permit ninety percent of her crew to be taken off by escorting destroyers. Abandoned as a hopeless salvage job, the ship was finally sent to the bottom by torpedoes from an American destroyer.

The *Wasp* went down on 15 September, 1942, during the period when the U.S. was beginning to shift from the defensive to the offensive in the Pacific, the period when the naval strength of Japan and the United States was about equal, and when some of the war's fiercest naval fights raged. Her loss was a great blow to our forces. The *Wasp* had figured prominently in the news practically from the very day of her launching in 1939. She earned much renown earlier in 1942 for her part in ferrying reinforcements to the British island of Malta in the Mediterranean, supporting the Marines when they landed at Tulagi and Guadalcanal, and provided air cover for convoys running supplies to all points of the Pacific.

Navy men will say that a name can make or break a ship. This is certainly true in the case of the *Wasp*. Since the days of the first *Wasp* (the carrier was the sixth U.S. ship to bear that name), it seems to have been the lot of every ship bearing that name to have a short, exceptionally brilliant career, followed by an unfortunate end. The *Wasp I* was the first of the magnificent sloops-of-war which did so much to establish American naval prestige in the War of 1812. She was the first to be built, the first to win a victory—in that action where she slaughtered the HMS *Frolic* and was captured by a British battleship before she was able to make repairs.

The *Wasp II* broke through the British blockade in 1814 to become the most efficient single ship the American Navy ever had. She ran into the English Channel, destroyed thirteen enemy merchantmen, fought down two enemy cruisers of her own weight, and sailed away, never to be heard from again. The norm was established for the *Wasps*.

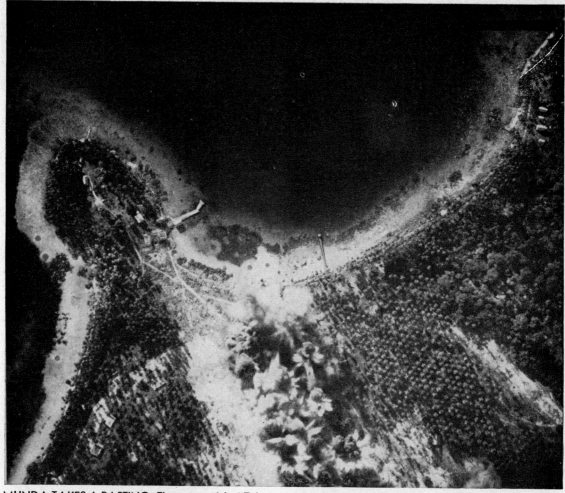

MUNDA TAKES A PASTING. The success of the "Tokyo Express" in rushing Japanese reinforcements to Guadalcanal, mainly during the night hours, prompted the South Pacific command to send in elements of the Army's Americal Division in October to reinforce the Marines, and the rest of the division during the following two months. While Navy and Marine Corps aircraft from Guadalcanal persistently attacked these night landing parties, air attack alone did not stop the operation. For this reason a task group of United States cruisers and destroyers, under Rear Admiral Norman Scott, was ordered to intercept enemy ships attempting further landings.

The "Tokyo Express" was "side tracked" near Cape Esperance, about midnight, October 11, when this task force engaged several Jap cruisers, destroyers, and transports to the westward of Savo Island. After a 30-minute battle, fought with both big guns and torpedoes, the enemy was forced to abandon his landing attempt and withdraw.

The whole situation was quite reversed from that of the night of August 8. Accurate and deadly fire from the cruisers *Boise, Helena, Salt Lake City* and *San Francisco*, and from other ships in our force, sank one Jap heavy cruiser (*Nati* or *Atago* class), four destroyers, and a transport of about 5,000 tons. Several of our ships received minor to moderate damage, and one U.S. destroyer was sunk.

By the time of the battle of Cape Esperance was fought, however, we had gained air superiority over Guadalcanal. The landing strip of Henderson Field had been considerably widened and lengthened, its surface improved, and revetments had been built to protect planes on the ground from strafing attack. Big bombers could now be brought in, and the air battle carried up the line to the enemy's new strong points in the north and central Solomons.

Some of these, under British rule, had merely been coconut plantations. The Japs moved in, took over the plantation buildings as headquarters, and levelled enough coconut palms to provide land for an air strip. Palm trunks were used for constructing revetments, ammunition dugouts, barracks and warehouses for supplies. Some plantations became seaplane bases, with ramps leading to sheltered water, and hiding places for planes under the trees.

ABOVE. Bombing planes from Guadalcanal blast the new Japanese airfield on Munda Point, one of the strongholds of the central Solomons.

JAP MORNING AFTER HANGOVER! So many Japanese and American ships were sunk in the sound between Guadalcanal, Florida, and Savo islands during 1942 and early 1943 that this placid stretch of water became known as "Iron Bottom Bay." The shoreline drops off steeply, however, and damaged ships that tried to beach themselves too often found that they were in the same predicament as the one shown above, a victim of the Battle of Cape Esperance. None of the cargo could be salvaged.

Following this battle, on the morning of October 12, Navy and Marine Corps torpedo and dive bombing planes took off from Henderson Field, Guadalcanal, to locate and attack the retreating enemy ships, many of which were believed to be in a damaged condition as a result of the punishment they had taken from our guns and torpedoes the night before.

At about 10 o'clock, two enemy cruisers were overtaken south of New Georgia Island, the Solomons. A torpedo hit was obtained on one cruiser, and several bombs were exploded near it. The cruiser was left dead in the water and burning badly. During the afternoon of October 12, an air group from Guadalcanal attacked an enemy cruiser and a destroyer, also in the area south of New Georgia Island. A direct bomb hit severely damaged and stopped the cruiser. When last seen her crew were hastily abandoning ship. This cruiser evidently had been damaged the night before in the action off Cape Esperance. A direct hit and several near misses set fire to the destroyer accompanying the cruiser, and she was left in a sinking condition.

Despite this drubbing, however, the Japs were back again in force the next night (October 13-14), when their surface ships bombarded our airfield and shore installations on Guadalcanal, causing considerable damage. This was a prelude to landing more troops early on the morning of October 15. Enemy transports, covered by naval units, disembarked a large number of men on the north coast of Guadalcanal, to the westward of our positions. An aircraft striking group attacked the Japanese ships, scoring three direct hits on one transport and leaving two other transports burning. A Japanese battleship was damaged and an enemy fighter plane shot down. U.S. motor torpedo boats also attacked these ships, and reported one probable torpedo hit on a cruiser. None of the motor torpedo boats was damaged.

DEATH OF THE *HORNET*. On the morning of October 26, 1942, United States Navy patrol planes contacted three enemy task forces off Santa Cruz Island. Our carriers *Enterprise* and *Hornet* launched attacks and scored several hits, inflicting serious damage. Enemy planes, however, torpedoed the *Hornet* and the destroyer *Porter*. The *Porter* sank immediately and the *Hornet* had to be sunk by our own forces. UPPER. The carrier *Enterprise*, a destroyer, and the battleship *South Dakota* (left to right) fighting off Japs at Santa Cruz. LOWER. A close-up of the destroyer *Smith* showing the damage suffered when she was struck by a flaming Japanese torpedo plane. In spite of this damage the *Smith* maintained her place in the battle line to the end of the engagement.

BEGINNING OF THE END FOR JAPANESE NAVAL AIR POWER—THE BATTLE OF SANTA CRUZ. After the tremendous Japanese air attacks which succeeded in sinking the destroyer *Porter* and irreparably damaging the carrier *Hornet*, both sides ceased attack and withdrew to lick their wounds. The two U.S. task forces retired independently. During the night they were pursued by the enemy surface units, but the Japs turned back when it became clear that their attacks were not succeeding. Between 170 and 180 Japanese aircraft took part in the attacks on the *Hornet* and the *Enterprise*. Of that number 56 were shot down by American anti-aircraft and an equal number by our planes. We sank no enemy vessels in this engagement, and our carrier strength in the Pacific was now dangerously low. On the other side of the ledger, however, we had put two enemy carriers out of action and cut to pieces four Japanese air groups. ABOVE. This picture of a *Chikama* class Japanese cruiser was taken from a U.S. dive bomber a few seconds before the bombardier released his bomb.

BAD LUCK FOR THE JAPANESE. The mascot of the Black Cat Squadron spelled bad luck for the Japanese in the air over Guadalcanal. In six months of hazardous night flying, which included bombing and strafing enemy bases, skimming torpedoes at Jap ships, and searching for enemy task forces, this squadron of Consolidated Catalina flying boats inflicted heavy damage without the loss of a single person and became one of the most decorated squadrons,

THE ENEMY'S TROPIC EMPIRE. UPPER. An aerial view of Guadalcanal Island shows the rugged terrain and dense tropical jungle covering the island. LOWER. An American examines a dummy Jap gun on a captured island. This gun, made of wood and camouflaged to simulate the real thing, is typical of the fake weapons with which the Japs hoped to delude our reconnaissance experts. Airplanes, built of wooden lattice work, were found spotted on airfields or partially hidden in revetments. Fake searchlights were installed to give a false impression of coast defenses.

DISASTER AT ALGIERS. A spectacular photograph, but one which illustrates the fact that all our losses were not due to enemy action. Here two liberty ships which had brought supplies to support our activities in the Mediterranean, burn at Algiers on 16 July 1943. The USS *Savannah* is in the foreground. It is only in rare cases that the trained men of the crews cannot cope with fire aboard ship with a minimum of damage to the equipment and cargo.

JAPS FAIL AGAIN. Following the naval battle of Guadalcanal, November 13-15, 1942, in which the Japs lost at least two battleships, four cruisers, six destroyers, and a dozen transports, two weeks elapsed before another serious attempt was made to reinforce their garrisons on Guadalcanal. This time the enemy was intercepted immediately north of the island.

In a spirited night action, which is known both as the Battle of Tassaronga and the Battle of Lunga Point, the Japs took another drubbing, losing six destroyers, two troop transports and a cargo ship. Several other ships, damaged, turned and fled. No landing on Guadalcanal was attempted. Our losses were one cruiser sunk and several other vessels damaged.

These two naval victories, together with the unceasing aerial attacks by Navy, Marine, and Army fliers on Jap strongholds and shipping throughout the Solomons, finally, discouraged all efforts to supply or to reinforce enemy positions on Guadalcanal. As the Japs slowly ran out of ammunition and food, our situation was becoming increasingly better. Complete conquest of the island soon became a matter of isolating scattered pockets of resistance, and of mopping up stragglers and guerrillas. This was slow, tedious, dangerous work, done mainly by patrols made up of volunteers who had been trained in jungle warfare.

ABOVE. Japanese transports, beached and burning at Tassafaronga, following the defeat of a large enemy force in the Battle of Guadalcanal, November 16, 1942.

THE INVASION OF
NORTH AFRICA
By Admiral H. K. Hewitt, USN

THE INVASION of North Africa, the beginning of the drive to make contact with Axis forces on continental Europe, was decided upon in July, 1942. The Allies hoped for light opposition, or none at all, from the French.

There were three main objectives in the Allied plans. Casablanca, on the coast of French Morocco, was to be taken by United States Army and Naval forces, while a Naval force, primarily British, was to land U. S. Army and British Army forces for the seizure of Algiers and Oran on the coast of Algeria. D-Day was to be November 8.

The U. S. Navy, except for one division of transports and other small units in the Algerian operation, saw most of its action in connection with the taking of Casablanca. The plans called for three landings, so that troops could close in on Casablanca itself from north and south, and so that the large airfield near Port Lyautey could be seized and utilized. The main landing was to be at Fedala, 14 miles north of Casablanca, just beyond range of the fixed defenses of that city. The secondary landings were at the mouth of the Sebou River, near Port Lyautey, 65 miles to the northward, and at Safi, a small port 190 miles to the southward. The capture of the latter port, with its docks, was essential to the prompt landing of tanks from the ships which carried them. (Special tank landing ships had not then become available.) The infantry division from Fedala was to advance south, and the armored force from Safi north, for the investment of Casablanca.

The large convoy of transports, supply ships, supporting battleships, cruisers, carriers and escorting destroyers sailed from ports in the U. S. (principally Hampton Roads), and Bermuda, effected rendezvous at sea, and proceeded by devious routes across the Atlantic, without loss from submarine attack. Radio silence was maintained throughout. At daylight of November 7, estimate of coastal surf conditions being favorable, the decision was made to land on the scheduled date, and the various task forces separated to take their assigned stations.

ZERO HOUR

THE ZERO hour for the landings was about three hours before daylight. All were made satisfactorily and very close to schedule. At Safi, where there was no beach outside the breakwater, two old world war destroyers, the Cole and the Bernadou, with masts cut down to give a low silhouette, loaded with specially trained assault troops, dashed inside the harbor and alongside the dock or breakwater, catching the defenses completely by surprise. At the River Sebou, a similar destroyer, the Dallas, rammed the harbor defense net and, ultimately, with the aid of a Port Lyautey pilot (who had been secretly brought to the U. S. for the purpose), proceeded up river to a point off the air field.

The French, unfortunately, resisted at all points, and it was necessary to return their fire. The shore batteries at Fedala were quickly silenced by the fire of the supporting cruisers, Augusta and Brooklyn, and by the pugnacious U. S. destroyers which went in to close range.

The French light forces in Casablanca, under cover of smoke screens, made repeated gallant efforts to attack the transports off Fedala. They were driven off, and eventually all were destroyed or severely damaged by gunfire, or air attack, or by a combination of the two. The immobile, partially completed Jean Bart, whose one quadruple 15″ turret was used as part of the Casablanca defenses, was hit by 16″ shells from the Massachusetts, and by air bombs. She was damaged and sunk at her dock, but her turret remained in action.

At 7:55 a.m., November 11th, five minutes before the opening of the final assault on Casablanca by combined sea, naval, air, and ground forces, word of an armistice was received, and hostile operations ceased.

On the nights of November 11th and November 12th, before they could be brought in to the wrecked harbor of Casablanca, four transports, engaged in unloading important supplies for the troops ashore, were torpedoed and sunk in the transport area off Fedala. A tanker, a supply ship, and a destroyer were also damaged by the assembling German submarines.

The U. S. Navy set up sea frontier forces (surface and air) based on Casablanca and the air station at Port Lyautey for the protection of convoys and allied shipping in the approaches to Casablanca and the western and southwestern approaches to the Straits of Gibraltar. The U. S. Navy also set up an operating base for the control of the port of Oran. Both of these activities subsequently became part of the "U. S. Naval Forces North West African Waters" when that command was established, in February 1943, with headquarters in Algiers.

H. K. Hewitt

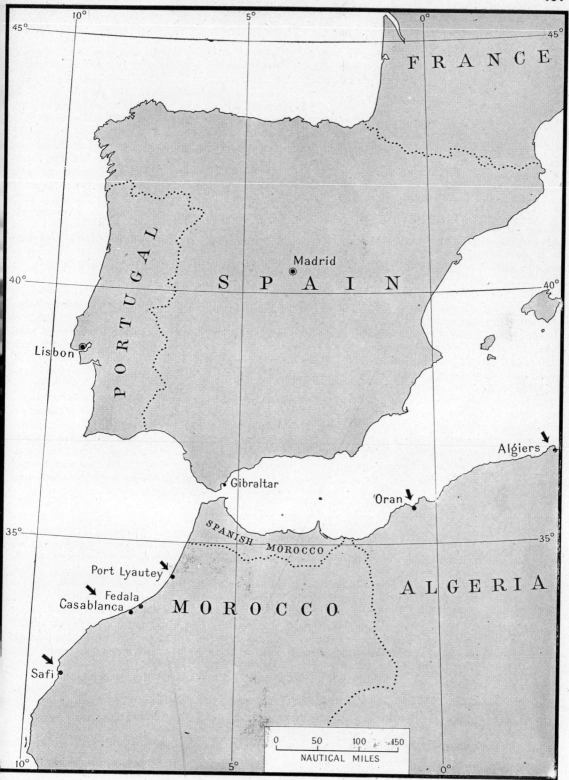

Chart showing the landings in North Africa.

SEAGOING WARHAWKS. UPPER. Her flight deck crowded and her hangar deck packed with U. S. Army P-40 Warhawk fighter planes, the escort-carrier *Chenango* plows through a calm sea enroute to North Africa. LOWER. Loading the starboard wing guns of an Army Warhawk aboard the carrier *Ranger*. These planes formed part of the air support on D-Day in North Africa. On the forward end of the flight deck rest the *Ranger's* own planes, TBF Avengers and F6F Wildcats, their wings folded to conserve space. Navy planes from the *Ranger* and other carriers in the task force provided aerial cover for the operation while the ships were at sea. Once the Army had captured local airfields ashore, the P-40's took off and flew to their new bases to begin operations.

AMERICANS LAND IN NORTH AFRICA. Under cover of the darkness on the night of November 7-8, 1942, the first units of an American Expeditionary force stormed ashore on the palm-lined coast of French North Africa. The landings were designed to keep the Axis forces from occupying any part of North or West Africa, and to deny the enemy a starting point for attacks on the East coast of the United States. They were also intended to provide an effective "second front" to relieve the heavy German pressure on our Russian allies.

The High Command timed these landings to coincide with the British Eighth Army's offensive against Rommel in the Western Desert. The initial success of the landings was due not only to the perfect cooperation between Allied forces, but also to the great secrecy which had surrounded it.

A fleet of 500 transports and 350 supporting Naval ships had been gathered and loaded and were well on their way before even the personnel aboard knew where they were to land. Powerful air cover protected the giant convoy the entire time it was at sea. Despite the dangers of the route across the Atlantic through the Western Mediterranean, all ships arrived safely.

ABOVE. The picture shows an anti-aircraft barrage put up against enemy night bombers in the harbor of Algiers. Enemy air activity was especially heavy in this sector. The intensity of the fire from guns aboard the transports and combat ships in this area alone accounted for 83 German planes between 8 and 20 November, 1942. A bare six months after these landings, the last German soldier in Africa surrendered.

AMERICANS LAND IN NORTH AFRICA. The principal Allied landings in Africa occurred at seven points, four in Algeria and three in Morocco. In the initial landings the Allies carried out flanking operations at Oran and Algiers. Later, as the American Army pushed toward Tunisia, new landings were made at Bougie and Bone, also in Algeria. Coastal batteries and small naval units held up the American occupation for two days at Oran. Two British-manned ex-American Coast Guard Cutters, renamed the HMS *Hartland* and the HMS *Walney,* went down in the Oran operation when they tried to crash the harbor boom.

Units of the American and British fleets officially occupied the city on November 10, 1942. Vichy acknowledged that in the action around Oran three French destroyers were put out of action and grounded, and that a fourth was sunk as it attempted to leave the harbor. The principal fighting took place around Casablanca. Our troops landed at Safi, 140 miles south of Casablanca, at Fedala, 15 miles north of Casablanca, and at Mahdia, 18 miles north of Rabat. Naval units supported army advances and bombarded defenses all along the coast. In a naval action off Casablanca a strong French destroyer force was "wiped out," and the incomplete French battleship *Jean Bart* was damaged.

On November 11, 1942, all French resistance came to an end in compliance with orders from Admiral Darlan, who represented himself as "Commander in Chief of All French Forces in Africa." His declaration stirred up a hornet's nest of political trouble but vastly simplified military problems. Within two weeks the strategic Atlantic base of Dakar was turned over to the Allies. This strongly fortified port had already repulsed landings by the Free French forces, and might have been a costly prize if military necessity had required its capture.

UPPER LEFT. A Navy Catalina patrol bomber of Patrol Bomber Squadron 63, the famous "Cowboys from Blitzville" soars past a Navy blimp while returning from a patrol flight over the Atlantic. These patrol squadrons flew convoy protection, scouting missions, and "Dumbo" rescue missions 24 hours a day for almost two and a half years. LEFT CENTER. Landing craft from United States forces offshore pour through the narrow entrance to Fedala Harbor, 15 miles north of Casablanca. LOWER LEFT. Aerial view of actual landing operations of U. S. troops in the Casablanca area, French Morocco. UPPER RIGHT. Ex-American Coast Guard Cutters *Hartland* and *Walney* shown crashing the boom in Oran Harbor.

PLANNING THE 1943 CAMPAIGNS. The success of the landings in French North Africa, the plans of which had been formulated by President Roosevelt and Prime Minister Churchill in June, changed the whole outlook of the war in the closing days of 1942. The time had come to review the progress of the war throughout the world and draw up plans to make sure that the Allies would keep the initiative in the campaigns of 1943.

Accordingly on January 14th President Roosevelt and Prime Minister Churchill opened a ten-day conference in Casablanca in which they laid plans for the United Nations offensive aimed, as the President said, at "unconditional surrender" of the Axis powers. They were accompanied by the Chiefs of Staff of the two countries who met in constant session two or three times a day to draw up the details of the general strategy.

Plans were drawn up for coordinating the resources and fighting power of the United Nations, for dispatching all possible aid to Russia and China, and for unification of the French in the war against the Axis. Nothing like this meeting had ever taken place before. Complete accord existed between the leaders and the Chiefs of Staff of the two Allies. ABOVE. General Honore Giraud and General Charles de Gaulle get together at the Casablanca Conference and shake hands as President Roosevelt and Prime Minister Churchill look on. The two French generals were invited to the Conference to discuss methods of healing the embarrassing breach between them.

CONFERENCE AT CASABLANCA. Premier Stalin was invited to the Casablanca Conference but replied that he could not leave Russia. The Red Army was at that time engaged in transferring their grim defensive into the sweeping advances of the winter offensive. But both Stalin and China's Generalissimo Chiang Kai-Shek were in constant communication with the Conference and were advised of the plans for giving aid to Russia and China. Stalin had openly expressed dissatisfaction with what he termed the Allies' repudiation of their commitments to open a second front in Europe and thus draw German troops away from the Russian front. Generalissimo Chiang Kai-Shek was advised of the proposed operations for opening up new and more efficient communication and transportation routes to China.

The entrance of the United States and Great Britain into the war against Japan actually weakened rather than strengthened China's position by allowing the Japs to cut the Burma Road. New routes had to be found. Meanwhile we had to give tangible evidence of our professed friendship for China. At the close of the Conference President Roosevelt gave a dinner party for Sidi Mohammed, Sultan of Morocco. Seated: Sidi Mohammed, President Roosevelt, Prime Minister Churchill. Standing: General George Patton, Robert Murphy, Harry Hopkins, the Crown Prince of Morocco, General Nogues, the Grand Vizier of Morocco, the Chief Protocol of Morocco, Lt. Col. Elliott Roosevelt, and Captain John L. McCrea. The dinner took place at the villa assigned for President Roosevelt's use.

A 525-MILLION DOLLAR DITCH. How many millions of man hours the Panama Canal saved in World War II, when even seconds were sometimes precious, will never be accurately counted. But certainly the $525,812,661 construction cost of the "Big Ditch," as figured by the Bureau of Efficiency on the completion of the Canal in 1921, has turned out to be one of the best bargains the United States has ever made.

In 1849 a United States Naval officer made the first United States survey of the isthmus. It was France that began the actual construction in 1882, but the French eventually gave up the enterprise, beaten by malaria and yellow fever. The United States took the task in hand in 1904.

ABOVE: The USS. *Bunker Hill* about to leave the last of the Gatun locks. There are three sets of locks in the water-

way. At Gatun three double locks raise Pacific-bound ships 85 feet above sea level to Gatun Lake. At Pedro Miguel one double lock lowers vessels a drop of 55 feet into Miraflores Lake. After the two double locks at Miraflores the ship again reaches sea level. From shore to shore the Canal is 40.27 miles long. From deep water to deep water, 50.72 miles.

All United States warships were formerly designed so that their width did not exceed that of the Canal. Modern carriers of the *Midway* class cannot pass through the Canal. Arguments are sometimes put forward for the construction of another and wider canal in Central America, a canal which would make use of Lake Nicaragua. But even such a canal would presumably become in time too narrow for the world's big ships.

STRATEGIC PIPELINE. Since the completion of the Canal, Panama has become one of the United States' most important bases. To lose the Canal would mean thousands of extra miles and weeks of extra travel whenever our ships sailed from one coast to the other. This would, of course, necessitate a much larger fleet for defense. Without the Canal, the commerce of the entire world would slow down appreciably. ABOVE. Here, under Panama's torrid sunlight, men and machines labor to complete work on a double-barreled fuel oil pipeline from Cristobal on the Atlantic side of the isthmus to Balboa on the Pacific. The pipeline was conceived as a secret alternate supply artery in the event that the Canal should be knocked out by enemy action. The line was laid originally with a single 20-inch pipe, but the needs of the Pacific fleet grew so great that workmen began a duplicate pipeline before the completion of the first. Daily capacity of the dual artery is estimated at 265,000 barrels of fuel oil, 60,000 barrels of gasoline and 47,000 barrels of Diesel oil. The pipeline was completed in 1945. Its total length is 46 miles. Since some of our larger ships such as the *Midway* class of carriers cannot negotiate the canal this fueling line may take on even greater importance as a supply center in the event of another war in the Pacific Ocean.

PLANTATION
BUILDINGS ON HILL

CLEARING

FROM COCONUT PLANTATION TO AIR FIELD TO RUBBLE. That is the story, in a capsule, of a once strong Japanese air base at Munda Point, New Georgia Island, in the central Solomons. For nearly eight and a half months Munda was one of the most famous of the so-called "milk runs" (regular bombing objective) of our Navy, Marine, and Army pilots in the Solomons. Enemy development of the airfield was spotted almost immediately.

The Japs moved into the plantation buildings in November, 1942, and for a short time worked, unobserved, on the preliminary steps forward setting up an airstrip. When they began to cut down trees to clear areas for the landing field and for revetments, however, bombing operations by our flyers began at once. Jap facil..ies that had sprung up by December 9, 1942, had already been blasted severely by January 5, 1943, and appeared to be almost untenable by March 30. But the fall of Munda did not come until August.

ABOVE. This is the way Munda looked shortly after the Japs had taken over the former British coconut plantation and its buildings, November 28, 1942. A trace of the clearing for the airstrip can be seen (right center) as well as the outline of revetments for plane protection and storage. Bomb craters (upper center) indicate that the recent airbase has already been under attack.

UPPER RIGHT. Five weeks later, despite terrific daily poundings, the Japs have succeeded in completing their main air strip, and encircling it with revetments large enough to shelter scores of planes. The photograph shows a stock of bombs from U. S. planes landing squarely in the middle of Munda's airstrip. Because the prevailing winds generally blow from one direction in the Pacific, most wartime airports had only one landing strip.

LOWER RIGHT. Symbols of revenge are these Navy Avenger planes along the runway on Munda after it fell to our forces. When U. S. air and naval bombardments were not able permanently to destroy Munda, and the other Jap base in the central Solomons near the Vila River (Kolombangara Island), American amphibious forces landed on the Russell Islands, sixty miles from Guadalcanal, to obtain an advanced base for our fighter planes. In a last ditch attempt to hold us there the Japs lost 107 planes (June 16, 1943) in one of the most furious air battles of the Southwest Pacific. We lost six.

The attack on Munda was preceded by the capture of Rendova Island, offshore, by the 25th Division of the Army while a simultaneous thrust was made at Viru Harbor by by the Marines. Repaired by Seabees, Munda became a major U. S. airbase.

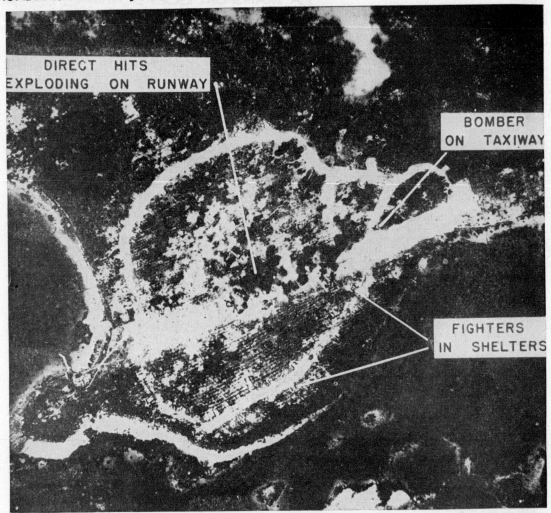

DIRECT HITS EXPLODING ON RUNWAY

BOMBER ON TAXIWAY

FIGHTERS IN SHELTERS

ABANDON SHIP. By rope and net, U. S. soldiers clamber down the sides of the SS. *President Coolidge* after the 22,000-ton transport struck a mine and sank on December 12 while on a war mission in the South Pacific. The proximity of the island in the background, coupled with prompt and efficient rescue methods, restricted the casualties to two men. At the opening of the war the greatly expanding fleet necessitated a like increase in auxiliaries, such as attack transports and cargo ships. The *President Coolidge* was chartered from the American Lines to be operated as a transport for the Army by the War Shipping Administration. Double inner-spring mattresses gave way to four high iron bunks, cream colored walls became steel gray, the ballroom became a storage room for oil-soaked machinery.

END OF THE U.S.S. CHICAGO. During the evening of January 29, 1943, a force of U. S. cruisers and destroyers, which was covering transport movements about seventy miles south of Rennell Island, was attacked by enemy torpedo planes. The cruiser *Chicago* was struck by two torpedoes, one in the forward magazine. Taken in tow first by another cruiser, she was later turned over to a Navy tug.

The following day, in the afternoon, the *Chicago* was again struck by thirteen Japanese torpedo planes, and, as a result of this attack, was sunk. U. S. aircraft shot down twelve of the thirteen enemy planes, but not in time to ward off the attack on the *Chicago*. Through war bond subscriptions, bought by citizens of Chicago, the gallant ship was replaced by another cruiser of the same name in 1945.

UPPER. Bow anchor down and stern lying low in the water, the stricken *Chicago* fights for its life following two attacks by Jap torpedo planes near Rennell, southernmost of the Solomons. Personnel casualties were light, and the men who fought so hard to save their ship eventually were awarded the Presidential Unit Citation.

LOWER. This vivid streak marks the end of one of the Jap torpedo bombers which attacked the U. S. task force off Rennell Island. It was believed at the time that the Japs were massing ships and planes for a showdown battle, but subsequent events showed that they were principally concerned with evacuating their own troops from Guadalcanal.

MOST SILENT SERVICE. The Navy, generally referred to as the "Silent Service," had a "super-quiet" branch of its own in the submarine fleet. Devices which our destroyers used against German submarines had to be kept from possible use by the Japs against our own submarines, and successful methods our underseas fleet employed against Jap shipping had to be concealed from Nazi U-boat commanders. So almost everything concerning the equipment and operations of America's submarine and anti-submarine warfare perforce had to be marked "Secret." Now many of these things can be told and shown in photographs, and the down-under boys in dungarees may get some of the credit they so richly deserve.

LEFT. Silently a U. S. submarine leaves its base for a long-range patrol of enemy waters. Ahead are monotonous weeks of hard work, slow cruising . . . and then, suddenly, the thrill of a "kill!" With only one per-cent of the personnel of the Navy, the submarine service sank 77 per cent of the tonnage lost by Japan in the first two years of the war. LOWER. The galley of a modern U. S. submarine is more compact than that of a dining car. Food on subs is the best in the Navy.

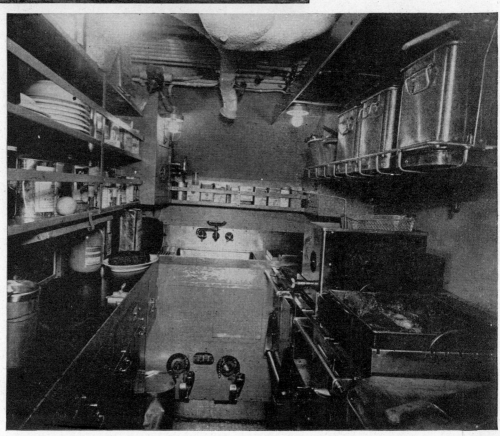

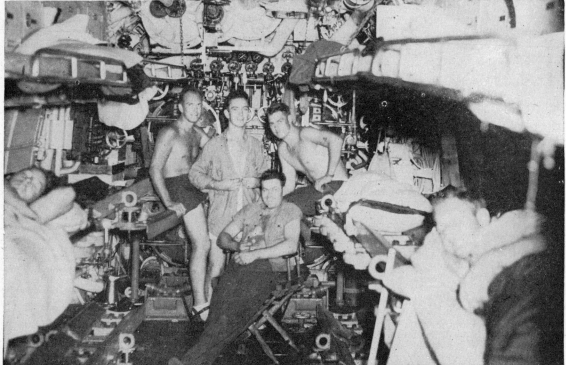

EXPLOSIVE BEDFELLOW. The men who go to sea in submarines are good men, good technicians, good sailors, and are justly proud to be a part of the submarine Navy. Eternal vigilance is the price of life aboard a submarine. Night and day in the engine room, in the control room, and in the conning tower or bridge, the watch is maintained. Everywhere the men are surrounded by equipment and machinery. UPPER. One of the men resting in his bunk over two torpedoes. LOWER. This photograph shows how the submarine utilizes every inch of available space.

THE SILENT SERVICE. The approach is stealthy, and finally the submarine is in the firing position. Then the captain gives the order, "Up periscope!" He checks the sight and every man waits. This is the moment that will justify the efforts of the men, their trials, the anxieties of loved ones in the States, and the expenditure that has gone into the mission. "Fire one!" With a slight jar the first "fish" slips from the forward tube. "Set 'em up in the next alley!" the skipper orders. "Fire two!" Another torpedo with hundreds of pounds of TNT in its warhead goes on its way. The seconds pass. Praying for hits and dreading the depth charge attack which may follow, the men listen. There's a dull shake, and then another. After a few seconds the captain orders, "Down periscope!" "We broke her in two," he says. The torpedoes have gone home and another Japanese merchantman joins its ancestors. There may be hours of depth charging and cold sweat ahead, but the submarine has done another job.

During World War II, U. S. submarines have done many jobs. They carried supplies to beleaguered Corregidor, supplied and reinforced guerrillas in the Philippines, rescued over 500 Allied aviators from enemy controlled waters, performed many valuable reconnaissance services. But the great justification of submarine warfare is the success they achieved in their major task of destroying the Japanese Navy and Merchant Marine. From December 7, 1941 to August 15, 1945 submarines sank 1,750 Japanese steel merchant vessels. This was over 56 percent of the total of Japanese merchant ship losses. In addition our submarines sank one Japanese battleship, eight aircraft carriers, fifteen cruisers, forty-two destroyers, twenty-eight submarines, and one hundred lesser warships for a total of one hundred and ninety-four combat vessels of all classes.

To appreciate the significance of this contribution to the war effort it must be realized that the Japanese were dependent upon ocean transport. The Japanese themselves attribute the breakdown of their war economy in major part to the American submarines. A Japanese War Lord said, "Submarines initially did great damage to our shipping and later the submarines combined with air attacks made our shipping very scarce." The Japanese are masters of understatement.

PULLING TOGETHER. Teamwork was the key to Allied success in World War II. The United States won the war in the Pacific by the combined effort of all forces, Air Force, Army, Navy, Marines, and civilians. Submarine operations profited greatly by the efforts of other forces. Submarines forced the enemy to concentrate his shipping in convoys. Air forces, particularly carrier air forces, found this concentration very vulnerable. In attempting to escape air attack, the enemy opened himself up to further submarine attack. The Japanese Navy and Merchant Marine found themselves in a dilemma. RIGHT. Crewmen of a United States submarine rescue U. S. Navy airmen from a Navy Patrol bomber. The rescue was effected off the coast of Japan. During the war, submarines rescued 504 Allied aviators from enemy controlled waters. Even a group of airmen who crash-dived in Tokyo Bay lived to see action again because an American submarine surfaced near them and literally snatched them up from under the nose of Japanese patrols. The services rendered by United States submarines and the men who sailed in them will rank among the most skillful and daring in history.

CONTRIBUTIONS TO VICTORY. When the Navy Department released these pictures the tide of battle had rolled very close to Tokyo. These photographs portray typical incidents in the war of attrition directed against the Japs by the United States submarines. UPPER. Crew members of the USS *Tambor* throw lines to survivors from the stricken Japanese merchant ship which is slipping under the surface off the *Tambor's* bow. LOWER. This first combat action photograph taken through the periscope of an American undersea raider shows an enemy destroyer after two torpedoes had found their mark. The Rising Sun insignia on top of the destroyer's turret serves as an identification mark for aircraft. The marks on the left and the center line are etchings on the periscope.

WHERE ANGELS FEARED TO TREAD. The stories of U. S. submarines that penetrated to the heart of Japan rank among the great adventures of all time. There were those who stalked the Japs at the mouth of Tokyo Bay, and some Americans navigated the Bay itself. Men of one submarine that operated off the coast of Japan and set a record of 70,000 tons of Jap shipping sent to the bottom during one patrol tell how they watched horse races at an amusement park in Japan. The pictures above were taken through the periscope of a U. S. sub. The picturesque junk is plodding along the coast of Japan. In the lower picture Mt. Fuji looms above an American submarine.

THE BATTLE OF TUNISIA, PRELUDE TO SURRENDER.
With the herding of the Axis armies into Tunisia, that last embattled corner of Africa became in effect an island battlefield. The two opposing forces which gathered their strength for the final test were entirely dependent for support on supply bases beyond the seas. The stores which they had accumulated in Africa would last through only a brief period of conflict, and if either side were deprived of its communications with other continents, its doom would be quickly sealed. The situation gave advantage to the side which possessed naval superiority combined with air support.

All through the struggle for North Africa the Allied fleets played an important part, striking blows against the Axis sea lanes, protecting Allied convoys against all but minor losses, and establishing a blockade which prevented the Axis from landing and reinforcing heavy equipment. Direct support of the Army advance was rendered along the coast from Gabez to Bizerte by small units of the Allied fleet. Planes were ferried to the scene of action on carriers, landing craft, and transports to combat the strong Axis air force and to be used as "tank-busters" to combat the Axis heavy armor.

ABOVE. A picture of a "tank-buster" in action. A British Hurricane fighter, fitted with 40mm high velocity wing guns swoops down to blast a Nazi mark IV medium tank. This type of attack accounted for a high score of enemy armored vehicles and helped to break the back of the Nazi armored forces, at a time when few, if any, armored replacements could be obtained.

SURRENDER IN AFRICA. By May, 1943, the end of the conflict in Africa was in sight. The swiftness of the final collapse tended to obscure the ferocity of the fighting that preceded it. Throughout Tunisia, the struggle for the heights had been waged against a tenacious and resourceful foe. In the south the Allies had been able to make only secondary gains. In the north the hill positions had been gained with the utmost effort. Even after the plains had been reached there had been stiff fighting before Tunis and Bizerte and at the entrance to Cap Bon.

The collapse which followed was less a sign of broken Axis morale than a tribute to the completeness of the Allied victory. The enemy troops on Cap Bon had little chance to resist and none to escape. Naval forces pounded them from offshore while planes hammered them from overhead. Tanks raced up both sides of the peninsula and heavy artillery kept up a constant barrage.

When organized resistance ceased in Africa on 12 May, 1943, it was a disaster for the Axis paralleled only by the destruction of the German Sixth Army before Stalingrad. In the whole of the Tunisian campaign the Axis had lost 266,600 captured, 30,000 killed, and 26,400 seriously wounded. Allied losses were under 70,000. For the three years of warfare in Africa the Axis paid a very great price. It is estimated that they lost 950,000 men killed or captured, 8,000 planes, 6,200 guns and 2,550 tanks destroyed.

ABOVE. An American 155mm "Long Tom" sends a torrent of hot steel whistling to German and Italian held positions in Central Tunisia.

"GREEN DRAGONS" OF NEW GUINEA. Not even American submarines were more feared by the Japs than the U. S. Navy's smallest combat ship, the PT, or Patrol Torpedo boat. Because of their small size and shallow draft, PT boats could be based in the inlets and river mouths that abound within the reefs of tropic island groups. Screened by overhanding foliage the PT squadrons could live in comparative safety during the daytime. Then, at night, they slipped out for sudden attacks on big enemy ships, earning for themselves the name "Green Dragon" from the apprehensive Japanese. UPPER. PT boat, silhouetted against the sunset, begins a night patrol near Lae, New Guinea. LOWER. A PT boat returns to its base, Morobe, New Guinea, with some natives as passengers.

LOADING THE STINGERS. Although PT boats are most famous for their torpedo attacks, they can also repell planes with anti-aircraft machine guns and assail submerged submarines with depth bombs. By the end of the war some of them were equipped also with rockets, and others could lay mines in enemy waters. In addition, PTs have been called upon to assist in commando raids, rescues of downed airmen, harbor surveys, escort trips, and in the laying of smoke screens. In fact, there are very few jobs which a ship can do that PTs have not been asked to do, and done well. From 70 to 80 feet long, PTs generally carried a crew of ten or eleven men. They were driven by three or more powerful motors, and depended upon their speed to save them from enemy fire, because their hulls were nothing but plywood. Top speed was about 70 knots, but they could be throttled down to a mere crawl,

"THEY WERE EXPENDABLE!" A rare pre-war photograph, showing the loading of a squadron of motor torpedo boats aboard a special auxiliary deck, built over the main deck, of a Navy oiler which carried them to the Philippines. Some of these boats, here ready to leave New York, became part of the famous Squadron Three, commanded by Lieutenant John D. Buckeley, USN.

At the outset of the war there were only three PT squadrons. One was stationed at Pearl Harbor and helped to fight off the Jap sneak attack. Another was in training, and the third, under Buckeley, was in the Philippines. Squadron Three had six boats. In his report of the Jap strike at the Philippines Admiral E. J. King, Commander-in-Chief of the U. S. Fleet, wrote: "On the evening of December 8, therefor, after the Japanese had bombed our airfields and destroyed many of General MacArthur's planes, our submarines and motor torpedo boats, which were still in Philippine waters, were left with the task of impeding the enemy's advance."

The PT's did their bit, and by sudden forays and surprise night attacks sent thousands of tons of Japanese shipping to the bottom. Two of the six boats struck coral reefs, and were too badly damaged for repair. But the other four carried on, and, finally, on March 11, 1942, they stole silently away from Corregidor with some twenty passengers. Enemy ships were lurking on every hand, and the gasoline supply was low. After several narrow escapes, however, the four PT's brought General MacArthur and his staff safely to an island to the south, where Army planes awaited to fly them to Australia.

PT BOATS WERE WELL EQUIPPED. For men who like gadgets, the PT is paradise. At times the riding is rough, and one must have a stout stomach, but there is more comradeship between officers and men, and less "spit and polish," than on the big ships of the fleet. Discipline is maintained, but it is discipline based on respect for the other man's ability and responsibility. Equipment is kept in first class condition, not just for the Admiral's inspection, but because the lives of every man aboard may depend upon it.

Those not familiar with PTs are usually amazed at the number of items of equipment, and the different kinds of deadly weapons that can be crowded into so compact a space. Much of it is in miniature, compared to equipment doing the same job aboard destroyers or battleships. But proof of the pudding is in the eating, and the PT has been truly the biblical David of this war; more than a match for enemy Goliaths. One PT operating in the South Pacific, for instance, sank 920 times her weight of Japanese shipping in six months—a total of 18,400 tons.

UPPER. The bee-hive above this PT is its "thinking cap," or radome, housing the antenna of the radar set. LOWER. Depth bombs, ready to be rolled over the side when submarines are reported.

ALWAYS IN THE THICK OF THINGS. The enemy must have thought we had far more PTs than we actually had, because our motor torpedo boats were on hand for every kind of action except battles on the high seas far from shore. UPPER. Friendly Filipinos come out to assist U. S. PT boats picking up survivors in Surigao Strait after the Battle for Leyte Gulf. LOWER. PT 321 picks up survivors of the Japanese warships destroyed in Surigao Strait by the U. S. Seventh Fleet in the Battle for Leyte Gulf, also known as the Second Battle of the Philippine Sea. Note machine gunners at battle stations, and torpedoes ready for use.

MUNDA AIRFIELD FALLS AT LAST. It was not until almost one year after our first landings at Guadalcanal that American forces captured the thorny Japanese airdrome at Munda on New Georgia Island. During this year, the airfield had been bombed almost every day. After U. S. troops made their original landings on New Georgia on July 2, 1943, they passed a month of agonizing jungle fighting, slowly converging on Munda. During this period, our aircraft made constant air attacks on the airfield. Fleet units supplemented the air bombings with accurate and devastating bombardments from the sea. At the cost of 93 of our own aircraft during the 37 days of the campaign, the Japanese lost an estimated 350. On August 5 our troops broke through and captured the airfield which was soon prepared for friendly use.

ABOVE. Just after the capture of the airfield, Marines inspect abandoned Japanese equipment. Now only one Japanese stronghold was left on the island. It was Bairoko Harbor on the northern coast. But with Munda airfield rebuilt and turned to our own use by the unstinting efforts of the Navy's Seabees and the Army engineers, American bombers soon made this harbor ineffective.

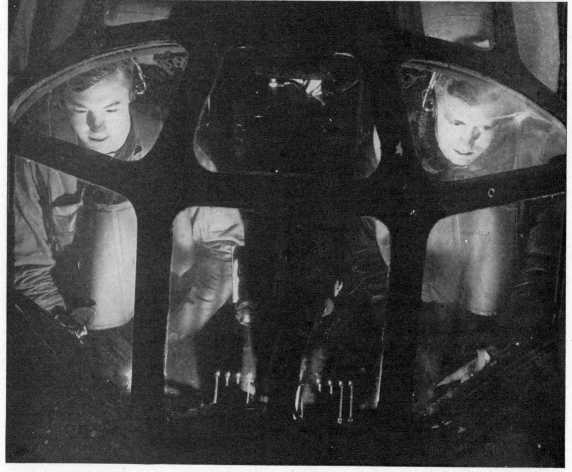

NAVY STALKS U-BOATS IN THE BAY OF BISCAY. In midsummer 1943, U. S. Navy Fleet Air Wing Seven, assigned to operate directly under the Royal Air Force Coastal Command, took over from the USAAF the task of patrolling the strategic Bay of Biscay. Thoroughly trained in naval warfare, U-boat tactics, and identification of ships, Navy pilots were particularly well-suited to the job. UPPER. A Navy Liberator, based near Exeter, England, heads out over the picturesque and rocky Devonshire coast on a patrol of the Bay of Biscay. LOWER. Pilot and co-pilot of a Navy Liberator, their intent faces lighted by the instrument panel, prepare to take off from their English base. Patrols were weary and tedious, often lasting twelve hours.

U-BOATS COWER UNDER NAVY'S EYE. It was summer 1942. The U-boat menace had become acute. From their fortified home bases in the French ports of Lorient, Brest, and St. Nazaire, German submarines sailed out into the Atlantic to prey in Allied sea lanes. The battle to maintain Britain's lifeline was at its most crucial moment. In order to ferret out the U-boats in their home waters, the RAF Coastal Command and the USAAF ran continued patrols over the Bay of Biscay.

The U. S. Navy took over the USAAF's share of the Biscay patrols in the summer of 1943, and set up an airbase at Dunkeswell near the historic city of Exeter in southwestern England. Here, for the next two years, a thousand men of the U. S. Navy worked in relative obscurity to combat the submarine menace. Patrols were increased and maintained constantly. They were tedious and nervewracking. Flying for twelve hours on end, week in, week out, many plane crews never even had the encouragement of sighting a submarine. Some patrolled for months before one was spotted.

When the great moment came it lasted but a few short minutes. But then, guns manned, depth charges armed, the Liberator would pounce down to the attack. And, more often than not, another U-boat never reached home. It was also dangerous work. Liberators patrolling the Bay were juicy bait for formations of German fighter planes that would swoop out of their French coastal bases intent on clearing paths for their homewarding submarines. Running a gauntlet of our watchful planes, U-boats approaching home bases were forced to remain submerged.

Navy fliers faced an equally dangerous foe in the weather, which in the Biscay region was quite often bad. But when ceilings were low, they still had to fly. For it was at just such times that the U-boats would take a chance of running for it on the surface. In these streaks of bad weather, many Navy pilots made it home by a gremlin's eyelash. Some, not so lucky, did not return. But the wearing patrols paid off. Hitler was finally forced to call in his hounds of the sea and save them against the day of the coming invasion.

A high spot of the Air Wing's English career came in December, 1943. In a desperate attempt to get crude rubber through the Allied blockade, the Germans assigned eleven destroyers to escort one blockade runner. An RAF Liberator sank the runner before she could rendezvous with her escorts, and a short time later a Navy Liberator spotted the eleven destroyers. Despite heavy anti-aircraft fire and attacks by enemy fighters, the Liberator doggedly held them in sight until two British cruisers steamed in to the attack. In the ensuing battle the cruisers sank three destroyers. The remaining nine, fleeing, were attacked by a special strike of Fleet Air Wing Seven Liberators. All pressed in to strafe the ships in face of heavy flak. The crews all won high praise for their day's work.

During the Normandy assault, patrols were augmented so that the Channel approaches were constantly covered by aircraft to prevent surface or undersea craft from attacking our forces. ABOVE. Intelligence officers brief a Liberator crew about to take off on a Biscay Patrol.

WAR IN THE NORTH. With the permission of the Danish government U. S. Coast Guardsmen landed in Greenland March 17, 1941, and were followed on April 9, 1941 by detachments of U. S. Marines. This was a half year before Pearl Harbor, but the Germans, in violation of the Monroe Doctrine, and in contempt of the Congress of American Foreign Ministers, were known to be setting up weather observation stations in Greenland that would jeopardize the safety of Lend-Lease shipments to Britain.

On June 7, the President approved the "Basic Joint Army and Navy plan for the Defense of Greenland," and set up a regular patrol of Coast Guard vessels. For three years this patrol broke up repeated attempts of the Nazis to set up bases along Greenland's bleak eastern coast. Sometimes the patrol overcame obstacles that would

have discouraged the most experienced Arctic explorers.

ABOVE. The Coast Guard cutter *Eastwind* turns over captured German supplies to the Danish Sled Patrol for the use of the Greenland government. The supplies were found in a cluster of huts on Koldewey Island, where the Germans had set up a meteorological station. First spotted by the *Eastwind*'s patrol plane, the base was raided by two platoons of men from the cutter. They captured also three officers and nine enlisted men, all of them wearing German uniforms. In the huts were discovered large quantities of meteorological and radio equipment, and ample stocks of food and clothing. Also confiscated was a collection of American phonograph records, many of them the newest jazz tunes, and German books, games, and pinochle cards.

ROUNDUP, GREENLAND STYLE. Because weather forecasts over the north Atlantic cannot be accurately made without data from Greenland the Nazis expended much time, money and ships in their efforts to establish bases along the island's bleak, uninhabited northeastern coast. Thanks to the vigilance and the perseverance of the Coast Guard, however, these stations were never long in operation. UPPER. Germans, in army uniforms, found at one of the radio-weather installations. LOWER. The German armed trawler *Externsteine* was captured by the Coast Guard cutters *Eastwind* and *Southwind*, off Cape Borgen, Greenland. Renamed the *East Breeze*, and manned by a prize crew of 28 Coast Guardsmen, the trawler was taken to Boston to be used by our own forces.

MIDNIGHT SUN PATROL. Exactly five months to the day before Pearl Harbor, an American Navy task force landed a detachment of United States Marines at Reykjavik, Iceland. Made up of twenty-three ships, Task Force 19 was our first naval foreign expeditionary force of the still undeclared war. The troops came at the invitation of the Icelandic government, which, while neutral in the world conflict, knew that the island was important to the Nazi scheme of conquest of England. To the United States, Iceland was an important sentry post along the convoy route to England, and a means of safeguarding Lend Lease supplies that already (May 1941) were piling up in some of our ports faster than ships could carry them away.

The United States, however, was not the first to undertake the protection of Iceland. When, in April 1940, the Germans invaded Denmark, Great Britain, whose respect for the neutrality of Norway and Denmark had made easier the Nazi conquest of both, sent a mixed force to Iceland. The force arrived May 10, 1940, a short time before a carefully planned but unexecuted German invasion, it was later learned. The British had no time to negotiate, but the Icelandic government, assured that its neutrality would be respected by the Allies, accepted the situation co-operatively.

In 1941, however, the British needed, desperately, the 15,000 troops of the Iceland garrison for their North African campaign. Iceland was confronted again with the alternatives of a possible, and very probable, Nazi invasion, or it could welcome friendly troops. It did not take long for President Roosevelt to negotiate the replacement of British forces with our own. Hard on the heels of the first American task force came a second, bringing in Army troops and Army Air Force units to supplement, and later replace, the Marines.

The base grew rapidly. In addition to quarters for troops, a naval air station was set up about five miles from Reykjavik, near the Royal Air Force and the Norwegian Air Force bases. From here a regular air patrol of the North Atlantic convoy lanes was operated. At Hvalfjordor, a deep safe anchorage about forty miles northwest of Reykjavik, shore facilities were set up to take care of the needs of scores of ships that began to use this harbor as a convoy forming ground. Finally, on November 8, Secretary of the Navy, Frank Knox, announced the establishment of "Naval Operating Base, Iceland," and placed the new base under the command of Admiral Ernest J. King, then commander in chief of the United States Atlantic Fleet. To the Germans Iceland was "enemy" country, and they continued to make nuisance raids and reconnaissance runs with long range planes.

The first U. S. navy casualty of the undeclared war, the U.S.S. *Kearney*, limped into Iceland in October 1941. The *Kearney*, a new destroyer, had been torpedoed by a German submarine, while escorting a convoy bound for Iceland 350 miles away. A gaping hole was torn in her starboard side, and the ship was almost cut in two. But, lashed to a sister destroyer, the *Kearney* made port, was patched up enough to proceed to the United States, and soon was out again with the fleet. ABOVE. A U. S. Navy plane on patrol near Iceland.

FIRE OF BATTLE BRIGHTENS THE NIGHT. War rends the calm of many a night with the ear splitting blasts of the big guns and the howling screech of crashing steel. In theatres of action as widely separated as Kula Gulf in the Central Solomons and Sicily in the Mediterranean the still of the night has been broken with the hellish noise of battle. To the fighting men of the fleet "night action" is more than a two-word description of a study in black and white photography. Night action means sweat and blood, and death streaking out of the sky. ABOVE. Manning a 1.1 anti-aircraft gun aboard a U. S. cruiser during the height of the Battle of Kula Gulf, July 5, 1943, these seamen are mometarily spotlighted in the flash of another of the ship's guns.

"CLEANING UP" AFTER THE BATTLE OF KULA GULF. ABOVE. Crew members of the USS *Honolulu* stack empty shell cases after the first battle of Kula Gulf. After being almost completely "derailed" at the Battle of Cape Esperance, the "Tokio Express," as the Japanese reinforcement convoys were called, for a time reverted to small numbers of fast, light ships to land troops in the Solomons. However by the end of June, 1943, the "Express" was beginning to operate again in force. The Japanese evacuation of Guadalcanal, in February, 1943, did not bring a halt to these forays. Troops were now being landed at Vila, and elsewhere in the northern Solomons. With U. S. landings on the New Georgia Islands, it became necessary to stop these nightly runs at any cost. On July 5, 1943 a cruiser-destroyer task force was dispatched to intercept these landing attempts, and early in the morning of the sixth contact was made with the enemy in Kula Gulf. U. S. forces opened fire with devastating effect on the first of the two enemy groups, and later took enemy ships in the second group under an equally effective fire. Return fire consisted chiefly of torpedoes. It is probable that at least two Japanese destroyers and several transports were sunk in this action.

MOVING IN AT DAWN. The Japs in the South Pacific were thrown off their stride by our simultaneous attacks on the central Solomons and on New Guinea. They apparently had been ready to deal with either campaign separately.

In the New Guinea theatre, after our successful landing at Nassau Bay, June 29-30, Allied troops moved up the coast to Mubo and Komistum. Navy planes and PT boats harassed enemy landing barges, and prevented the reinforcement of the nearby Jap base of Salamaua. On September 3, our amphibious forces moved into Huon Gulf, and landed the Australian Ninth division near Nopoi. Salamaua fell September 11, and five days later Lae surrendered, giving our forces two fairly good bases.

The next objective, Finschhafen, was captured by a flanking movement October 2, and our PT boats sank a number of barges loaded with enemy troops trying to escape from the island. The next day we suffered a loss, however, when the destroyer *Henley* was torpedoed and sunk. An Allied landing at Saidor, January 1, 1944, met no resistance, and, finally, on February 13, the occupation of the strategic Huon Peninsula was completed by the meeting of Australian units, coming from the eastward, with the 32nd U. S. Division. Thus our left flank was secure, and the way paved for moving along the north caost of New Guinea toward the Philippines and Japan itself. ABOVE. PT's and landing barges come ashore at Nassau Bay, New Guinea.

THE INVASION OF SICILY

By Vice Admiral Richard L. Conolly, USN

BY MID-MAY of 1943, the Germans and Italians had surrendered in North Africa, and our military forces in that area were powerful enough to justify planning a major offensive operation against "Festung Europa," the fortress Europe.

Unique features of this operation were that it was to be mounted largely in North Africa from ports extending from Oran to Alexandria, and it was to employ in addition to the usual large transports with their embarked landing craft, a host of newly constructed landing ships, intermediate sized self-sustaining landing craft and support craft. All this armada had to be assembled in small North African ports, trained, organized, and rehearsed with the troop units to be landed.

The whole tremendous operation, air, naval, and ground force, was planned under the aegis of Allied Force Headquarters. The combined naval force with embarked troops was commanded by Admiral Sir Andrew Browne Cunningham, the Commander-in-Chief, Mediterranean, a British flag officer of pre-eminent record and vast experience in those waters. It was divided into Eastern and Western Naval Task Forces, commanded respectively by a British and an American vice admiral. Each of these major subdivisions was further divided into three subordinate task forces, each in turn commanded by a rear admiral. Included in the general plan were vast air forces and powerful naval covering forces, the latter for protection against the beaten, but still potentially dangerous Italian Fleet.

THE LANDINGS

ALL THE many naval components took a preliminary staging disposition and later departed from staging ports on a vast and intricate schedule. The seamanship of the newly organized naval forces was tested severely by the rough weather encountered en route. However, the attack was delivered simultaneously and the troops were landed successfully and with complete tactical surprise during darkness of the early morning of 10 July 1943. Major landing forces were put ashore at five principal positions. Three of these objectives, Scoglitti, Gela, and Licata, on the south coast of Sicily, were attacked by the American task force (Western).

The landing at Scoglitti, preceded by bombardment by our naval units, was accomplished with comparatively little opposition, the Italian troops abandoning their defense positions during the pre-invasion bombardment.

At Gela the troops landed exactly on schedule, and the first waves encountered slight opposition. The second wave met stiff resistance and suffered heavy casualties until shore batteries were silenced by the naval gunfire from the U.S. cruisers *Savannah* and *Boise*.

At Licata the larger part of the assault infantry were transported to anchorages off the landing beaches in thirty-six new LST's which had been converted by the installation of six landing craft, each of which landed an assault platoon. Heavy opposition was encountered on the left flank, but all beaches were captured and the unloading of supplies began.

After the landings, the participating naval forces were subjected to intense enemy air attack for three days. The enemy also launched violent counter attacks on our troops, spearheaded with tanks which threatened to drive our forces near Gela into the sea. Accurate naval gunfire broke up these attacks and served as antitank fire for the men on the beaches. Had there been no naval support, these attacks might have succeeded in destroying our forces in that area.

SUPPORTING FORCES

AS THE combined troops drove ahead from the landing beaches they were supported, whenever possible, by our naval forces. At Porto Empedocle and Agrigento this support contributed greatly to the capture of those positions. The resistance met by our ground troops consisted mainly of small arms fire, since almost every large gun was spotted and destroyed by well directed naval fire.

Destroyers and small craft took a major part in the protection of transports against the almost continuous German air attacks. These small craft also protected captured harbors, swept enemy mines, performed necessary salvage, and opened up ports essential for the support of the Seventh Army.

This operation was a triumph of planning and an example of what can be accomplished by a generous spirit between the Army and Naval Forces and between two allies, all working enthusiastically toward the same end on approved plans. The Invasion of Sicily was the prototype of large-scale amphibious landings that were to prove so irresistibly effective throughout the ensuing campaigns of the war.

RLConolly

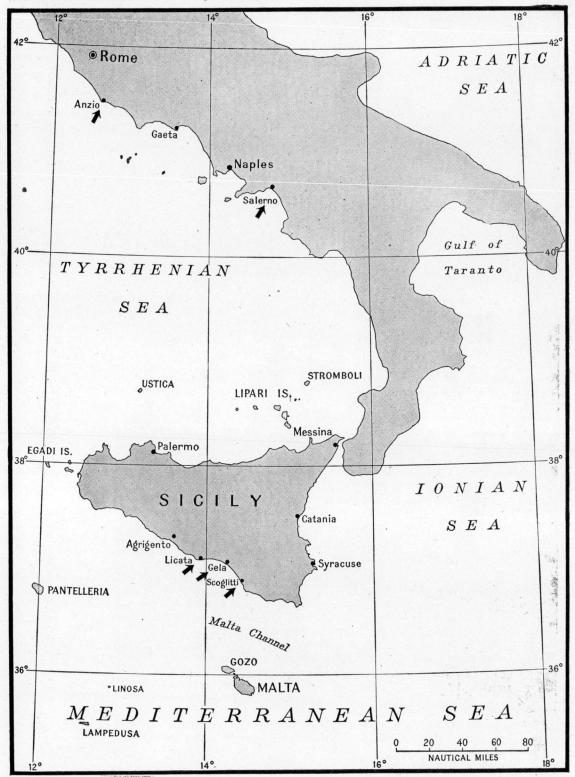

Chart showing the American landings on Sicily.

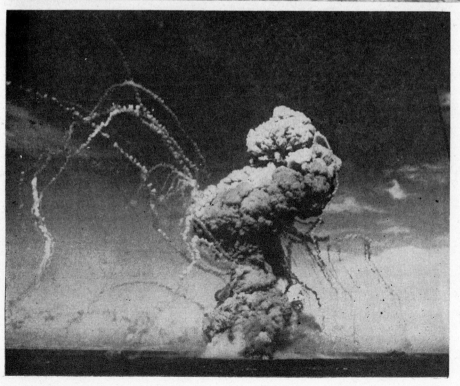

"OPERATION HUSKY." As a prelude to the Sicilian landings battleships, cruisers and destroyers softened up the beachheads with a terrific night bombardment July 9-10, 1943. H-Hour was 2:45 a.m., July 10, and the sea was rough. Most of the troops, however, were landed on schedule. Naval forces supported landings at Gela, Scoglitti, and Licata, and bombarded Porto Empedocle and Agrigento.

UPPER. A bird's eye view of one of the Sicilian beachheads, showing landing craft broached by the heavy surf. Salvage crews soon had them back on the job. LEFT. One of our ammunition ships goes up in a spectacular blast. The vessel was hit by a Nazi aerial bomb, which started fires. Most of the crew escaped.

RIGHT. An LST (Landing ship, tank), her bow doors open, takes on a complement of troops for the Sicilian campaign. The LST had its combat premiere in the landings on Sicily. The famous Seabees also had their baptism of fire.

SICILIAN BEACHHEAD SECURE FROM ENEMY. The invasion of Sicily was a joint U. S.-British operation in which a two-pronged thrust was aimed at southern and eastern ends of the triangular island. U. S. forces went in on the western sector, the British on the eastern. Our troops ashore on D-Day made good progress, supported by accurate fire from Navy cruisers; and destroyers, a scant 800 yards from the coast near Gela, actually beat off a desperate thrust made by tanks of the crack Hermann Goering division. It was the last ground attack the enemy made, and later in the day, the other two objective towns of Licata and Scoglitti fell. ABOVE. LCT's, which had been delayed by buffeting seas the night before, ply into Licata harbor to unload. In the foreground a Navy crewman scans the skies for enemy planes. LCT's performed workhorse tasks following the first assault. After depositing their own cargoes on the beach, they worked day and night unloading transports. On the northern coast of the island, after the fall of Palermo, LCT's ferried men and supplies for ground forces as they advanced in leap-frog landings toward Messina. The Sicilian invasion was a proving ground for new amphibious vehicles and techniques.

SICILY FALLS. The Sicilian campaign lasted six weeks. It was a campaign in which the Army and Navy, British and American, worked together as one team. When the U. S. Army called for help to reduce enemy batteries impeding the capture of Porto Empedocle and Agrigento, our cruisers *Philadelphia* and *Savannah* sailed immediately to the scene and pounded the city's defenses into rubble. In late July, Mussolini and his Fascist regime resigned, and on August 17, 1943 Messina was captured. The entire island was in our hands. As the battles passed on, Seabees —the Navy's skilled construction battalions—worked under constant pressure to turn the captured ports back into serviceable harbors. During the period of rehabilitation, one great problem was that of feeding the civilian population. To help relieve this situation, the Navy assigned several Coast Guard officers to aid in restoring the island's fishing industries. UPPER. Sicilian fishermen pour their difficulties into the receptive ear of an officer assigned to this duty. LOWER. Navy men in Sicily inspect a stripped Messerschmidt left behind by the fleeing Germans.

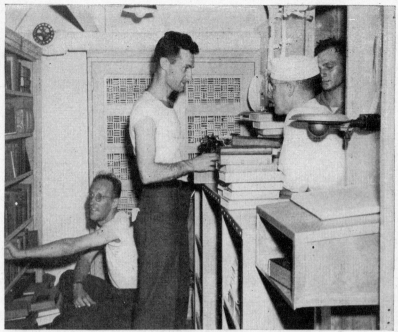

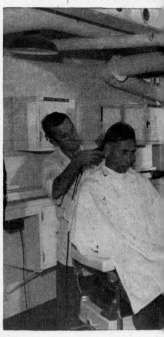

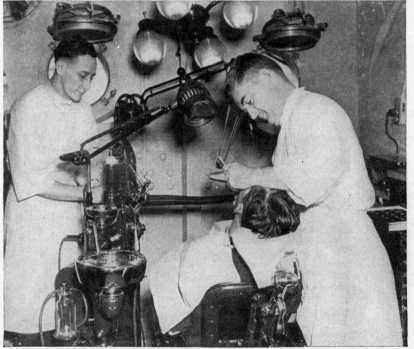

ditions the yeoman-librarians man assigned positions at gun stations. LOWER LEFT. Sound teeth are essential to good health in keeping the efficiency of the fighting man at its peak. Here a Navy dentist and his pharmacist's Mate assistant examine the teeth of a sailor aboard the USS *Pennsylvania*. Naval doctors come from the foremost medical colleges in the country to work in shipborne sick bays which have the latest equipment known to medical science. UPPER CENTER. Good grooming may be considered nonessential for living, but when men live in close quarters it is a "must" that they keep clean. In the barber shop aboard the USS *Iowa* the continuous activity of six barbers keeps the clippers working constantly, but it doesn't seem to cut into the line of customers. Shaves, shampoos, manicures, etc., are luxuries left ashore. In addition to the services shown here, laundries, tailor shops, soda

SOME REASONS WHY SOME SAILORS LIKE BATTLESHIPS. Life aboard a large ship is not too different from life on a shore station. There are movies, athletic facilities, libraries, and other recreational opportunities to make life more enjoyable. In this spread of photographs some inkling is given to the multiple and varied professional talents required to keep life livable. UPPER LEFT. Sailors crowd to the door of the library aboard the USS *Missouri*, the Navy's 45,000 ton superdreadnought on which Japan formally surrendered. Aboard the larger units of the fleet there are libraries available to all hands. Stocked by contributions from the Navy's Welfare and Contribution Fund the men frequent them in their leisure hours. Under battle con-

fountains and ship's stores are maintained. Each ship also carries an allotted amount of athletic equipment, and whenever the opportunity presents itself the men are encouraged to participate in competitive sports. Competition becomes keen among divisions and goes a long way toward building morale and making a happy ship. And a happy ship is an efficient ship. It has been said by many a commander that he would rather have a wooden ship and iron men than an iron ship with wooden men. Our Navy is the greatest in the world today because services like these have made men of steel to fight ships of steel. Our totalitarian enemys, whether Germany or Japan, have never been able to instill the same spirit into their men.

SUPER-FED FIGHTERS. One of the most important factors in maintaining the morale of the Navy is the quality of its food. Despite the jokes about the Navy's menu, the fighting sailor gets a properly balanced and appetizing diet. Much care and effort goes into the procurement and preparation of food. There are complete and modern galleys which would be the the envy of the best chefs at the finest hotels. They are fitted with electric ranges, dishwashing machines, dough mixers, coffee urns, cake mixers, and many other modern appliances. The crew of a battleship on a typical day consumes 1500 pounds of meat, 3,200 pounds of fresh fruits, and a corresponding quantity of other foods. Through the course of a year one of these ships will consume 900,000 eggs. Whether on large ships, where there is a cook for every 75 men, or on small ships, where there are but 2 cooks, the food turned out in every general mess is always healthful, wholesome, and tasty. UPPER RIGHT. Navy cooks are in the process of preparing lemon pies for evening chow aboard the USS *Missouri*. LOWER LEFT. The Boatswain's Mate of the watch aboard a battleship pipes the crew to attention over the public address system prior to general quarters. At this signal, all hands including cooks and bakers and ship's service personnel move on the double to their respective battle stations. The seemingly peaceful city then becomes a huge and terrifying dragon capable of belching fire and death to the enemy.

"THIS IS A DRILL." No order aboard battleships is more despised than one preceded with "this is a drill." Yet no order other than "man all battle stations" is more vital. A battleship is the most destructive piece of machinery built by man. And man is the very life that manipulates its great powers of propulsion and destruction. Like a newborn babe, learning to walk and talk, so the nervous system of a battleship—its crew—must be trained to command these powers.

ABOVE. The crew of this 5" 25 cal. dual-purpose gun is put through its paces. Innate qualities are important factors. To begin with, the gun-captain must know his gun and the job of each member of his crew. Mensuration for the sight-setter, above-average coordination for the pointer and trainer, and endurance and agility for the shellman are prerequisites. But the ability to work as a team—that is the reason for "this is a drill."

NEW GUNS FOR A VETERAN. From the spitting minor calibre machine guns to the roaring major calibre rifles, constant care is necessary to keep them all in tip-top operating condition. The ballistics of every projectile is altered by each successive firing of a gun. The degree of alteration becomes appreciably noticeable as the size of the gun increases This is partially due to heat developed by rapid firing which at times becomes so great that the paint blisters on the barrel. It is also caused by wear and chemical deposits left in the bore as each shell passes through.

Before securing a gun after firing, the bore must be swabbed out, dried, and polished. Then a damp oily cloth is passed through to form a protective coating against corrosion. But with all this care, ships must come to port and have the guns overhauled. When this becomes necessary, the guns are taken out of the turrets and replaced by others with new liners. This system of holding extra guns in readiness greatly bolstered our first line of defense, and helped our Navy to heed the orders of the Joint Chiefs of Staff at all times.

ABOVE. Linings worn out by frequent firing, the 14-inch rifles of a veteran battleship are replaced by guns with new linings at the Navy Yard in Bremerton, Washington. Guns like these are what heralded our landings in the many amphibious assaults on Japanese held islands in the Pacific. And guns like these are what pinned the Germans to their fox-holes, blasted their coastal defenses, and splattered their very dreams of world conquest into the mud at Normandy.

THE "LUCKY LOU" TAKES A HIT. During the second week of the New Georgia campaign our ground forces consolidated their positions at Rendova, Rice Anchorage, and Viru, and began to close in on Munda. The job of the Navy at this time was twofold: to pace American ground troops with sea bombardment, and to prevent the enemy from reinforcing his Munda garrison. On July 12, 1943, a U. S. task group of cruisers and destroyers again intercepted a Japanese troop convoy bound for the northern Solomons. The Japanese units were disposed in two groups of transports ringed with combat ships. The first enemy group was badly shot up. At least one cruiser and several transports were probably sunk. The stronger, second group, however, inflicted considerable damage on our forces. Tor-

pedoes damaged the cruisers *St. Louis* and *Honolulu,* and gunfire set afire the destroyer *Gwin.* The New Zealand cruiser *Leander* also suffered a torpedo hit while engaging the first enemy group. ABOVE. The bow of the "Lucky Lou," as the crew members called the *St. Louis,* after the battle. The "Lou" earned her nickname in several other engagements, each a more miraculous escape than the last.

In February, 1944, she took six Japanese bombs—one direct hit and five near misses—while operating north of Bougainville, but returned to action three days later. While supporting landings on Leyte the "Lou" was attacked by six Kamikaze planes, one of which scored a hit on the ship. But in each case the damage was repaired and the ship returned for vengeance.

ALL ASHORE THAT'S GOING ASHORE. REN-
DOVA. UPPER. The Japs were caught flat-footed when
American blue jackets landed soldiers and Marines (shown
coming up the beach) on Rendova Island in the New
Georgia group, at dawn the 30th of June 1943. LOWER.
Troops and equipment were being unloaded for fully an
hour before the Japs stirred from their sleep. Formerly the
Grace liner *Santa Barbara*, the USS McCauley, APA 4,
disgorging her cargo, was severly damaged in air attack
that afternoon and abandoned that evening. As we were
about to destroy her, a Japanese submarine ironically
saved us the trouble. Hit by three Jap torpedoes, the
"Wacky Mac" exploded violently and disappeared. All
records for handling amphibious cargo were broken at
Rendova. Our ships took only four hours to unload upwards of 600 tons of combat equipment.

ASHORE AND STILL GOING—RENDOVA. Surprised and stunned, the enemy reeled and collapsed in the face of the furious dawn assault at Rendova Island. UPPER. Soldiers and Marine jungle fighters hit the beach, take cover and, when organized in strength, moved inland. Rain was incessant and the mud so thick that it practically sucked their shoes off. LOWER. In the wake of their advance came the medical corpsmen setting up an emergency battle dressing station. The man lying on the cot in the foreground was more than likely carried in on a poncho stretched between two rifles. The stretchers leaning against the tree were deluxe. Munda was seven miles across the inlet. In five hours Army patrols, having moved to vantage points inland, were subjecting its defenses to artillery fire. . The Munda airstrip was the next objective.

NIGHT ACTION OFF VELLA LAV-ELLA. The Japanese in the Solomons were faltering. Desperately the "Tokyo Express" attempted to supply and reinforce their beleaguered garrisons in Vila and elsewhere in the Kula Gulf. Under the cover of night, their destroyers, piled high with men and materials, tried to run through our naval defenses and then withdraw quickly. Although a destroyer is limited in its capacity, and therefore cannot transport as many troops and as much equipment as might be desired, the Japanese counted on the destroyer's speed and mobility for success in these desperate missions. At times they were successful.

In order to stop these blockade runners, our Naval command dispatched Group X to make a sweep of Vella Gulf and to engage any enemy encountered. Group X was composed of about five destroyers. One night in August they picked up four Japanese ships steaming in column—three were destroyers, the fourth was a cruiser, designed to afford heavier gun protection to the gauntlet-running ships. Group X took them by surprise. Apparently the Japanese did not make as efficient use of radar as our ships did.

Group X closed in for the kill. On the command to fire, twenty-four torpedoes went racing through the dark waters, leaving thin strategic lines of white wake behind. Balls of red flame went shooting skyward. Violent explosions followed which blew two enemy destroyers to pieces. The cruiser burst into a mass of flame. The waters reflecting this ghastly light outlined the third Japanese destroyer which had escaped severe torpedo damage and was not pitifully attempting to elude its attackers. The destroyers in Group X trained their guns on it and sank the ship within minutes. The entire battle had lasted only a half-hour. Vella Lavella was one of the many actions which contributed to the decimation of the Japanese Navy.

LEFT. A destroyer of Group X bellows a flash of hot flame from one of the guns which sank that last Japanese destroyer.

"NOBODY HOME" AT KISKA. On August 15, 1943, United States and Canadian forces reoccupied Kiska. Men from a large amphibious fleet, assembled at Adak, jumped ashore set for battle. They found that the Japanese, like the Arabs, had folded their tents and silently stolen away into the night. They found quartermaster houses bulging with clothing, food, fruit, vegetables, fish, ammunition, and even some big guns and midget submarines. They found a sign from the Japanese that said, in effect, "out to lunch." On the wall of the main Japanese command hut was scrawled, "We shall come again and kill out separately Yanki jokers." They found myriads of booby traps and souvenirs, but they found no Japanese. For seven months the Japanese in the last enemy stronghold in the Aleutians had been pounded by sea and air. 4,000,000 pounds of bombs had rained down on them. They had been shelled until every one of their coastal defense guns was put out of action and many of their installations were mere rubble.

JAPS RUN AWAY FROM A FIGHT—THE AMPHIB-IANS REOCCUPY KISKA. On 13 August 1943, a large American-Canadian task force, which had been forming in Adak Harbor, in the Aleutians, began to slip out to sea. There were battleships, cruisers, destroyers, landing craft, tank lighters, oil tankers, and troopships. But there were no soldiers, no sailors. There were only Amphibians. Each man who landed wore upon each shoulder the mark of the Amphibious Forces. And the men who wore the mark came from both the Army and the Navy. When they landed at Kiska, they found a deserted island. UPPER. Japanese trucks, copied from American models, wrecked near the harbor. LOWER. A Japanese float-plane hangar, bombed out by American planes.

BITTER MEDICINE FOR THE ENEMY—THE JAPS "TAKE A POWDER." Even though the Tokyo radio broadcasts stated that the withdrawal from Kiska had been "according to plan," and that it was successful "without parallel in military history," the fact remained clear, even to the Japanese, that they had run from a fight. For the first time in the war the enemy had fled without attempting to defend a conquered position. The Japanese escape was made from Kiska across 70 miles of sea in barges and submarines to Buldir Island where ships were waiting to take them to Japan. Since the barges had a maximum speed of about 5 knots, it is supposed that the evacuation of the garrison, of between 7,500 and 11,000 men, took place under cover of the heavy July fogs. ABOVE. When the Japs left Kiska they left equipment behind, including this ship, the *Nozima Maru*. An American bombardier made sure this ship would not be used to take Japanese troops to, or from, Kiska.

NATS DELIVERS THE GOODS. An emergency call from a submarine, thousands of miles from the nearest repair base, for repair parts sent a plane winging 10,000 miles in 72 hours. An urgent request for detachable wing tanks for Wildcat fighters at an advanced base in the Pacific sent a plane loaded with these tanks from New York to San Francisco where they were transferred to another plane and flown to the outpost in time to break up a Japanese attack. These are two instances of the hundreds of chores performed by Naval Air Transport Service, the "errand boys with wings" of the Navy.

NATS grew from a single flying boat of uncertain vintage at the time of Pearl Harbor to 10 full transport squadrons, several ferry units, and large contract operations by Pan American Airways System and American Export Airlines. Annually NATS transported hundreds of thousands of pounds of urgently needed war materials. NATS planes flew some 3,600,000 plane miles per month.

During the war its planes flew to the fringes of battle zones, operated through tropical and Arctic blizzards and fogs. They flew a majority of the routes without radio navigation aids, the use of which would have betrayed them to the enemy. In spite of the difficulties and hazards of wartime flight, NATS achieved an efficiency and dependability equal to that of the pre-war civil airlines.

NATS operates under three Wing commanders, one each for the three main areas of naval activity: the Atlantic, the West Coast, and the Pacific. The Naval Air Ferry Command is under a fourth Wing commander.

NATS' greatest job during the war was the transportation of high priority materials, raw and finished, from the factory to the fighting front, and from the mine or mill to the factory. Transports returning from overseas flights brought cargoes of strategic materials for American war industries: industrial diamonds, mica, beryl ore, rubber, quartz crystals, platinum, quinine and totaquine, block talc from South and Central America, from Africa, and from thousands of remote places. NATS became, in a few short months, a lifeline supply for our forces in all corners of the globe. UPPER. A plane load of military men and civilian technicians bound for the Aleutians. Although the "bucket seats" are uncomfortable, the time saved is well worth while.

SALERNO BEACHHEAD ESTABLISH-ED. Five hundred British and U.S. ships hove into the Gulf of Salerno in the early hours of September 9, 1943 to launch a two-pronged assault against the Italian mainland. Unfortunately most of the troops expected to make unopposed landings. Reason: Italy's surrender had been announced over public address systems to all hands the night before. But the Germans were still waiting. All hell broke loose. Until accurate fire from off-shore destroyers could silence enemy batteries and tanks it was touch and go on the beach. Our casualties for the day were extremely heavy. Enemy fire also took heavy toll of equipment on the beaches, and German planes, making continuous air attacks, damaged several ships, including the cruiser *Savannah* LEFT. Rear Admiral Richard L. Connoly, USN, and Maj. Gen. J. L. Hawksworth, British Army, watch the landing from the flagship *Biscayne*.

SALERNO BUILDUP. An LST shrouds herself in her own smokescreen. In the foreground a British sapper searches the beach for mines. Here, LST's heavily laden with men and gear discharged load after load onto the Salerno beachhead. Some carried long sections of pontoon causeways, over which tanks and equipment poured when LST's could not get up on the beach. After unloading their assault cargoes, they plied back and forth between North Africa and the beachhead, bringing in troops of all Allied nationalities.

GERMAN SECRET WEAPON APPEARS. Slowly and gruelingly the Allied Armies widened the Salerno beachhead. The Germans fought a bitter retreat, and we suffered many casualties. In the evening of September 13, the Germans launched an all-out counterattack in an attempt to drive the Allies back into the sea. They nearly succeeded.

It was during the Salerno campaign that the much-touted German secret weapon finally appeared in the form of radio controlled flying bombs. German heavy bombers, coming in for a high level attack, would release these winged machines, which would start off on a long glide. Suddenly the bomb would change course into a roaring dive, headed straight for a ship. These were precursors of the later V-1 and V-2 bombs. Ships off Salerno were under continued attacks by these new bombs for many days.

UPPER. A command post on the beachhead covered with camouflage netting. LOWER, An Italian submarine, which surrendered in Salerno Bay, draws alongside an American ship. In the background a British Motor Launch s ands by.

OUR HEART WAS NOT IN NAPOLI. We had won a victory at Salerno. But the ultimate objective still lay ahead: Naples. For in the final analysis, deep water harbors, with their piers, cranes, and safe anchorages, are as essential to campaigns as beachheads. As in previous Mediterranean operations, the Army called upon the Navy to aid with naval bombardments. When we finally entered the harbor, it was a sickening scene of devastation and ruin. ABOVE. The Germans had cunningly scuttled or sunk every large ship in such a way as to impede our progress, shut off all docks, and foul the channels. Dock installations lay in ruin. Everywhere mines and booby traps lay hidden. This was the harbor of Naples, beauty spot of the continent, teeming port and pride of Italy, home of laughter and song. But incredibly, within four months, Naples harbor was receiving a major amount of Allied shipping. Credit for the tremendous task of rehabilitation went to Commodore William A. Sullivan, USNR, and his harbor clearance Seabees.

ITALY SURRENDERS BUT FIGHTING GOES ON. The ironic news that Italy had surrendered made little impression on the men in the foxholes at Salerno or on the sailors in the ships offshore, under repeated air attack.

ABOVE. Somehow, in the scramble of the surrender, five cruisers and two *Littorio* class battleships of the Italian fleet escaped from German-held ports in Northern Italy, and steamed for Malta. But with the exception of these fleet units, the surrender of Italy made little difference. For the next few months it was a campaign of mud and rain for the American Fifth and the British Eighth Armies, driving for Rome, a campaign that was stalemated until the summer.

In the early morning of January 22, 1944, in an attempt to outflank our own Armies driving for Rome, and establish a beachhead behind the enemy lines, Allied troops launched an assault on the small port city of Anzio, just 30 miles south of Rome. Code name for the operation was "Shingle," and it had been planned to coincide with a general attack along the Fifth and Eighth Army's front.

The assault convoy sailed from Naples the morning of the 21st, and in order to deceive any lurking reconnaissance planes, headed in the direction of Corsica. During the night, the convoy turned and headed for the invasion point. At two o'clock in the morning, H-Hour, the first waves of landing craft headed for the beach. All ships were at general quarters waiting for enemy fire from inland, but none came. The first landings by the assault boats were made with no enemy opposition, much to the troops' surprise.

BITTER FIGHTING ON ANZIO BEACH. At dawn the morning of the Anzio landing the anticipated German resistance finally came. The enemy opened up with his heavy artillery, shells began to fall on the beach. ABOVE. A geyser of water plumes upward as a German shell narrowly misses an amphibious DUKW plowing in with supplies. German aircraft also appeared, but our fighters soon came up from Naples and drove them off. The Germans had mined the beaches thoroughly and casualties from mines in the British area were especially heavy. By the afternoon of D-Day, however, the resort towns of Anzio and Nettuno had been occupied. The Germans had prepared to carry out extensive demolition But the surprise was complete. They had no time to effect the destruction. Anzio beaches presented several problems not previously encountered in Mediterranean operations. Sand bars parallelled the beaches some distance out, and had to be bridged by pontoon causeways.

STALEMATE AT ANZIO. Within a week after D-Day at Anzio the weather turned bad, and remained that way for the next two months. The troops ashore dug in and sat out the long stalemate. During this entire period a screen of cruisers and destroyers patrolled offshore, acting from time to time as a fire support group as well. Not all the attacking Luftwaffe planes were driven off before they let go their weapons of destruction. UPPER. The destroyer *Plunket* after being hit by a German bomb on January 24. LOWER. Looking over the battered roofs of Anzio harbor out to sea. In the background, landing craft and ships are anchored offshore.

ROCKY HARBOR, EXPERT SEAMANSHIP. The entrance to tiny Anzio harbor lay between the end of a jagged seawall and the hulk of a sunken ship. German shelling had eaten away the last twenty feet of the seawall, narrowing the harbor entrance, and leaving a number of jagged rocks just below the water's surface. Trips in and out required smart ship handling, as the weather was usually squally, and a sudden gust of wind might mean a hole in the side of an LCI or LST. As holding the Anzio Beachhead was a touch-and-go-play, LST's and LCI's had to make constant reinforcement convoys. During the five days after D-Day, some LST's and LCI's made as many as five trips. UPPER and LOWER. LST's, LCT's, and LCI's pour supplies into Anzio harbor.

FRIEND AND FOE. Some units of the Italian fleet managed to evade the Germans and surrender to the Allies. UPPER. The Italian submarine *Nichelio* surrenders to the Headquarters Ship, USS *Ancon*, in Salerno Bay. LOWER. Conspicuous in its white paint, a U.S. Navy Hospital Ship lies in a fleet anchorage in the Pacific. By international convention, hospital ships of all nations are painted white and display the red cross prominently.

ROCKETS IN FLIGHT. One of the oldest of modern weapons, and one of the most spectacular, rockets came into their own in this war. Because of the lack of recoil in their launching, they give fire power to smaller vessels far in excess of what could be obtained from guns which require more stable mounts. ABOVE. Rockets streak from a U.S. Navy support ship during the early stages of the invasion of Brunei Bay, Borneo.

BATTLE IN BOUGAINVILLE. The retreating Japanese in the Solomons finally entrenched themselves in Bougainville. On the morning of November first, heavy guns of the fleet and hundreds of planes began battering the shoreline of this island, the biggest and the last stronghold of the Japanese in the northern Solomons. Then a typical amphibious assault was made by our forces. Hundreds of planes in the air covered troop transports and smaller craft. What was far from typical, though, was the lack of Japanese resistance to the initial landings. Not a single shore battery answered the thunderous bombardment. Nor did any Japanese plane appear to challenge the attackers. Apparently, they had been taken by surprise. Marines of the Third Division landed and the struggle began. Months later after bitter fighting, our forces controlled the island, but still many Japanese troops remained hidden in dismal jungles and swamplands. UPPER. Marines, trudging through jungle mud, seek out the fighting Japanese remnants.

THE BATTLE FOR
TARAWA

By Major General Julian C. Smith, USMC

TARAWA—a tiny v-shaped atoll in the vast Pacific—and Betio, a miniature island of the atoll, containing the air field—these were names until recently unknown to most Americans.

With its formidable fortress Betio, Tarawa was of strategic importance because it was the nearest point to our travel routes—San Francisco to Hawaii to Australia—and because it was the first obstruction on the road to Tokyo.

For fifteen months the Japanese had perfected their defenses in the Gilberts, and the heart of their efforts was Betio. They had transformed its flat insignificance into one solid fortress which they felt, with considerable justification, would prove impregnable.

Its beaches and reefs were lined with obstacles and mines. Its shores bristled with coast defense guns, anti-aircraft guns, field artillery, and machine guns. Its flat surface was covered with emplacements, pill boxes, and rifle pits, all scientifically constructed to withstand the heaviest bombardment. Its defenses were manned by 4,000 men of the imperial Japanese landing forces. The admiral in command said, "A million men could not take Tarawa." His confidence was based on realism but failed to take into account the quality of the men who would be taking it.

THE BATTLE BEGINS

BY THE light of a waning moon, the battle of Tarawa began. Warships and planes poured more than 3,000 tons of explosives on tiny Betio. After dawn, three battalions of Marines started ashore in amphibious tractors followed by supports in landing boats. The leading waves in the tractors made the beach with light losses and seized shallow beachheads. Men from the landing craft waded waist deep across the reefs.

In bitter fighting the beachheads were first held, then expanded until artillery and reserves could land. Battleships closed the range until salient targets could be pin-pointed with 16 inch guns. Cruisers and destroyers delivered supporting fires with deadly accuracy at pointblank ranges. Planes bombed and strafed from dawn 'til dark—but the decisive factor was the fighting spirit of the United States Marines on shore.

Desperately, they engaged the enemy with tanks, mortars, rifles, grenades, and flame-throwers—overcoming strong point after strong point, gaining ground by yards and grimly holding every inch of their gains.

In 76 stark and bitter hours an island was taken; its 4,000 defenders slain, and American history was enriched by a new name to stand beside Concord Bridge, Bon Homme Richard, the Alamo, and Belleau Wood.

Tarawa was a battle for which there was no precedent. Precedents were made, not followed. It was a battle of firsts: the first American assault on a fortified atoll; the first reef impassable to landing craft to be crossed under fire: the first use of amphibious tractors as troop carriers. It set the pattern for future amphibious operations in the Central Pacific. It was the beginning of the end of Japan's dream of empire.

Tarawa was a great shock to the American people who had come to believe that wars could be won without bloody fighting. It cost the lives of nearly a thousand American boys and brought sorrow to as many homes. It brought home to the American people the grim reality that there is no cheap, short-cut to win wars. It showed definitely that men well entrenched and determined to fight to the last ditch cannot be destroyed by bombardment alone but only by other men imbued with greater determination to cross that ditch.

THE RESULTS

TARAWA proved, as it never need be proved again, that Americans can hold their own with the best fighting men in the world. The enemy was Japan's best, fighting from behind cover against our men in the open, yet their dead lay four to one in the dug-outs. After witnessing the valor of the men who took Tarawa, I shall always have for every Marine a feeling of reverence and respect.

As the war moved westward, Tarawa lost its military significance except as an inter-island air stop. It became a shrine where those who walk among the rusting tanks, the silent guns, and the torn palms, pause in silent reverence as they view the graves in Betio's white and shifting sands.

Today it has lost even its utility as an air base but it will stand forever a landmark on the road to Victory. Natives tend the 37 cemeteries on Betio where those men lie who died perfecting the pattern of amphibious warfare.

"So there let them rest on their sun-scoured atoll,
The wind for their watcher, the waves for their shroud,
Where palm and pandanus shall whisper forever
A requiem fitting for heroes so proud."

Julian C. Smith

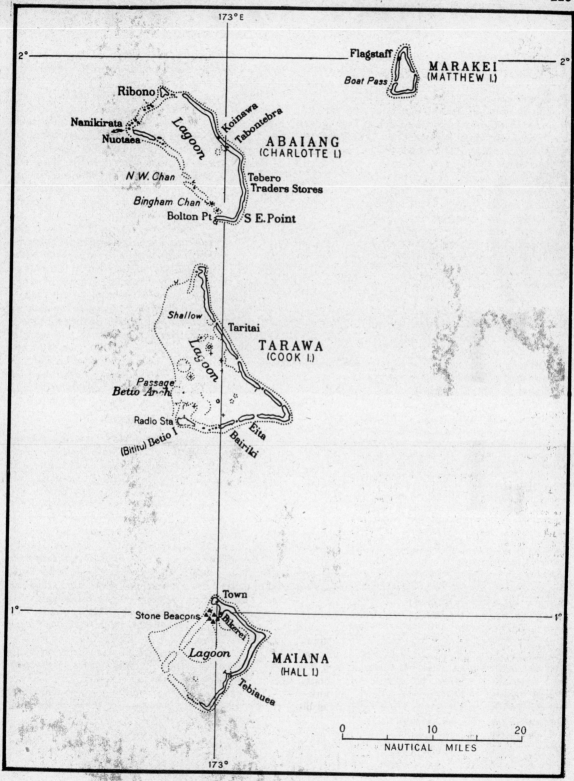

Map of Tarawa and adjacent atolls.

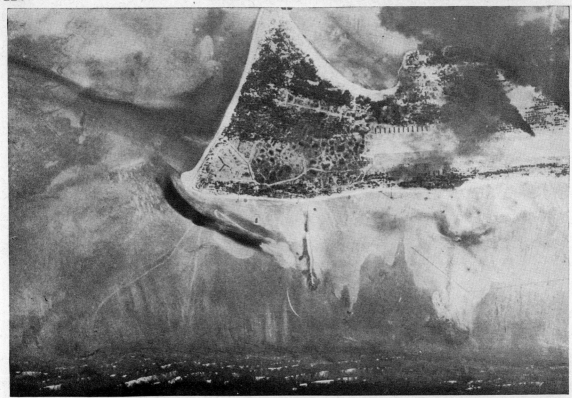

"BLOODY TARAWA." While the joint arm—longe range Army bombers and planes of the U.S. Navy carrier force—pounds the ground installations of the Japanese stronghold of Tarawa from the air, the big guns of the fleet standing off-shore lay down a heavy barrage. Within a few hours, streamers of smoke, like those depicted here, clouded the atoll from aerial reconnaissance. Besides wrecking numerous pillboxes, blockhouses and gun emplacements, the deluge of explosives sank two medium-sized Jap steamers and numerous smaller vessels and destroyed nine medium bombers on the ground. The attacking force lost four carrier-based planes.

UPPER. An aerial photograph of the coast of Tarawa. LOWER. Despite the devastating bombardment which preceded the landing of the U. S. Marines on Tarawa, the enemy was ready and waiting. The landing was further complicated by treacherous offshore reefs and man-made under water obstacles of concrete and cable which forced Marines to disembark with their equipment from landing boats 500 to 900 yards from the beach. Wading toward land, and sometimes swimming, they made easy targets for Jap sharpshooters.

Finally, however, combat teams of the first wave made the sandy beach and dug in. Then, a few hours later, the forward push began. It was slow going. The enemy contested every foot of land stubbornly. Surrenders were rare. Death was everywhere and bayonets and hand grenades were death's weapons. Tarawa will go down in history with Belleau Wood, Chapultepec, Guadalcanal, Saipan, and Iwo Jima as one of the Marine Corps' most gallant fights.

VICTORY AT TARAWA. UPPER. U. S. Marines paid a high price but won a great victory over deeply entrenched and fiercely resisting Japanese on Tarawa. The enemy was destroyed almost to the last man—only a few hundred of the attacking force escaped injury or death. Sprawled bodies testify to the ferocity of the struggle for this little stretch of land on the road to Japan. **LOWER.** Though an inferno for 72 hours beginning November 20, 1943, quiet now reigns over a particularly hot sector on Tarawa. Bodies float in the water and lie along the beach. An "Alligator," Landing Vehicle Tracked, hangs on the sea wall where it was stopped. Another LVT stands in the water at the right,

BATTLE'S END. On Tarawa's narrow and littered beach U. S. Marines, some wounded and all exhausted by battle and the suffocating heat, take it easy after being told that the atoll is secured. A few hours earlier, all organized Japanese resistance ceased. Nevertheless individual enemies turned up again that night to make personal war against the victorious Americans. One Jap managed to gain the lip of a shell hole being used as a regimental command post before a sentry dropped him with a bullet.

Others, after abortive attempts to infiltrate through Marine lines, retired to their own dugouts and committed suicide rather than surrender. Here on Tarawa the Jap suicides largely abandoned the traditional hara kiri. Instead, they removed their shoes and used their toes to pull the trigger of a rifle whose muzzle was held in their mouths. Dozens of the enemy died this way. Hundreds of others had sacrificed their lives as fruitlessly in frontal assaults earlier in the day in attempt to crack the invaders. Hand-to-hand fighting was commonplace.

Story after story drifted across the blackened battlefield of men who killed Japs with their rifle butts or, when the rifle was shattered, with their bare hands. Then, too, there were those other stories . . . stories of the Jap officer who sabered a Marine in the back, of the Marine who was shot in the back as he was in the act of carrying a wounded comrade to safety. ABOVE. A section of the beach on Betio Island, Tarawa Atoll, Gilbert Islands, a resting place for the Marine Corps wounded after the battle.

"COMMENCE OPERATIONS." A Navy torpedo bomber circles her carrier while on an anti-submarine patrol. The carrier and the South Dakota class battleship in the background are members of the task forces that took part in the offensive operations in the Marshall Islands during the early weeks of 1944. Two years had passed since February, 1942, when the first American strikes had occurred there, but by January, 1944 the American forces were ready to take over in this area and tear away the Marshalls from Japan's empire.

THE MANDATES ARE BLASTED.

It was the 30th of January, 1944 when the American task forces struck the Marshall Islands with the intention of seizing them from the Japanese. Simultaneous attacks were directed at Kwajalein, Roi, Taroa, and Wotje by U.S. carrier forces. Navy shore-based aircraft bombed the four islands and two others, Mille and Jaluit, as well. Cruisers moved in and bombarded Taroa and Wotje.

The bombings continued for two days, and on February the 1st the landing commenced. Troops went ashore on Majuro and occupied the island. Landings occurred on Roi and Namur on February 2nd, and by the afternoon the 4th Marine Division had overcome all Jap resistance and had the situation well in hand. The Army's 7th Division landed on Kwajalein, and against increasing resistance moved ahead until the 8th when the entire atoll was in their possession.

In the days following, U S. Naval Forces continued the strikes at the remaining Jap-held islands of the Marshall Group. February 17th and 18th saw the daring and devastating attack on the islands of Truk, Japan's "Gibraltar" of the Pacific. The initial phase of the strike involved carrier-based aircraft. Then the battlewagons steamed in with many cruisers and destroyers. Together they pummelled the island's installations. On the 17th an expeditionary task group of United States Marines assaulted Eniwetok Atoll, which had received a treatment of bombs and shells for several days. Engebi Island fell to American forces on the 18th, Eniwetok on the 20th. With the capture of Eniwetok, control of the Marshall Islands passed into American hands.

LEFT. This striking photograph shows the effects of the opening phase of the Pacific Fleet bombardment of Wotje, one of the eight Japanese bases in the Marshall and Gilbert Island groups blasted by fleet guns and planes in the raid of 1 February. Carrier-based bombers have already set an ammunition dump, and two fuel dumps afire.

COMMITTED TO THE DEEP. Two enlisted men of the ill-fated escort carrier *Liscome Bay*, torpedoed by a Japanese submarine in the assault on the Gilbert Islands, are buried at sea from the deck of a Coast Guard manned attack transport. Other *Liscome Bay* survivors and Coast Guardsmen witness the service.

The CVE's (Navy official designation of escort carriers) were originally designed for anti-submarine warfare, but they proved themselves effective in providing air support during amphibious operations in the Pacific. The invasion of the Gilbert Islands brought the first "Jeep Carrier" casualty in the Pacific War. Just how the Jap torpedo managed the fatal hit is still somewhat of a mystery. Two theories have been advanced: (1) The Japanese submarine commander launched his deadly fish at one of the screening ships and it missed its target, continued on its way and lodged in the *Liscome Bay*. (2) The other theory is that there were one or more submarines in the area, and when a screening destroyer pulled out of line to investigate a contact, the enemy slipped a torpedo through the hole and aimed it at the CVE. The little flat-top burst immediately into flame from a midships hit, was rocked by other explosions and sank quickly.

Casualties were heavy. Included among those lost were Rear Admiral H. M. Mullinix, USN, whose flag flew on the *Liscome Bay*, the ship's commanding officer, and a large number of officers and men. Many were officially listed as missing in action because there was no definite information as to whether they actually went down with the ship or escaped only to die in the water.

DOWN THE RAMP. Out of the jowls of an LST, manned by the Coast Guard, Marines pour down the ramp to wade ashore at Cape Gloucester, New Britain. They are part of one of the many amphibious landings made on December 15. At other points, soldiers of General MacArthur's Army were also landed. In invasions such as this, the Japanese were slowly but surely pushed out of the southwest Pacific.

Most amphibious assaults made by American forces in these islands followed a rather regular pattern, but in the invasion of New Britain, a gigantic number of small amphibious tractors were used. They were necessary because of the formidable coral reef barriers and shallow swamps of New Britain's coast and its dense jungle further inland. Landings had to be made at a great many points scattered throughout the island.

ABOVE. One of these tractors being unloaded. They served many varied purposes excellently. At Arawe, amphibians, loaded with infantry men and supplies, were launched into the sea five miles from their landing beach, under cover of pre-dawn darkness. Their speed, mobility, and compactness which made them small targets permitted them to land many Army assault teams without the loss of a single soldier, despite enemy fire from shore and Japanese dive-bomber attacks. After landing infantry, amphibious tractors, mounting .50 caliber machine guns, spearheaded drives which secured beachheads at several landings. They were also used as tanks and as substitutes for bulldozers in bowling over brush and trees and clearing wooded areas,

THE INVASION OF NEW GEORGIA. Guadalcanal in the south Solomons was taken, so was Rendova. New Georgia was next in the steady American drive to capture the Solomons. On July 5 a Navy task force battered the island with heavy guns and opened the way for the landing of troops by a destroyer group.

The landing was made before dawn on a remote part of the island. It was a land movement from the rear, not a direct assault from the sea. Troops landed and waited for daylight to begin the fighting march overland. During the night a heavy downpour fell and in the morning the jungle floor was a sea of mud. Huge fallen trees with slippery moss, and myriad roots of giant banyans slowed the progress of the Marine raiders and soldiers. Further inland the terrain became worse. Sharp, corral-like rocks, thick, overhanging vines and creepers, and prickly plants that pierced jungle suits, added to their hazards. After three days of marching, the raiders were in the thick of enemy area. A series of bitter engagements took place. There was a heavy opposition. Enemy machine gun nests and snipers concealed in the roots of big trees and overhead foliage took a severe toll of our troops. But the island was captured and quickly converted into a base for the forthcoming American campaigns.

ABOVE. Seabees who performed most of the building are working on a tough patch of coral while the sun streams through dust laden air. They are using pneumatic hammers and dynamite to hew a jungle road after it was cleared by charging bulldozers.

ALLIES ON GREEN ISLAND. The assault and occupation of Green Island in the southwest Pacific was truly an allied campaign. Fiji natives, inhabitants of neighboring islands and born jungle fighters, joined American and New Zealand forces in battle against the Japanese.

ABOVE. Members of the First Fiji Infantry race off a Navy landing barge at a deserted plantation on Kukudo River. These wily fighters contributed much to the discomfit of the Japanese troops—to put it mildly. The capture of Green Island greatly bolstered the allied position in the Solomons. Our forces there cut off Japanese supply lines from Truk to Rabaul, thus preventing the enemy troops on New Britain from being reinforced. Our airpower was strengthened, too, when Seabees with machete knifes and bulldozers cleared jungle land for an airbase.

The story of how these fighters with great engineering ability accomplished prodigious building feats while overcoming many obstacles in record-breaking time is an epic in itself. To build the roads and airstrips on Green Island Seabees worked 24 hours a day. Tractor operators, truck drivers, riggers, dynamiters, excavating shovel operators all worked on eight-hour shifts throughout the day. The problems of terrain were tremendous. Top soil had to be removed along the runway area to reach the hard coral. Then additional quantities of large coral had to be transported from pits on the island. Heavy diesel-powered rollers crushed this to form a smooth, weather-resisting surface for our dive-bombers which wreaked havoc on enemy supply lines.

THE CAPTURE OF
KWAJALEIN

By Admiral Richmond K. Turner, USN

BLOODY Tarawa had fallen, but any further progress toward Japan was blocked by the Japanese-held Marshall Islands. Comprising some 37 atolls and islands with a combined land-sea area of 375,000 square miles, they lay halfway between Hawaii and New Guinea. They were heavily fortified; and with numerous airfields, and with harbors large enough to moor the fleets of the world, they could not be by-passed. But being practically the eastern extremity of the Carolines, once in our hands they would give us the first of a series of stepping stones almost all the way to the Philippines. Planning for their capture was begun as early as October, 1943, and the actual assault was made at the end of January, 1944.

The decision was made to capture most of the western of Ralik chain of the Marshalls, including mainly the islands of Kwajalein, Roi, Namur, and Eniwetok, and simply leave the eastern chain, containing strongly fortified Wotje, Maloelap, Mili, Jaluit, and Nauru, by-passed and neutralized. For the task a force was assembled strong enough even to match the main Japanese fleet if it appeared. In addition to transports, landing craft, minesweepers, etc., this force contained 8 battleships, including the *Iowa* and *New Jersey*, two of our very latest superdreadnaughts; 6 large aircraft carriers, including the *Saratoga*; 5 small carriers and 2 escort carriers; 12 heavy cruisers and 5 light cruisers; and over 50 destroyers.

During the entire month of January the whole Marshalls group was plastered by air attacks, getting consecutively heavier. Meanwhile the assault troops and bombardment ships were assembling both from the West Coast and Hawaii. By January 28, they were all in position.

THE FURY STARTS

TERRIFIC air strikes were made on both the eastern and western chains on January 29, and also on January 30. At the same time surface ships were told off to bombard the eastern chain, especially Wotje. As a result the eastern chain was so badly battered that it could give no help to Kwajalein and the rest of the western chain when the real assault struck there.

But the real fury of the assault fell on the western islands. On January 30 everything from the sixteen inch shells of the *Iowa* and *Massachusetts* to the five inch guns of the destroyers and the rockets of the rocket ships burst upon Kwajalein, Roi, Namur, and the surrounding atolls. At the same time hundreds of planes from the carriers dived and strafed, hitting with everything from bombs to machine-gun bullets. Not even the long-prepared, reinforced concrete gun emplacements, bombproof shelters, and barricades could withstand the tornado of explosives. Thick concrete bombproofs were rent apart, huge guns blown from their emplacements, and concrete barricades smashed to rubble. Japanese soldiers exposed in trenches and foxholes had their necks broken from the blasts. Reconnaissance planes had previously photographed the islands so thoroughly that almost every pillbox and gun emplacement was hit with pinpoint accuracy. At Roi the battleship *North Carolina* attained as high as 95 percent hits.

Kwajalein Island is only 2½ miles long by 1,000 to 2,500 feet wide; Roi and Namur are even smaller. Practically every foot of terrain was swept with gunfire. But beneath their coconut shelters and amid the ruins of their concrete bombproofs the Japanese prepared to put up a desperate resistance.

KWAJALEIN ITSELF

EARLY on February 1, 24 LCI's equipped with rocket projectors moved to within 600 yards of the shore and deluged the landing beaches with rockets. Then from the transports outside, the LVT's and DUKW's crossed the reefs and landed the assault troops on the beach. By nightfall we had 11,600 troops ashore, as well as tanks and other equipment, and they had already fought well inland. With their usual tactics the Japanese made suicide attacks and night infiltrations. But by nightfall of February 4, the capture of Kwajalein was complete. And by nightfall of February 5, we were in complete possession of the lower 26 islands and atolls of Kwajalein at a loss to ourselves of only 174 killed and missing, and some 712 wounded. The Japanese casualties totaled 4,650 killed and about 50 prisoners.

Roi and Namur had fallen even before Kwajalein Island. Eniwetok fell on February 21. The way lay open ahead to the west—toward Saipan, Guam, Tinian, and then on to the Philippines, Iwo Jima, Okinawa, and the shores of Japan. It was not necessary to capture Wotje and the rest of the eastern Marshalls. Cut off from the rest of the Japanese Empire, constantly pounded by air attacks, they were reduced to impotency, to fall into our hands ultimately.

R. K. Turner

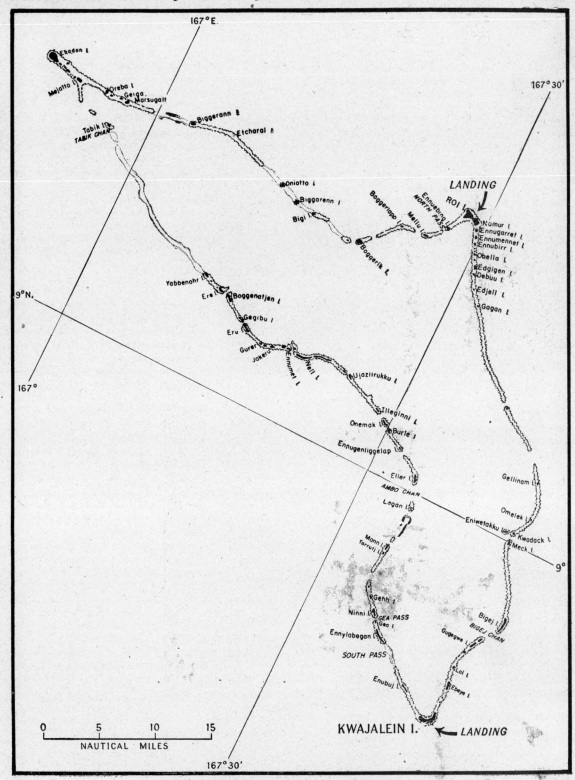

Map of Kwajalein Atoll, indicating landing points.

ANOTHER STEP TOWARD TOKYO — KWAJALEIN.

The Marshall Islands are a strange, sandy battleground. Kwajalein lies in the western "Sunset" group. For two months before our attack, the principal atolls in the Marshalls had been smashed and softened from the air. The invasion of Kwajalein came in the form of a tremendous two-pronged attack from the north and south.

Two days before the actual invasion, the pounding of the islands was stepped up to unprecedented volume. For hours before the troops went ashore the explosions sounded almost like a symphony of giant kettledrums. Japanese artillery was blasted out of existence. The airfields were turned into rubble. Gun emplacements, underground shelters, log and concrete pillboxes—all were pulverized by the barrage.

UPPER. U.S. ships bombarding Roi and Namur Islands. LEFT. A reconnaissance view of the Japanese stronghold on Kwajalein atoll as it looked the day before the bombardment opened. Less than twelve hours after this picture was taken all structures in area had been demolished.

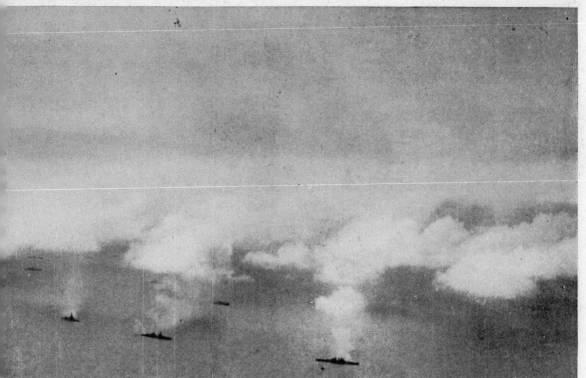

THE OLD "ONE-TWO" IN THE MARSHALLS. When the landing forces hit the beaches of Roi, Namur, and Kwajalein they encountered stiff resistance at some points. But pre-invasion bombings had done their job well. Islands flanking Roi and Namur were captured on January 31, 1944, while close inshore, the fleet continued to pound the main targets.

Landings at Namur had been scheduled for 1100 on February 1, 1944. Despite the handicaps of heavy rain and clouds of smoke the landings were made exactly on schedule. They drew light matching gun fire and rifle opposition from the smashed and shattered pillboxes. The going was tougher on Namur. Marines crossed over from Roi in the afternoon and, later, another landing was made on Namur from the ocean side. The Marines, paced by dive bombers and artillery from adjacent islands soon wiped out all resistance.

RIGHT. Japanese installations on Namur go sky high as demolition squads go into action. Marines return enemy sniper fire on Roi Island beach in the foreground.

JAPAN'S "PEARL HAR-BOR." Hard on the heels of the smashing amphibious victory at Kwajalein came the devastating trip hammer blow to Japan's proud naval bastion at Truk in the Carolines. UPPER. From the flight decks of the *Yorktown, Essex, Enterprise, Bunker Hill, Intrepid,* and *Belleau Wood* came this two day shuttle service of Dauntless and Avenger bombers.

LOWER. Plumes of smoke testify to our Naval pilot-bomber's skill as docking facilities are pummeled with more bombs. Task Force 58's ships and planes sank 2 light cruisers, 3 destroyers, 1 ammunition ship, 2 oilers, 2 gunboats, 8 cargo ships, and 5 unidentified vessels; 204 planes were destroyed in combat and over 50 damaged on the ground. Six additional ships were listed as probably sunk and 11 damaged.

We lost 19 planes but recovered several of their pilots and crewmen. During a night attack, the *Intrepid* was hit near the stern by a torpedo. It was a part step in avenging Pearl Harbor.

THE WHITE MAN RETURNS TO TRUK. The Carolines are situated approximately 3,000 miles from Hawaii and about 1,500 miles north of Australia. In land area they would equal about ⅔ the state of Rhode Island but if superimposed over the United States they would extend from Baltimore to Denver. Originally called the New Philippines after their discovery by the Portuguese in 1527, the islands were renamed the Carolines in 1685 after Charles II of Spain.

Germany bought the group in 1899 after the Spanish-American War but lost them in World War I to Japan who got them under the mandate of the League of Nations. The mandate specified that the islands were not to be fortified. Contrary to agreement the Japanese moved into the islands and closed them off from all foreign eyes. It wasn't until February 4th, 1944, when the Marines sent two B-24s over Truk at 20,000 feet with "super-eye" cameras, that the United States Navy was able to find out what was really going on at Truk. Photo reports visaged a great enemy fleet at anchor. Fully recovered from Pearl Harbor our Navy was ready to vindicate the very reason for its existence—to seek out the enemy fleet and destroy it. And that is exactly what it set out to do on the 17th and 18th of February, 1944.

ABOVE. Eten anchorage in the Truk atoll under attack. Great as the devastation was, what the white men found at Truk was not the Jap fleet but a collection of vessels that would scarcely have made a respectable task force. Because of the Marine visit on the 4th the Japanese had decided to evacuate their major fleet units.

UNSINKÁBLE CARRIERS. Japan had boasted in prewar days that she would control the Pacific by airpower based on coral islands and islets bespeckling it. For the first two years of the war it looked as though she was making good her brag. Some people in the United States even held that the only way to wrest Japan's command of the sea was by land-based air power. ABOVE. Not sunk, but useless to the enemy, these bomb-pocked runways at Truk littered with the wreckage of planes and gun-emplacements expose the fallacy of Japan's strategy. When Admiral Spruance withdrew on February 18th, 1944, his Fifth Fleet had sealed the fate of Truk. With 75 to 100 thousand tons of enemy shipping and over 200 planes destroyed, the myth of mutually supporting insular bases proved to be no stronger than the fleet and air forces based upon them. Thus the Navy's carriers proved the unsinkable island theory wrong.

ACTION IN THE WEST. Eniwetok atoll is on the fringe of the Marshall Islands group, about 285 miles northeast of Kwajalein. The entire atoll is only 21 miles long and its highest peak is barely 16 feet above sea level. A coral atoll is by all odds the most difficult objective to attack by amphibious operations. It offers no cover. It must be reached by navigation through dangerous reef formations and exposed approaches. At Eniwetok, shelling and bombing on an incredible scale were the answers to these basic problems.

The landings at Kwajalein had the element of tactical surprise. They were a blow at the most important base, well in the center of the atolls, and apparently came as a complete surprise. Victory at the center virtually neutralized the enemy strongholds on the outer fringes of the island group.

The Japanese got another surprise when U.S. troops landed on Eniwetok. The enemy expected us to consolidate our position in the Marshalls by attacks on the eastern group of the atolls. Instead, our forces, as part of their drive toward Tokyo, hit at the westernmost atoll in the group. To confuse the Japanese, our forces bombed and raided many islands in all sections of the group before setting out to bomb and bombard Eniwetok. Four weeks before the actual assault, swarms of carrier based planes slashed and tore at the island defenses. Days before the landings, guns of the vast support armada joined in the shelling.

UPPER. First, second, and third waves of landing craft with Marine assault troops approach Engebi Island, Eniwetok Atoll, under smokescreen cover on February 18,1944 The effectiveness of the pre-invasion bombing is evident by the condition of the airstrip on the island.

"...THE TUMULT AND THE SHOUTING DIES..." UPPER. While his buddy covers him from a distance, a Marine armed with a tommy-gun fires at a Japanese straggler in a fox-hole.

Eniwetok was invaded on February 17, 1944, and by the 22nd had been completely secured. The fighting, while fierce, was sporadic and limited to minor engagements. The Japanese troops found on the island were stunned and shaken by the ferocity of the naval bombardment which preceded the actual attack. While the battle they put up was determined, it was disorganized.

LOWER. These Marines, begrimed and weary from two days and two nights of fighting, are relaxing with a cup of coffee aboard a coast guard manned assault transport. These men swept the Japanese from Engebi Island in six hours and then went on to Eniwetok Island proper, where they blasted the enemy out of his stronghold in five days.

Almost overshadowing the actual invasion of Eniwetok was the covering operation, the first aerial strike at the Japanese base at Truk. This strike, an overwhelming success, was carried out to forestall any possible Japanese counter attack on Eniwetok by Jap fleet units from Truk. The invasion of Eniwetok and the attack on Truk inaugurated a series of far-reaching blows which emphasized the extent of the retreat which had been forced upon Japan by the U.S. Pacific Fleet. The main Jap lines had been reached and pierced.

THE NAVY LOSES A LEADER. Early in the afternoon of April 28, 1944, radio messages to all Navy ships and shore stations carried the news of the death of the Secretary of the Navy, Frank Knox. Frank Knox was named Secretary of the Navy in 1940. In the subsequent four years as the Navy's civilian head, he supervised the Navy expansion program, saw the Navy fight back from the bitter defeat of the first months of the actual war, and led it to its present power as the mightiest seaforce in history.

ABOVE. Secretary Knox on tour of inspection. In the early days of the United States offensive in the South Pacific, he toured the Navy "front lines" in the Pacific and underwent enemy bombing attacks on several occasions. Frank Knox was one of the greatest proponents of a "Two Ocean Navy" that the United States has ever had. To this end he worked tirelessly from the time he took office till the day he died.

Among the hundreds of tributes and condolences which poured in from Allied leaders, his former military associates, and prominent Americans, were these words by Admiral Ernest J. King, Commander-in-Chief U.S. Fleet. Said King: "Well done, Frank Knox. We dedicate ourselves, one and all, to what surely would have been his last order—'Carry On!'"

HITTING THE BEACH. During the Marianas operation, forces under General MacArthur made various amphibious landings all along the North Coast of New Guinea. The purpose of these landings was to prevent the Japanese from making air or troop movements in Western New Guinea, and from making approaches from the southwest to our lines of communication.

To secure airports for the support of further westward operations, an unopposed landing was made at Arara on the Dutch New Guinea mainland. Extending their beachhead along the coast from Toem to the Tor River, the troops made shore to shore movements to the Wakde Islands on May 17 and 18. By May 19 all organized enemy resistance had ceased.

ABOVE. LCI's reach the beach in the second wave of the invasion of Sarmi, Dutch New Guinea. A Coast Guard combat photographer, coming in with the first wave, was able to catch this striking beachhead picture. Stretcher bearers are shown going down the ramps and plunging through the surf in the amphibious assault which resulted in the capture of Wakde and Sarmi—important for their strategic air strips. In the distance, the dim light of early morning discloses an American destroyer keeping vigil for enemy aircraft and surface craft. This scene at dawn was re-enacted time and again until a series of stepping stones had been established which enabled the United States forces to move westward and bring the war right up to the Japanese home islands.

THE INVASION OF
NORMANDY

By Vice Admiral Alan G. Kirk, USN

TO MANY Americans the expression "D-day" means but one thing—June 6, 1944. It was on that day that the greatest aggregation of land, sea, and air forces ever assembled hurled themselves against the Normandy coast and struck the combined blow that was the beginning of the end for the Nazi military machine.

As early as January 1933, the Combined Chiefs of Staffs at the Casablanca Conference had projected this invasion. Almost from the beginning military leaders everywhere had realized that, regardless of Russian victories or long-range bombing, sooner or later the German fortress of Europe would have to be invaded and the Nazis decisively beaten on their own soil before complete victory could be achieved.

That resistance would be bitter had already been proved in the Allied commando raid on Dieppe in 1942, which resulted in almost complete annihilation of the attacking troops. The outer fringes of the bastion of Europe were studded with steel and concrete, beach obstacles, and mines. From Wilhelmshaven to Bordeaux enemy troops and millions of political slaves had labored four frantic years, pouring the concrete and digging the caves, making the "western wall" of Europe the most formidable barrier ever known to fighting man. The Germans themselves called it "impregnable."

Early in 1943 advance units of the U. S. Navy amphibious forces began to arrive in the British Isles to prepare stage for the Invasion. After the establishment of "Base 1" in Ireland, our sailors and Seabees began the construction of other bases in England as "jumping off" points for the great attack. "Base 2" was in Scotland; then came amphibious bases at Pernarth and Milford Haven in Wales, at Falmouth and Plymouth, at Poole and Weymouth and Southampton and Fowey. At every cove and bay which could conceivably be used for harboring and loading naval vessels, the Royal Navy and the U. S. Navy set up installations and began readying the landing craft and transports which were to carry our troops to the shores of the enemy. Intensive training operations were instituted in every phase of amphibious warfare from boat-handling to gas-mask drills. In January 1944, General Eisenhower arrived in England to take supreme command of all the invasion forces. By March had begun the three months of continuous pounding by the U. S. 8th Air Force, the U. S. 9th Air Force, and the Royal Air Force at targets along the coast and in northern France, the Low Countries, and Western Germany.

WHEN AND WHERE

EVERYONE knew what was coming—even the Germans. But what only a few men in all the world knew was *where* the blow would come and *when* it would come. The answers to those questions were among the most closely guarded secrets of the entire war, and were known only to a few of the highest commanders in the Allied forces. As D-day approached, the air attacks were intensified. Actual loading of assault troops began on June 1. The men were briefed and the ships "sealed," and the great armada hung poised on the southern cost of Britain, waiting only for the final "this is it" message from Supreme Allied Headquarters.

D-day had originally been set as June 5, but due to adverse weather conditions there was a last postponement of 24 hours. Then on the night of June 5, our last-minute air attacks rose to a crescendo, paratroopers made their jumps far inland, and the great armada moved across the Channel. And for the next 24 hours the fate of Europe perhaps lay in the hands of the United States and Royal Navies.

But almost every contingency had been anticipated in a masterpiece of far-sighted planning. From long months before, things had been figured to the last inch and last second. A fleet of 4,000 ships, converging from half the points of the compass, and of varying sizes and varying speeds, reached the rendezvous with split-second timing. And from that point on, all those vessels continued to operate with split-second timing.

THE LANDING

THE site selected for the landing was a stretch of beach on the Normandy coast between the Seine and halfway up the Cotentin Peninsula. British troops were to land on the eastern beaches, and American troops on the western beaches. Complete direction of the operation while crossing the Channel lay in the hands of the naval commanders: Rear Admiral Alan G. Kirk, USN, commanded the U. S. Naval forces and Admiral Sir Philip Vian, RN, commanded the British Naval forces.

Minesweepers were already far ahead, sweeping channels right in to the beach and dropping lighted buoys to mark the swept channels. Reference vessels were posted at every turn in the courses, to guide traffic into the proper lanes. Inside the 1,000-yard line off shore special control vessels would guide the assault boats in the final dash.

All across the Channel the great armada stretched, with the battleships, cruisers, and destroyers guarding the van and the flanks. A veritable umbrella of air coverage gave protection against air attack. Air patrols as well as surface vessels kept down any U-boat that might venture near. Then the bombardment ships moved in and began hurling an avalanche of shells against the surprised Nazi pillboxes, entrenchments, and gun emplacements. The old U. S. battleship *Texas* opened fire at 12,000 yards; the old *Arkansas* moved in to 6,000 yards—a bare three miles. The destroyers delivered their fire at such close range that, as one observer put it, "they had their bows against the beach." That avalanche of shells beat down German 88's and 105's high up on the bluffs above Omaha Beach; it hammered the concrete gun emplacements amid the dunes and swampland of Utah Beach.

Then the transports, reaching the Transport Area, lowered their assault craft, the LVCP's and LCM's; the troops swarmed down, and the amphibious craft chugged off toward shore with their loads. Already, ahead of them, the Navy and Army Demolition teams were driving in through the shallow water, blowing up underwater obstacles under a hail of enemy bullets. Too, enemy mobile 88's and 105's and other Nazi guns which had lain outside the zone of fire of the bombardment vessels, began to open up with a heavy crossfire, and casualties were heavy. Offshore vessels were struck, to flame up or lie helpless and sinking. Now the U. S. Coast Guard rescue craft, especially equipped and trained, plunged in under the fire and made sensational rescues as they pulled men from the water or from sinking wrecks. Then bombers and ships' gun fire searched out the hidden guns and put them permanently out of commission.

THE FIRST DAY

BY LATE afternoon our troops had secured the landing beaches. At the end of the first 24 hours, 66,000 troops had been landed on the two American beaches; at the end of seven days, almost 250,000 Americans were ashore. The supply ships were now moving across a steady stream of supplies, ammunition, and reinforcements. Block-ships were sunk to form breakwaters in the open roads. The secret "Mulberries"—huge floating harbors constructed in sections and towed across—were assembled to form the long piers so necessary for the countless supplies needed for the drive through France and Germany. By September 1, over 2,000,000 men, 440,000 vehicles, and 2,480,000 tons of stores had been landed by the Allies, and all but a small portion of them had gone in over the beaches.

For the ultimate battle of Germany, however, permanent harbors were needed. Cherbourg offered an ideal solution, but Cherbourg remained in Nazi hands. And to Cherbourg's previously powerful defenses the Nazis had in four years added tremendous strength. Driving across the peninsula, our ground troops attacked Cherbourg from the rear. From the Channel our naval forces attacked the seaward side. Against the enormous coast defense guns in the land forts of Cherbourg our battleships and cruisers and destroyers matched their own naval guns. Down they swept, in plain view of the coast, and with amazing skill dropped their shells on enemy gun emplacements with pin-point accuracy. With their forts beaten down around their ears, the Nazis finally surrendered. And the U. S. Navy at Cherbourg as well as at Normandy had proved that what had been regarded for two hundred years as a military axiom was just another fallacy—i.e., that naval ships cannot engage on equal terms with strong coast defense guns in permanent fortifications. The U. S. Navy had not only engaged the Nazi land fortresses on equal terms, they had overwhelmed them with superior gunfire.

Alan Kirk

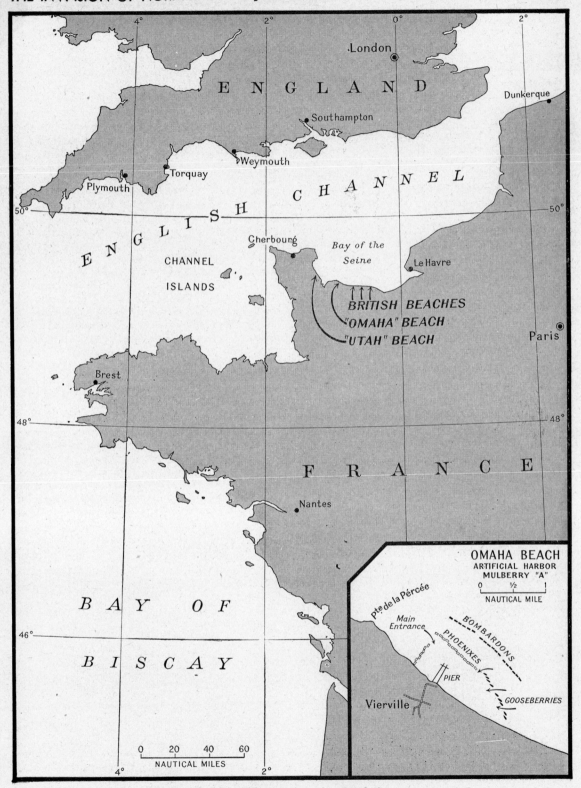

ENGLAND

London

Dunkerque

Southampton

4°

Weymouth

Torquay

Plymouth

50°   50°

E N G L I S H   C H A N N E L

Cherbourg   Bay of the
                   Seine

CHANNEL
ISLANDS   Le Havre

BRITISH BEACHES
"OMAHA" BEACH
"UTAH" BEACH

Paris

Brest

48°   48°

F R A N C E

Nantes

B A Y   O F

46°

B I S C A Y

OMAHA BEACH
ARTIFICIAL HARBOR
MULBERRY "A"

0   ½   1
NAUTICAL MILE

Pte de la Pêrcée

Main
Entrance   BOMBARDONS

PHOENIXES

PIER   GOOSEBERRIES

Vierville

0   20   40   60
NAUTICAL MILES

Chart of the Normandy invasion with a detail of
Omaha Beach.

GREATEST AMPHIBIOUS ASSAULT. Two years of planning and preparation went into the great invasion of Normandy. A system of 15 U.S. Naval bases in English south coast ports supplied and harbored nearly 2,500 U.S. Naval craft assigned to the assault. UPPER. An LCI, with historic Dart castle on the starboard beam, passes through the submarine net at Dartmouth harbor on the way to Normandy. Squally weather delayed the assault convoys' sailing by 24 hours. Any further delay would have caused the operation to be called off for two weeks. LOWER. Barrage balloons floating overhead, an LST disgorges supplies onto a powered "Rhino" barge, which enabled LSTs to unload without beaching, a complicated process in Normandy due to 19-foot tides,

TREACHEROUS UNDER-WATER OBSTACLES. UPPER. Germans had laid underwater obstacles such as these along the entire coast of Normandy. Exposed at low tide and covered with water at high tide, they presented dangerous obstacles to landing craft and difficult barriers to surmount.

Scant minutes before H-Hour, specially trained Navy Combat Demolition Teams crept ashore in LCVP's. Each man carried 40 pounds of TNT strapped to his chest. Working in small groups, these men were under constant peril from hostile fire, and some units suffered heavy casualties. But by D-plus two days, 85 percent of all the enemy obstacles had been removed.

LEFT. Carrying heavy packs and rifles, Army troops trying to get to shore through the heavy surf find it hard going. Aboard the Coast Guard LCI 675, one crew member, foreground, swam through the heavy enemy fire to carry a line ashore. Wrapping the line around himself, he then served as a human anchor in the midst of enemy fire. Many of the troops that followed him did not reach shore.

NAVY GUNS JOIN IN CHERBOURG ASSAULT. By 20 days after D-day, U. S. troops had reached the environs of the port of Cherbourg and were preparing for a final assault on this prime objective. To assist in the land assault, the Army called for a naval bombardment. Three old U. S. battleships, the *Texas*, the *Arkansas*, and *Nevada*, together with British and American cruisers pounded the heavy enemy fortresses around the harbor into defenseless rubble. UPPER. Mute testimony to the accuracy of Navy fire. Debris lies around a hole made by a direct hit in the mine control room of Fort de l'Ouest. LOWER. Two Navy Beach Battalion men hit the sand for protection as a German plane swoops over to strafe the beach. The camera has failed to stop their speed of their precipitate dive.

LANDING SHIP—TRAINS. LST's, which in previous invasions, had demonstrated their adaptability by carrying such conglomerate items as men, tanks, trucks, supplies, mountain mules, and Cub airplanes for spotting, went one step further in the Normandy operation and carried rail equipment as well. Planners in SHAEF realized that French railroads would be in a devastated condition when our troops finally reached a point at which they would be required. In order to supplement the regular pre-war rail ferries which had served on the Dieppe-Newhaven run, SHAEF therefore ordered a handful of LST's to be equipped with special rails for carrying rolling stock. Orders for equipping these LST's came through late in the planning phase, and work for installing the equipment had to be rushed through on a top-priority basis, jamming even more the already overworked British and American base repair units. After the capture of strategic Cherbourg, rail-equipped LST's began pouring army rail equipment into port. As our troops advanced in France, Army engineers rapidly rebuilt the devastated rail lines, and the use of the transported equipment then paid high tribute to the mobility of American ingenuity.

NORMANDY BREAKTHROUGH. During the first week in the invasion of Normandy we landed 250,000 troops, a vast number of vehicles, and mountains of supplies. Even after the capture of Cherbourg, the major amount of supplies moved over the beaches until the port could be placed in operation by Seabees and Army port engineers. By the beginning of July an average of 30,000 men and tons of supplies moved across the beaches every day. On July 25, American troops under General Bradley broke through the enemy lines at St. Lo and Avranches, and advanced rapidly to the Meuse River. This was our first definite blow, and General Eisenhower lost no time in exploiting his advantage. General Patton's heavily armored divisions swept across the Brittany peninsula, cutting it in two, and on August 13, Patton's Third Army swept northwards from LeMans at the same time that Canadian Forces were driving south from Caen toward Falaise. This created the famous Falaise gap in which 100,000 German troops were captured. ABOVE. One sad-faced Japanese German in uniform.

ACTIVITY ON THE BEACH. UPPER. Hospital Corpsmen of the Navy Beach Battalion's Medical Section hit the beach with other sections to administer first aid to the wounded. LOWER. The beachmaster of a Navy Beach Battalion uses a "walkie-talkie" to maintain contact with other sections of his outfit. In the background other communications men are ready to use either blinker or signal flags on an invasion rehearsal in England.

DESTRUCTION AND RECONSTRUCTION. UPPER. Firing as it heads in toward land, a PT boat shows a brilliant burst of flame as it supports an amphibious landing. LOWER, A Sea Bulldozer rests briefly during its roadbuilding after the recapture of Guam. Moving in with the early stages of assault, the Seabees lost no time in starting the work of reconstruction which was to give us a system of far flung island bases from which to operate.

MAN'S NEW DEVICES AND THE TEMPEST. Out of an attempt to protect the open beaches from the elements came one of the sensational creations of the war: artificial harbors, or "Mulberries," made by sinking a number of old ships and concrete caissons off the beaches. Constructing the equipment in secrecy as well as towing the units to the assault area for assembly was a gigantic task. At Omaha Beach the weather took a hand. In a three day gale which ended June 22, the entire beach was left in a shambles, and the Mulberry so badly torn apart that it was abandoned. UPPER. The newly completed pier leading ashore from the Mulberry at Omaha Beach. LOWER. The littered beach after the storm. More than three hundred craft were damaged.

THE ROCKET'S CEMENT LAIR. New, ingenious German devices took many forms. RIGHT. A pilotless miniature tank operated by remote control. This contraption was captured before it could get into action and U. S. troops promptly dubbed it a "Doodlebug." It was powered by two electric motors, carried a load of explosives, and was supposed to play havoc with the landing troops.

Weapons of a more serious nature were the V-bombs, which, since the first week following the invasion, the Germans had been launching against London from the Pas de Calais area.

LOWER. An immense rocket-launching site under construction; long rows of steel rods stand ready to receive cement. Capture of the emplacement came at a strategic time, as V-bombs were beginning to present one of the most serious dangers to the English south coast.

SKYWARD AGAIN BY JATO. Jet-assisted takeoff, a recent development in the art of carrier warfare, is slashing the takeoff run of this F4U Corsair in half. The innovation allows a flattop-fighter complement increase, and augments the facility of large flying boats to carry increased load—in short, gets the planes into the air sooner, a vital factor in a split-second business.

Jet units look very much like bombs, except that they are fastened to the plane's fuselage, as shown above. Easily mounted and replaced, each unit delivers thrust equivalent to about 330 horsepower which is available through the takeoff period. Each jet unit is an engine in itself—a cylinder full of a solid propellant which includes oxygen in the mixture so it can burn without air. It has an electrically controlled spark plug which sets it off, and a rocket-like vent from which the jet gases give their thrust. In JATO use with the Navy's big flying boats, like PBY's and PBM's, four, six, or eight of these units must be used in salvo or in series. This is of particular value in the activity of these ponderous ships in the Pacific where small flying-boat harbors are often necessarily confined.

The Navy started its jet-assisted takeoff experimental program back in 1941 at the U. S. Engineering Experimental Station, Annapolis, Maryland, under the direct supervision of Captain Calvin M. Bolster, USN. With the experiments underway, the Guggenheim Aeronautical Laboratories at the California Institute of Technology were requested by the Navy to build the first small jet units.

"ALL TICKY-DOO." His own expression meaning that everything is in perfect order characterizes the demands that Lord Louis Mountbatten required of himself and everyone under him. Appointed Chief of Combined Operations in March of 1942, England's No. 1 Commando at the age of 43 had the unusual distinction of holding the triple rank of Vice Admiral, Lieutenant General, and Air Marshal. Outstanding capacity for applying himself to whatever he has to do, unswerving will to master whatever job he undertakes, and a firm memory for details are characteristics that chiefly determined his selection as the Supreme Commander in Southeast Asia. ABOVE. He pays a visit to the American carrier Saratoga, then assigned to his command.

WORKING WITH THE BRITISH. Admiral Mountbatten's arrival in India on 7 October, 1943 heralded preparations for the ultimate offensive to drive the Japanese out of Burma and thus open the road to China. In this he was successful, but with the tempo of the Japanese death rattle approaching crescendo, he focused his attention more to bolstering Allied sea power in the Pacific with units of the British fleet. UPPER. In July of 1943 the HMS *Victorious* swings at anchor with the USS *Saratoga*. LOWER. Looking across Trincomalee Harbor, Ceylon on March 31, 1944 from the deck of the USS *Saratoga*. The HMS *Illustrious* is shown backed up by two British cruisers, the HMS *Renown* and the HMS *Cambia* part of the joint British-American task force.

NAVY RECUES NATIVES STRANDED ON JAP HELD
ATOLLS. UPPER. Daring rescue missions by the Navy in
the Marshall Islands group accounted for more than 2,000
natives being successfully withdrawn from by-passed Jap
strongholds. In most instances the evacuation of the natives
met with stiff Jap resistance. Here a Navy bluejacket
watches intently from aboard his LCI as native men, women,
and children brave the surf and Jap gunfire to swim to the
safety of the United States ship. A total of 590 natives
were evacuated in this daring rescue off Jaluit, an island
of the Marshall group. LOWER. Wreckage of Japanese
installations in the Northern Marshalls inflicted by Navy
bombers is shown in this picture made by reconnaissance
units of the fleet.

NAVY'S ADVANCED BASE SYSTEM. ABOVE. A bulldozer clears the gutted terrain of Eniwetok for an American base after its capture in 1944. In the Pacific the war involved not only guns, planes, tanks, and ships, but also the great volume of material and equipment that went into the shaping of America's "war empire," a domain consisting of more than 400 bases hewn from the jungle or built on coral. The larger of these bases were the equivalent of good sized industrial cities. To install the extensive facilities, such bases required the efforts of many skilled Americans and large amounts of material. The omnipresent bull-dozer, piloted by naked and sweating Seabees, pushed the tropical jungles back and leveled the slopes of Pacific islands to turn them into airfields, supply depots, and roads. If troops and planes and ships cleared the road to Tokyo, the bull-dozer and machinery paved it.

ACTION IN THE ATLANTIC. "The submarine had already been depth charged by the destroyer escort *Baker* when she broke the surface like a huge whale coming up for air. It was sudden, like that," said a sailor who had been aboard the little destroyer escort USS *Thomas* that day in July, 1944. "We were going full ahead to join the *Baker* and then that big U-boat surfaced right off the bow. Without swinging away, the skipper plowed head on into the sub's conning tower. The bow of the U-boat shot up in the air. We had broken her in two. Then with full power astern we backed down from the submarine just as she slipped under for the last time. What a kill that was! We came out with our bow ripped open, but the old *Thomas* was still seaworthy."

ABOVE. The *Thomas* backs down, leaving the sub broken and sinking. When action came in the Atlantic, it came hard and fast, usually after many monotonous days and nights of search. The Atlantic Fleet's record speaks for itself. From the outbreak of the war until victory, ships of the American Navy escorted 16,760 ships across the Atlantic. Of these, less than a score were sunk in convoy.

The Atlantic Fleet and ships in convoy cruised more than 50,000,000 miles in the battle against the U-boats, to say nothing of the millions of miles flown by American pilots patrolling the stretches of ocean. At any given moment there were at least 450 cargo ships at sea and 75 escorts with them. During the war, 126 U-boats went to the bottom due to the activity of the Atlantic Fleet, and there were many more probable "kills."

"BOARDERS AWAY!" On June 4, 1944, for the first time since 1815, a Navy boarding party captured an enemy warship intact and towed it to port as a prize. A task group made up of the escort carrier USS *Guadalcanal* and five destroyer escorts first contacted the U-boat in the waters off French West Africa. The skipper of the *Guadalcanal* had issued orders to capture the first sub sighted. The USS *Chatelain's* sound gear detected the submerged undersea craft. From the bridge of this destroyer escort, word passed to the *Guadalcanal*, and seconds later her planes roared from the flight deck.

From the air the pilots could see the U-boat lurking under the surface. They commenced their runs spraying the water with machine gun fire, marking the spot for surface craft. The *Chatelain* swung in and dropped depth charges which apparently exploded close to the submarine, for within a few minutes the U-boat surfaced in the middle of the task group. Small-arms fire and severe strafing forced the Nazis to remain below. Finally they decided to open the scuttling valves and abandon the craft, leaving it circling at full speed.

From all the task group's ships boarding parties in whale boats raced for the sub. It was a matter of minutes before the submarine would sink. The boarding party from the *Guadalcanal* rushed to the bridge and down the hatch to shut the sea cocks. Then the captain of the *Guadalcanal* went below to check for boobytraps.

ABOVE. The U-boat lies alongside the USS *Guadalcanal*. Men of the boarding party are visible on the raider.

OLD GLORY FLIES OVER THE U-505. ABOVE. Following the capture of this German undersea raider, the stars and stripes were hoisted over the Third Reich's swastika flag. After foiling the attempt by Nazi crewmen to scuttle the vessel, the U.S. Navy boarding party secured a towline on her prow, and the USS *Guadalcanal* took her in tow. Navy men set the sub's screws so that they would recharge the batteries. Then, with the batteries back in shape, the U-boat's own equipment pumped out the water remaining in her hull. This was but one of the many actions that cut down Grossadmiral Doenitz's U-boat wolf packs and won the battle of the Atlantic for the Allies. The Captain of the *Guadalcanal* presented the U-505's flag to Admiral Jonas H. Ingram, Commander-in-Chief, Atlantic Fleet, and the trophy now hangs among the Navy's treasured archives at Annapolis.

THE MAN BEHIND THE SCENES. One of the least publicized but most important "behind the scenes" jobs of the Navy's Port Director Offices is the Port Liaison Officer. Diplomat, paymaster, counselor, and general intermediary between men of the U. S. Navy and the Allied peoples, these men have been honored by the countless authorities with whom they have come in contract.

A Liaison Officer's job is seldom an easy one, but when added to the normal woes of this type of work you have the added discomfitures of language barriers, custom differences, and political and civil regulations, the job becomes one for a man with the utmost in tact, diplomacy, and understanding of the niceties of Allied relationships. His duties may entail almost anything involving shipping,

Armed guard crews, and supplies. Among the multiple and diversified tasks he must handle are advising Armed Guard crews of the local customs, laws, and prohibitions; routing American shipping; contacting officials of other members of the United Nations and our own Army officers, and helping settle disputes between Navy personnel and civil authorities.

Port Liaison Officers were stationed in all corners of the world where American ships came into contact with people of the Allied Nations. ABOVE. One of the duties of the Port Liaison Officer is to see that the men on the incoming ships get their pay. At an English port, a crew is being paid in English pounds and shillings. These men will have plenty of "folding money" to make their stay enjoyable.

THE MARIANAS

By Lieutenant General Holland M. Smith, USMC

WITH the decision to seize and occupy the Marianas Islands of Saipan, Tinian and Guam, the Pacific war jumped 1,200 miles from the Marshalls into the first land mass fighting of the Central Pacific campaign.

Behind us lay the flat and bloody atolls, ahead lay mountains, caves, jungles and plains. Also ahead lay the still formidable Japanese fleet and a sizable air force.

But the Marines and soldiers of the Fifth and Third Amphibious Corps were confident of victory because they were backed by the fighting might of almost 800 Naval ships manned by a quarter million sailors. Against enemy effectives were approximately 150,000 amphibious battle tested American troops.

The objective was the usual one— to land upon, seize, occupy, and defend the three islands in order to deny their use to the enemy and convert their flat spots into air fields for attack upon the home islands of Japan. From these bases would be mounted future offensives aimed at the continued annihilation of the reeling enemy.

Like most Central Pacific real estate, the price came high. But the war across the Pacific had to move and the price had to be paid in order that the way might be made easier for those who came after. The Marianas cost America 25,000 land casualties including 5,000 killed and missing in action. The Japanese lost 48,000 of their defending troops.

Against superior weapons, aggressive troops, closely coordinated air and sea support fire, the Jap fought stubbornly and died horribly.

THE LANDINGS

ON JUNE 15, July 21 and July 23 amphibious landings were made effectively on Saipan, Guam, and Tinian respectively in the sultry summer of 1944. The long twenty-five day continuous attack against strongly entrenched and fiercely resisting troops on Saipan proved the most bitter battle in the Pacific up to that time. Guam was secured in 20 days and that lone American out-

post returned to the Stars and Stripes. Tinian was won in nine days by one of the most perfectly planned and daringly executed shore to shore operations in world history.

Protected by the Navy surface forces and air arm, which sought out and partly destroyed penetrating forces of the Japanese fleet, Marines and soldiers were blessed with friendly skies free of enemy aircraft. What comparatively few planes got through did little damage with their supply lines protected, their skies free, with naval gunfire and close air support, the foot soldiers and Marines devoted their full attention to the extermination of the enemy.

BASES AGAINST JAPAN

UNDER heroic and brilliant leadership of officers and non-commissioned officers, our troops suffered heavy casualties from the enemy and the climate, but gained the inevitable triumph to forge in blood and fire a most important weapon, a base for B-29's. In the year that elapsed between the securing of the Marianas bases and the capitulation of the enemy, thousands of B-29 missions were flown against the Japanese homeland from these three island air bases. The capture of the Marianas was one of the most decisive actions against the enemy in the Central Pacific.

Today Guam is again a proud American possession. The Guamanian school children play under the American flag, worship in the church of their fathers and place flowers on the graves of Marines of the 3rd Division and the 1st Brigade and soldiers of the 77th Army Division. On Saipan and Tinian Christian Chammoros enjoy the blessing of freedom while beneath the soil lie the bodies of Marines of the Second and Fourth Divisions and soldiers of the 27th Infantry.

The Marianas, paid for in courage and blood, shall remain American possessions as a promise to those who died that their sacrifice was not in vain.

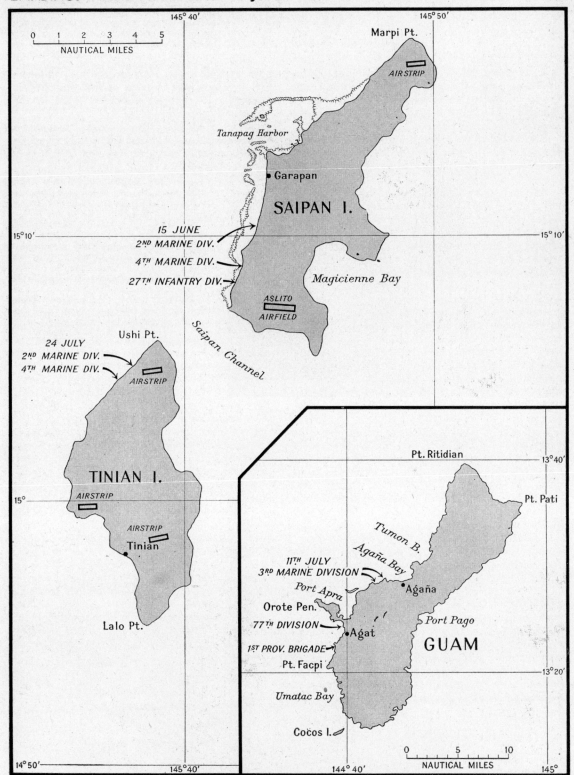

Chart of the invasions of Saipan, Tinian, and Guam.

SUICIDE ATTACK. When a Japanese plane sustained a fatal hit, its pilot usually did his best to dive it into a ship of the U. S. Navy The bigger the ship, the better the target. But more often than not, anti-aircraft batteries aboard the prospective target of the suicide diver battered the zooming plane to so much flying debris before it reached the ship

LEFT. An enemy torpedo bomber has been dealt a deadly blow by one of the anti-aircraft batteries aboard the carrier escort *Sangamon* which is lying off the shores of Saipan in the Marianas. Twisting and turning, the stricken plane plunges seaward, barely escaping the deck. Meanwhile, the unscathed carrier waits for the return of its own planes which are busy bombing and strafing Saipan and Tinian, preparatory to ship-to-shore operations by Marines.

The weight of bombs and shells thrown at the Marianas was the greatest, up to that date, of any pre-landing assault in the Pacific. Guam, particularly, underwent a terrific shelling. However, when the green-garbed Leathernecks went ashore, they met withering bursts from Japanese mortar and artillery fire. As at Tarawa, the landings were further complicated by treacherous reefs and rapidly changing tides

LOWER. D-Day for the seasoned Second Marine Division and the untried Fourth who went ashore on Saipan. Opposition to the landing was so fierce that the first wave was pinned down in some sectors with the feet of the men still in the water and only elbows resting on sand. Jap defenses covered the island from every angle.

TWO MAN ADVANCE. By July 9, 1944 the 2nd and 4th Marine Divisions and the 27th Army Division had smashed all organized resistance on Saipan. RIGHT. Concealed from nearby Japs by a sand-bagged dugout, two U. S. Marines prepare to go over the top in the last hours of the Saipan campaign. One of the men, holding a bandoleer of ammunition and a carbine, obviously will take the jump first. He is waiting only for his comrade to hurl the grenade into the Japanese positions. Carbines and hand grenades proved invaluable as close-quarter weapons in all the battles of the Pacific. Marine combat teams used both with unusual skill and telling effect.

LOWER. Perched on the rocky edge of a sheer cliff on the island of Tinian, just across the channel from Saipan, stands the dreaded 75mm pack howitzer. It was carried from the beach by its crew, piece by piece, and assembled on the height for action. From this vantage point the gun crew has an unobstructed view of Japanese cave defenses, now ready for heavy shelling. This picture was taken five days after Tinian was declared secured. The howitzer crew was charged with mopping up a pocket of resistance. As elsewhere, Japs rarely surrendered even when the battle was clearly over.

WARMED OVER. UPPER. A Marine flame throwing tank turns a Jap pillbox into a flaming hades on Saipan while an interested lone Marine watches the proceedings from his ringside foxhole in the foreground. Light tanks, fitted out experimentally with flame throwers, made their debut under Marine control at Saipan. As one of the answers to the enemy "tunnelling tactics" they were used extensively in all Pacific amphibious operations thereafter, and added the burning of captured enemy war planes to their list of functions. **LOWER.** After the Marines captured this mountain gun from the Japs on Saipan, they put it into use during the attack on Garapan, administrative center of enemy government for the entire Marianas island group. To offset the concussion effect as the toy cannon goes off, one Marine is holding his ears, another is shouting to equalize the pressure on his ear drums, and the man in the foreground has stuffed his ears with cotton.

WHERE WAS JAP AIR FORCE ON SAIPAN? Here's the answer. LEFT. Much of the Jap air force was destroyed on the ground before it could rise to do battle. In this view of Aslito airstrip on Saipan, taken by a crewman on the first Navy Consolidated Liberator to land on the captured field, a staggering number of Jap planes can be seen in the wreckage. Note the U. S. planes spotted on the airstrip between the debris of the Jap aircraft. LOWER. To play its role in the crushing of Japan, the Navy constructed what amounted to an attenuated "island empire" in the Pacific; a domain consisting of more than 400 bases hewn from the stubborn jungle or erected on coral. The larger of these bases are the equivalents of good-sized industrial cities; and even the smallest of them is a unit into which a staggering amount of planning, material, and personnel has been funneled. Here we see the Naval Air Base at Marpi Point, Saipan, a hitherto primitive island prior to Marine occupation.

THE BATTLE OF
THE PHILIPPINE SEA

By Admiral Raymond A. Spruance, USN

WHEN the operations for the capture of the Marianas were begun early in June 1944, most of the Japanese fleet had been basing— according to our best intelligence—on Tawi Tawi, in the extreme south of the Philippines, whence they could pour into the Philippine Sea and threaten our Marianas landings by several routes. Watching the Japanese even in their own waters, however, were our submarines, and one of these just off Tawi Tawi informed us on June 13th that a strong Japanese force had left that base and was heading northward. The possibility that this force might attempt to block our Saipan landings immediately appeared.

Our original plans had included a strike on Iwo Jima by two of the four carrier groups which with battleships, cruisers, and destroyers composed Task Force 58. The strike was to be made as soon as possible after the enemy air in the Marianas had been knocked out. I considered canceling this strike, because these two task groups might not be able to rejoin before the Japanese fleet could attempt a blow against us at Saipan. However, the risk had to be taken. The strike was successfully conducted on June 16th, and the two task groups making it were able to rejoin in time to oppose the Japanese fleet.

Our landings on Saipan started on June 15th and were strongly opposed. That night we received contact reports from two of our submarines. One of them reported an enemy force steaming to the eastward at high speed from San Bernardino Strait. The other reported a second force about two hundred miles to the northeastward of Mindanao headed to the northeast. These reports removed all doubts as to the Japanese intentions to oppose our landings on Saipan with all their available naval strength.

Unloading of troops, equipment and supplies continued at Saipan on June 16th and 17th, while Task Force 58, reinforced by such cruisers and destroyers from the Joint Expeditionary Force as could be made available, operated in a covering position to the westward of Saipan, with carrier planes making searches to the limit of their range to look for the enemy fleet. During this time Japanese land based search planes were able to keep up good contacts with us in spite of their losses.

THE SEA BATTLE BEGINS

ON THE forenoon of June 19th began the Battle of the Philippine Sea. The Japanese carriers launched their attacks from outside the range of our planes, with the apparent intention of having them land on their airfields on Guam and Rota, in the vicinity of Saipan. This day, June 19th, will be remembered by Navy men everywhere as the "Marianas' Turkey Shoot." The result of the day's action was 408 enemy planes destroyed out of 545 sighted, as against 32 American planes lost and negligible damage to 4 ships. There was nothing else like it in the whole of World War II.

Our fleet now headed westward, hoping to bring the main Japanese fleet to action. On the afternoon of the 20th our search planes made contact with the enemy, and, immediately, heavy strikes took off from our carriers. The enemy force was at extreme range. Late in the day, our air groups struck, sinking 1 enemy carrier and 2 fleet tankers, and inflicting heavy damage on 2 carriers and lighter damage on 1 battleship, 1 carrier, and 1 destroyer. Our losses amounted to only 23 planes.

With darkness practically upon them, our pilots started back to their carriers 300 miles away. The returning planes had difficulty in locating their carriers in the darkness, and many ran out of gasoline after reaching our fleet. It was our responsibility to make a decision, either to remain in darkness secure from enemy submarine and air attack, or give our fliers a better chance to land by lighting up the carriers. We chose the latter. Searchlights and flares enabled many pilots to land, but a total of 80 planes were obliged to make crash landings on the water. Our cruisers and destroyers managed to rescue 90 per cent of the personnel from those planes.

The Battle of the Philippine Sea broke the Japanese effort to reinforce Saipan. It gave us control of the eastern portion of the Philippine Sea and ensured that our later landings on Guam and Tinian could go through without further Japanese naval opposition.

R. A. Spruance

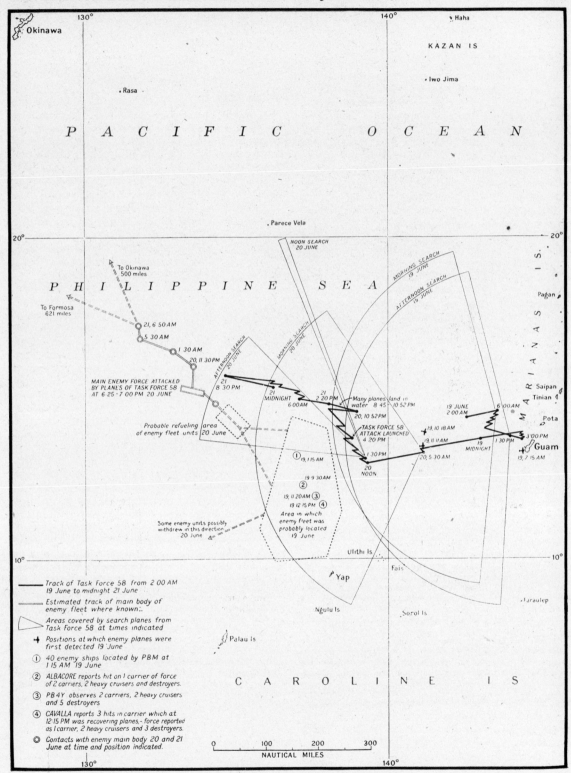

Chart showing the Battle of the Philippine Sea.

"THE MARIANAS TURKEY SHOOT." The bitterness with which the Japanese defended Saipan reflected the Japanese intention of retaining the island at almost any cost. The enemy, for the first time in over a year, sent out a strong naval force to attempt to break up the invasion.

The task force that was sent was stronger than the Japanese could afford to lose, yet too weak for the task assigned to it. It consisted of at least 4 capital ships and half a dozen carriers. The only way the Japanese could have accomplished their objective of crippling our landing coverage was to score a sudden, spectacular, surprise attack. The Japanese commander attempted just this. While still remote from his goal, he launched his planes at extreme range, timing their departure so that they arrived at the scene of action at the same time that Jap planes from the Marianas went into action. The Japanese had banked on two things to give success to their venture, neither of which, to the Jap's dismay, was realized.

The enemy had counted on the prolonged bombardment in which the American ships would expend their supplies of fuel and ammunition. They had also counted on being able to use the fields on Guam and Rota to refuel and rearm their planes. U. S. carrier planes neutralized the fields at Guam and Rota, and the U. S. fleet still had plenty of ammunition and more than enough fuel left to pursue the Japanese task force for two days. ABOVE. Twisting and turning to avoid bombs from U. S. planes, a Japanese carrier takes near misses off her bow and stern.

THE SECRET OF THE "FLEET THAT CAME TO STAY." Unheralded by the press, all but unknown outside naval circles, Pacific Fleet Service Squadron Six, (Servron Six to the Navy) was the factor which gave the Third and Fifth Fleets their astounding mobility and endurance, qualities earning them the collective nickname of the "Fleet That Came to Stay."

Consisting of a staggering array of tankers, ammunition ships, escort carriers, tugs, storeships, and other auxiliaries, Service Squadron Six put to sea and met the Fighting Fleets at specified rendezvous a few hundred miles from the battle areas. There they quickly refueled and re-supplied the fleets, enabling them to wheel about and strike the foe again—thus adding consternation to chaos. Many "deter-

mining factors" are being credited with turning the tide of battle; but few will dispute that the great element in our overwhelming naval power was the mobility and staying power supplied by "Servron Six."

Actually the Fleet Train is not a new idea; since 1916, the Navy has had a Fleet Auxiliary for such purposes. It was not until this war however that the Fleet Servrons have been developed to a point where combat ships can operate almost indefinitely at sea.

ABOVE. Small besides the Iowa class battleship it is refueling, this tanker of Service Squadron Six is responsible for much of the giant battlewagon's success by providing oil to feed ever hungry power plants; the tanker saves the battleship a long trip to a shore base.

"...AND PASS THE AMMUNITION..." All materials necessary for a naval operation must be provided long before the actual operation commences, and most it of is made in the continental United States. In consequence the naval supply system for the Pacific Ocean areas consists of a "pipe line," beginning hundreds of miles inland from the West coast of the United States and extending across the Pacific to the Philippines, with branches to our many ocean bases. The carriers on this "pipe line" were the ships of the Fleet Train consisting of a staggering array of tankers, ammunition ships, tugs, and other auxiliaries, which re-fueled and re-supplied the fighting ships at sea. ABOVE. Ammunition being transferred from the ammunition ship in the foreground to an *Essex* class carrier, one of the hundreds of such operations conducted by ships of the Fleet train in keeping the Fleet fighting.

SEEING IS BELIEVING. ABOVE. Three Marine Corps Officers study one of the Navy's new terrain models prior to the invasion of Guam. These terrain models are a three-dimensional model of a portion of the earth's surface. Military personnel planning strategy have found that they can learn far more about an area of operations by studying models than they can by studying contour maps of the same area.

These models, developed by the Hydrographic Office of the Navy in cooperation with the Bureau of Aeronautics, were first used by pilots in preparing for air attacks. The pilot could rehearse an approach from his assigned angle sliding his hands or a model of his type of plane in and out of the valleys and dropping "bombs" on his objective. He could actually get the "feel" of the land. Commanding officers in the field soon began to use these models to familiarize all their personnel with their objectives. In landing operations, photos of an accurate model of a stretch of coastline taken from an angle which enabled beaches, cliffs, rocks, and other important landmarks to be recognized promptly from sea level, were issued to every landing craft taking troops ashore.

Construction of terrain models is based on information derived principally from maps, aerial photographs: and ground information such as Hydrographic Office charts, Army and Navy Intelligence data, and guide books. Models are divided into types according to their scale. Those at scales smaller than 1 to 20,000, presenting an accurate reproduction of the coastline, and indicating the general character of the terrain under consideration, are called Planning Terrain Models and are useful for over-all planning tactics. For planning air attacks, models at 1 to 25,000 or 1 to 50,000 are most useful. Since hardly any detail can be shown at small scale, the result is actually a three dimensional relief map, representing the geological form of the area with its most outstanding features such as rivers, railways or towns indicated. Assault models are larger in scale, ranging up to 1 to 5,000.

Target, or Low-Level Models, are used to brief pilots in strafing or bombing attacks on specific enemy installations. They are large models, 1 to 5,000 or larger, and show details of combat terrain. Buildings and military installations appear as they are actually related to one another. Mobile objectives, guns, ships, planes, and the like, their position determined by daily aerial reconnaissance, can be placed on the model to show their latest disposition. These models in addition to the Navy's maps and charts, have had a profound effect on invasion strategy.

THE STARS AND STRIPES RETURN TO GUAM. Our landings on Guam, originally scheduled for mid-June, were delayed somewhat by the unexpectedly stiff resistance on Saipan Island and a sortie of the Japanese fleet. This delay permitted a period of air and surface bombardment which was unprecedented in severity and duration. U. S. surface ships first bombarded Guam on 16 June 1944. From 8 July 1944 until the landings on the 21st, the island was under daily gunfire from battleships, cruisers, and destroyers. This incessant bombardment was coordinated with air strikes from Saipan and from fast carriers.

The destruction of airfield facilities on Guam and on Rota, as well as the neutralization of more distant bases, gave us uncontested control of the air. Troops were landed on Guam on 21 July 1944. The beach conditions were poor, and the surf running high. Landing craft were forced to transfer their personnel to "Ducks" and "Alligators" to accomplish the scheduled landings. The assault waves, however, did land on schedule.

There were two simultaneous landings, east and south of Apra Harbor. Resistance on the beaches consisted chiefly of mortar and small arms fire, the bombardment having knocked out enemy heavy guns. Heaviest enemy opposition was encountered in the Apra Harbor area proper. RIGHT. The Stars and Stripes return to Guam. LOWER. At Guam a Seabee-manned bulldozer churns up the surf as it maneuvers a section of a pontoon causeway into position to facilitate the movements of equipment and supplies from a reef to the beach.

THE RECAPTURE OF GUAM. Since a reef at the site of our first landings prevented craft from reaching the beaches it was found necessary to capture Apra Harbor. Heavy enemy opposition in the harbor area held up its capture until we controlled the heights on both sides of the bay, but, with Apra Harbor in our hands, supplies were landed far more easily, and with much greater speed than had been possible before.

Then the troops pushed inland and drove the Japanese to the northern end of the island. After overcoming stubborn enemy resistance our forces were able to claim possession of the island by 10 August 1944.

LEFT. Marine attack dogs being fed on board ship on the way to Guam. These dogs were invaluable as sentries on the South Pacific islands. UPPER· The Guam-Midway communications cable is repaired. This cable, the second longest in the world, was severed by Navy technicians as a security measure before the Battle of Midway.

"...SHOES AND SHIPS AND SEALING WAX..."
With Guam recaptured by our forces in August of 1944, the Navy took immediate action to help the civilians on the island who had been Japanese prisoners at large for almost four years. Food and livestock were vital necessities for these people.

RIGHT. Cattle are transferred from the deck of an LCT to waiting trucks at Guam. These animals are part of the first cargo of livestock sent to a forward area in the Pacific. The cargo included dairy cows, chickens, hogs, and turkeys intended to restock the Jap-gutted island.

LOWER. Cans of powder and 14" projectiles being loaded on board a battleship to replace ammunition expended supporting the invasion of Guam. The hundreds of rounds fired by ships in this action kept a fleet of ammunition ships busy replenishing fired rounds. The Navy's supply lines, far flung though they were, delivered everything from shoes to shells to every port from Pearl Harbor to Palau.

BUILDING A RUNWAY FOR SUPPLIES TO CAPE SANSAPOR. On July 30, 1944, the Navy landed in the Cape Sansapor area on the Vogelkop Peninsula in western New Guinea. The main assault was made without either naval or air resistance by the enemy and within a short time secondary landings were made at Middleberg and Amsterdam Islands a few thousand yards off shore. Since there was hardly any opposition there was as a result no naval bombardment, and supporting Army aircraft from Owi and Wakde were released for duty elsewhere. Casualties were very light; one man killed and minor damage to small craft.

This move brought United States forces to the western extremity of New Guinea. It effectively neutralized New Guinea for enemy operations and rendered the Japanese more vulnerable to air attack in Halmahera, and the Molukka passage, and Makassar Strait. Due to the absence of roads, most enemy transport was necessarily water borne. Here United States' PT boats operated and did admirable work, roaming east and west along the coast, harassing enemy barge traffic, and preventing reinforcements from being put ashore.

ABOVE. The beach at Cape Sansapor was not made to order for the American invaders so troops turned to build a ramp out to the yawning bow doors of a coast-guard manned LST. A bulldozer in the foreground was put to work constructing the dock. Coast guard gunners are ready to meet any interference from Jap planes, while a PBY swoops low in its reconnaissance assignment.

THE INVASION OF
SOUTHERN FRANCE

By Rear Admiral Calvin T. Durgin, USN

ON AUGUST 15, 1944, a giant Allied Naval Task Force landed U.S. and Free French Army divisions on the beaches of Southern France in the last of the great landings that crushed Hitler's boasted Fortress of Europe. After four months' preliminary bombing, culminating in a terrific 1300 Allied plane attack on a 40 mile coastal front, the predominantly American armada of 880 ships started the troops ashore in 1370 ship-borne landing craft. Confident after their successful operations in North Africa and Sicily, at Naples and Anzio and in Normandy, the Allies landed in broad daylight which allowed extensive use of underwater demolition teams and shallow water minesweepers. Under the protection of the terrific land bombardment of the 53 naval gunfire support ships, these latter operated effectively even close-in under the guns of powerful enemy coastal gun positions, including the great forts at Toulon and Marseilles.

So well-planned and unexpected was the attack, and so wrecked was the Luftwaffe by the battering it had received on the Normandy front, that the enemy air opposition which had been so strong in the previous Mediterranean landings did not materialize. As a result our naval carrier-based air, which had been assigned to give air protection to the bombardment and landing ships during the operation, found itself with a new unexpected role.

Just as they were already proving in the Pacific that carrier-based land and Marine planes in force could completely sweep even the enemy's land-based planes from the air, in the Southern France operation they now proved that they could wreck enemy forts, demolish his railroad and motor vehicle transport, and totally disrupt his transport and communications.

CARRIER-BASED OPERATIONS

ORIGINALLY it had been planned to do much of this air work by landbased planes from the island of Corsica and airfields seized in Southern France. But the difficulties of operating landbased planes from Corsica, at ranges of from 100 to 300 miles from the rapidly changing front, demonstrated the tremendous advantages of the carrier planes which operated from only 30 miles offshore and moved along the coast as the armies progressed.

In two task groups totalling but nine British and American escort carriers, the carriers began operation on D-day with reconnaissance and attack of enemy positions, combined with their important function of spotting for the bombardment ships. The carrier planes were intended to do this work at 6,000 feet altitude, but low clouds and poor visibility forced them often to operate only a few hundred feet above the enemy positions. Their excellent spotting enabled the bombardment ships to wipe out the enemy coastal guns with pinpoint accuracy, and their reconnaissance revealed almost every aspect of the enemy's positions and movements. With no enemy air opposition except a few enemy planes which were downed far inland, the carrier planes took up their new role of destroying enemy forts, railroads, bridges, trains, and motor vehicle concentrations.

Navy Hellcat fighters with bombs, rockets, and bullets smashed at everything enemy in sight. In a swoop at one enemy fort, four Hellcats dropped four 500-pound bombs within the 50-foot square fortifications without a miss. They pounded locomotives and cars with rockets, and strafed enemy troops with bullets; they knocked out bridges and highways and motor vehicle convoys deep behind the lines. One carrier pilot even skip-bombed a tunnel entrance almost at tree-top level.

RESULTS

THE results were spectacular. Within some 15 days of operation, some 100 planes from the 4 carriers of task group 88.2 alone accounted for 9 enemy planes, wrecked 1389 trucks and other motor vehicles, destroyed or immobilized 57 locomotives and 395 railroad cars, damaged 17 bridges and made 61 cuts in railroad tracks and highways, smashed 6 railroad roundhouses and train sheds, hit a fort, destroyed 7 gun emplacements and neutralized 4 more, and wiped out 22 fuel tanks and 2 ammunition dumps.

With such terrific damage and disruption around and in their rear German resistance became demoralized. Marseilles and Toulon fell on August 29, and the triumphant armies swept on into France with the carrier planes still striking deep ahead of them up the Rhone valley. It was almost the speediest of all the land invasions. But for direct air support even more significant was the superiority of carrier-based planes, operating from mobile flight decks close inshore and moving as the land troops moved, over landbased planes operating from fixed airstrips far behind the rapidly changing front.

C T Durgin

Chart showing the landings in Southern France.

SOUTHERN FRANCE ASSAULT FORMS UP. Originally planned to coincide with the invasion of Normandy, the Southern France operation was delayed in order to assemble a larger striking force and to include some of the ships that had taken part in operation "Neptune." The invasion itself was one of the worst kept secrets of the war; shoeshine boys in Naples could, and did, discuss the place and approximate date of the coming attack. In a four-pronged assault designed to capture important southern French ports, convoys made up in far-flung ports. LST's sailed from Naples, LCI's, LCT's from Corsica. UPPER. Line after line of vehicles in Naples await loading. LOWER. LST's, packed with Army equipment, loading for the invasion in Naples harbor.

GERMAN RESISTANCE WEAK. German resistance in Southern France was so unexpectly weak that troops ashore by the end of D-day were already a day ahead of schedule. One German air attack occurred the evening of D-day, destroying an LST, but that was all. In addition to U. S. troops, 300,000 French troops under General de Lattre de Tassigny took part in the campaign. More difficult objectives, however, were the ports of Toulon and Marseilles which were defended by heavy German artillery. UPPER. Victorious American troops head into Marseilles Harbor in an LCVP. Fort St. Jean lies directly ahead. LOWER. Troops and equipment pour ashore from an LST onto a beach where once gay vacationers sunned themselves in the halcyon days before war came again.

MARSEILLES. FINALE. In defending Toulon and Marseilles the Germans fought a battle born of desperation, as they knew they could never hold out. At Toulon, the French attacking troops were forced into the situation of having to destroy a fortress which they themselves had built. The great fortress of St. Mandrier guarded the entire harbor, and its guns, with a range of over 20 miles, dominated the surrounding water approaches.

The battleship *Nevada* and the cruiser *Quincy*, together with the French battleship *Lorraine*, tackled the problem of reducing the fort. Beginning August 19 they ran bombardment runs every day for a week, alternated with low level bombing attacks from the air. Even so the fortresses did not surrender until three days after the city fell. Wreckage in the harbor was almost as extensive as at Naples, but Seabee salvage teams went to work at once, and within three weeks the port was receiving shipping. Marseilles was taken by ground forces August 29. UPPER. Secretary of the Navy James Forrestal gets a first hand view of the Southern France landings. Left to right, Brig. Gen. G. P. Saville, USA, Maj. Gen. A. M. Patch, USA, Vice Admiral H. K. Hewitt, USN, who commanded the Navy operation, Mr. Forrestal, and Rear Admiral Andre LeMonier, French Naval Commander. LOWER. Captain Ansel, USN, of the cruiser *Philadelphia*, passes by sullen stares and Nazi salutes as he goes to the surrender conference.

TANKS TAKE PELELIU AIRFIELD. On March 29 to 31, 1944, carrier forces under the command of Admiral Spruance heavily attacked the Palau Islands group in the Western Carolines, sinking 29 Japanese ships. Peleliu was bombarded several more times by air and surface units in the next five months.

On September 14, the first Marine division, supported by naval and surface units, landed on the island. The ground opposition was stiff, and not until October 12 was it announced that organized resistance on Peleliu had ceased. Even then, many Japs fought on in numerous caves which had been concrete reinforced and supplied with food, ammunition, and guns. Since hand grenades and flame throwers would not penetrate the winding underground passages, caves that had been cleaned of Japs on one day would sometimes prove to be filled with them the next. On October 18, the Army relieved the Marines, but not until November 27 was the island declared secure.

Peleliu's principal value was as a stepping stone for aircraft between the Marianas, New Guinea, and the Philippines. The Japanese had built a good airport on the island, and this was converted for the use of the United States.

ABOVE. Amid the debris of Jap planes and equipment battered by the pre-invasion bombardment, Marine tanks take up positions on the enemy built airport on Peleliu. This field, largest on the island group, was captured after the Marines repulsed several counter-attacks by Japanese tanks. In order to maintain the usefulness of the base, the remainder of the islands had to be neutralized by subsequent action and patrols.

THE U.S. COAST GUARD
IN WORLD WAR II
By Admiral Russell R. Waesche, USCG

THE Coast Guard had become part of the Navy only a month before Pearl Harbor, but its larger cutters had already been armed and were soon protecting our convoys from enemy submarines in the Atlantic. The *Campbell* rammed one of a wolf pack after depth charging five others, picked up survivors and was towed to St. John's with a flooded machinery compartment. The *Spencer* and *Icarus* brought theirs to the surface and captured their crews before they sank. Dozens of other submarines never reached the surface again after Coast Guard depth charges found their target. One of the larger cutters, the *Alexander Hamilton*, was torpedoed off Iceland. A smaller one, the *Acacia*, was sunk in the West Indies, while a third, the *Escanaba*, was blown up while returning from Greenland.

It was in Greenland that the Coast Guard established a patrol and ultimately destroyed Weather Stations which the Germans had set up there, depriving our foes of advanced weather information on the European battle fronts.

As the war progressed Coast Guardsmen who had gained invaluable experience in the handling of small boats in surf, were sent to man the strange new landing craft which the transports first carried to Guadalcanal. Later these men helped land the Marines and Army in the Gilberts, the Marianas, the Marshalls, the Admiralties, on New Guinea, in the Halmaheras, the Carolines, the Philippines, and finally at Iwo Jima and Okinawa. They also manned landing craft at the invasions in North Africa, Sicily, Italy, Normandy, and Southern France. Continuing the life saving tradition of the Coast Guard, thousands of lives were saved when troop ships were torpedoed in the Atlantic, and on D-day in Normandy the 83 footers saved nearly 1500 lives.

THE RESERVE

MEANWHILE at home new recruits, Temporary Reservists and Spars were freeing the fighting Coast Guard from home security patrols. As beach patrols relaxed in 1944, with the driving of the German submarines farther from our shores, thousands of these fighting men were released to man Navy attack transports, destroyer escorts, frigates, LST's, LCI(L)'s, and Army freight and service boats and tugs that were coming down the shipways. Coast Guardsmen were fighting off submarine attacks in the Mediterranean or shooting down Japanese suicide planes in the Pacific. Some of them died but more of them piloted thousands of Marine and U. S. Army troops safely to enemy-held beaches. Their deeds of heroism are legion.

While nearly half the 173,000 Coast Guardsmen were in the thick of battle, the other half were performing equally important if less spectacular tasks at home and abroad. It was the Coast Guard that built and manned LORAN stations on many a lonely island in the Pacific. As the offensive mounted, hundreds of newly garrisoned islands had to be serviced by Coast Guard manned Army boats. At home the millions of tons of newly constructed merchant shipping were being inspected by the Coast Guard, their officers licensed and their seamen certificated while merchant marine hearing units, established throughout the world, aided merchant marine personnel. The lights on our coasts had to be blacked out or dimmed. Ice was broken on the Great Lakes to permit earlier spring movements of iron ore to the steel mills. Thousands of vessels were loaded with explosives under expert Coast Guard supervision. Shipyards were guarded and waterfront property protected from sabotage and fire. Finally with the upsurge of ocean flying, Air-Sea Rescue called for Coast Guard planes and cutters. "On the eve of the return of the Coast Guard to the Treasury" said a recent message from the Chief of Naval Operations "I desire to commend the officers and men of the Coast Guard for their superb performance of duty throughout the war."

LIFE SAVING, COAST GUARD STYLE. During the war the U. S. Coast Guard took its place alongside the Navy, patroling and fighting on the seven seas. One of the most important jobs assigned to the Coast Guard was air-sea rescue. The vigilance and tenacity of these rescue units paid off dividends in the form of thousands of pilots' lives— lives which would have otherwise been lost. After the inception of the service, the efforts of one Coast Guard station alone resulted in the saving of more than 200 crash victims. This composite photograph reveals what a Coast Guardsman often saw through his binoculars at the end of a successful search for a survivor at sea. Due to the Coast Guard rescue mission, American fliers who were forced down at sea had a better than 50-50 chance of cheating the ocean and returning to fight again. The monetary value of a trained pilot was great; to the Coast Guard, the value of an American life was even greater, and if it could be saved, they would do it.

HURRICANE! UPPER. A Coast Guardsman clutches at a fuel hose and a chain life line as he struggles to "dig his toes" into the deck of a tanker swamped under savage seas in a hurricane off the north coast of Cuba. For three days the crew of this Coast Guard-manned tanker fought to survive the hurricane's violence. LOWER. Coast Guardsmen to the rescue. The Coast Guard operated nine air stations along the coasts of the United States. These stations (along with the ships of the Coast Guard) served in the conduct of air-sea rescue. During 1945 Coast Guard aircraft assisted in 686 plane crashes and the saving of 786 lives. "Always Ready," men of the United States Coast Guard saw action in every theatre of operations in World War II.

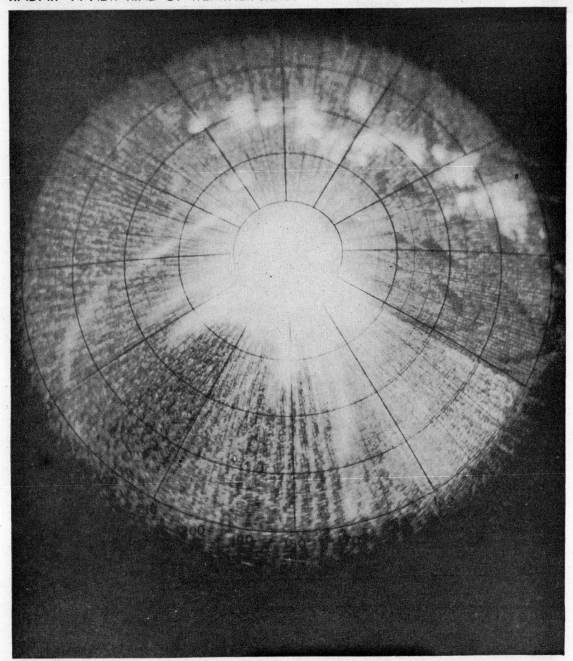

RADAR PICKS UP A TYPHOON. Even before the war, British and American scientists learned that certain radio impulses would "bounce back" after striking a solid object, and would reflect the outline of that object on a screen. This discovery led to a new field of electronics—radio direction and ranging (RADAR).

Ranking alongside atomic energy, radar has emerged as one of the greatest discoveries of the war. So valuable was the discovery, our security regulations prohibited publication of any information concerning it or even public mention of the word "radar." The Navy soon realized the value of the "all seeing eye" and has led the way in the development of radar equipment and techniques. All combatant ships of the U. S. Fleet were equipped with radar devices and specially qualified experts to operate them.

These sets made it possible for our surface vessels to detect the presence of enemy aircraft more than a hundred miles away.

ABOVE. The radar screen of the USS *Ticonderoga*, showing the registration of a Pacific typhoon. The white area in the center is called "sea return" or "grass" due to reflections from the heavy sea. The typhoon is the white opaque area at the top of the screen.

The Germans were aware of the military value of radar and set up huge stations along the French Coast in Normandy and the Pas de Calais to intercept allied bombers. The Japanese also employed radar, although it is conceded that their sets were inferior to those of the United States. Today the Navy is continuing radar research and is converting its principles to peacetime uses.

ANGUAR BEACH SMASHED BEFORE LANDINGS BY THIRD FLEET. D-Day, September 17, 1944. Battleships and cruisers of Admiral Halsey's powerful Third Fleet and planes from his aircraft carriers make a roaring inferno of the Japanese beach defenses at Anguar Island, one of the Palau group.

ABOVE. Small landing craft cluster around the LST in the foreground awaiting Zero hour and the mighty push by Marine and Army assault forces toward the beach.

LEFT. Skeleton framework of buildings and other installations at Anguar, is evidence of the accuracy of the Navy bombers that struck the Jap base on July 26 and 27, 1944, in an effective and devastating softening-up operation before D-Day. In the background underwater obstacles can be seen as the tide is on the ebb. These barriers had to be cleared away by Underwater Demolition Teams before a landing could be made.

NOT A FIREWORKS DISPLAY, BUT A NIGHT PICTURE OF ACTION ON BLOODY NOSE RIDGE. About five hundred yards from a Marine encampment where a movie is being shown, terrific action is taking place.

The white streaks in the center of the picture are star shells, being fired over the Japanese positions to outline them. The thin white streak in the upper right section of the picture is also star shells. Horizontal white streaks and also the straight lines going diagonally right are tracer bullets. The horizontal lines across the foreground by the hill are the lights of a jeep enroute to the movie. The projection booth may be seen in the lower right section. The irregular curving white light across the bottom is made by a flashlight carried by a spectator bound for the show.

The incident took place on Peleliu Island in October, 1944. After much fighting, whence the name "Bloody Nose," American forces took the ridge.

WARRIORS IN TRUNKS. THE UNDERWATER DEM- OLITION TEAM IN AC- TION. UPPER. Members of a Navy Underwater Demolition Team, wearing rubber suits and "web-feet," demonstrate how they placed explosives on concrete and steel beach ob- stacles in pre-invasion opera- tions against Jap-held Pacific islands. Expert swimmers, they secured sachels of TNT against the obstacles, then retreated to small boats before the ex- plosion was set off. Concrete and steel blocks like these would have knocked holes in the bottoms of our landing craft if the daring "demos" had not accomplished their mission.

LOWER. Having plunged over the side of a landing boat, members of the Under- water Demolition Teams begin the swim toward their assigned areas. At the right the charges that the divers are to use float on the surface of the water.

BACK FROM A SWIM, MISSION ACCOMPLISHED.
An Underwater Demolition Team crewman, armed only
with a knife, is pulled over the side of a pick-up boat after
a mission off Balikpapan. The UDT man carries mine deton-
ators and a knife at his waist. One of the most dangerous
and most difficult assignments of the war was undertaken
by the Navy's Underwater Demolition Teams.

Clad only in swimming trunks, members of these teams
swam into action—braving enemy fire and sharks to clear
out natural or man-made obstacles located off the beaches
or in the surf where future American landings were to occur.
From Normandy in the Atlantic to Balikpapan in the
Pacific, they led the way, blasting the sea roads clear of
barriers. These photographs depict the various steps in the
operations followed by the "warriors in trunks." The work
of the "demos" was vital to the success of landing operations. Because of the nature of their work this branch of the
service was one of the most closely guarded secrets of the
war.

The sacrifices of the UDT men, amounting to as many
as 40 percent casualties at Normandy, kept down the
casualties among the fighters who arrived on D-Day and
after. They obtained information concerning mines, obstructions, and the nature of beaches where future American
operations were to take place. They eliminated beach defenses when necessary. On several occasions the Japanese
declared that the first American assault wave had been
repulsed. Actually the "demos" had paid them a visit, so
that when the first wave actually did come, it came to stay.

SAVING SUNKEN SHIPS. "A penny saved is a penny earned" is a saw usually learned in childhood. The Navy early learned that a ship saved is a ship built, so it has developed an efficient salvage organization. When it becomes necessary to blast your way into a harbor, many ships are sunk.

The salvage teams inherit the job of raising these ships, not only to clear the harbor for shipping, but to re-use the sunken ships. Mostly the ships as such are useless, but as scrap they help feed the great steel mills back home in their steady business of grinding out new ships, guns, and shells. Salvage work is dangerous, for sometimes a wily enemy will scuttle ships and affix underwater booby traps in an effort to prevent salvage.

ABOVE. Here a Navy diver prepares to go down to carry out salvage operations on an oil barge scuttled by the Germans in Naples harbor. In right foreground is radio used for communication with the diver.

SECRET WEAPONS. One big reason why the Navy was able to maintain constant, ever-increasing pressure on the Japanese in the vast reaches of the Pacific was its ability to make quick repairs in the forward areas without the long haul back to Pearl Harbor or a West Coast shipyard. The Navy was able to do this because it developed floating repair facilities.

One of these facilities was the floating drydock. Some floating drydocks, constructed in sections, were capable when tied together of accommodating the largest battleships afloat. A ship wounded in action was towed or limped back under its own steam to the drydocks where repairs were made.

Sometimes a ship could come out of a floating drydock ready for the line again, sometimes the drydock merely made such repairs as would permit the ship to reach an anchorage and a ship repair unit, or come back to Pearl Harbor. In the event that further repairs were needed, the drydock enabled the cripple to reach the final repair base much quicker than otherwise, and much valuable time was saved.

ABOVE. This picture shows a floating drydock traversing the Panama Canal. Too wide for normal passage the dock was passed from one ocean to another by a novel device conceived and directed by Seabees. Riding on the beam, the dock is towed through Culebra Cut. This dock has the capacity to accommodate cruisers and large auxiliaries, or several small warships at the same time. The plan of careening the dock on its beam and towing it through the canal was simple, but daring.

BACK TO THE PHILIPPINES. By October, 1944, Admiral Nimitz's campaign extended more than 4,000 miles from Pearl Harbor to Peleliu, while General MacArthur was more than 1,000 miles away from Port Moresby at Morotai. Only a few more operations remained scheduled before the return to the Philippines. Admiral Halsey of the Third Fleet, acting on information from one of his fliers, survivor of a crash landing recommended a speed up in strategy which was acted upon. UPPER. Protective smoke-screen is laid around U.S. warships during 20 October invasion of Leyte as enemy planes approach. LOWER. LST armada lands Army equipment at Tacloban Airstrip on Leyte. Note the hurriedly built causeways and bomb craters which have not yet been repaired.

DIGGING THEM OUT. It was a part of Japanese tactics throughout the Pacific campaign to let U. S. Marines and troops come ashore, only to be harassed by snipers hidden in caves, trees and undergrowth. For the Marines, Soldiers, Coastguardsmen, and Navy Beach battalions this practice was extremely uncomfortable and interrupted the unloading of vital supplies necessary for a push into the interior. At every beachhead it was necessary to send out scouting parties to rout and kill, one by one, the enemy snipers, cleverly camouflaged and concealed behind natural barriers. Here two Yanks cautiously inch their way toward a cave.

LEYTE DOG-HOLE. When war came to the United States Fido, Rover, and Rex answered the call as patriotically as Jack, Jim, and Joe. For the Coast Guard these faithful household watch-dogs became faithful national watch-dogs, participating in beach patrols and helping patrol shore stations. Marines and soldiers found man's best friend a best friend indeed in the jungle islands of the Pacific, braving great danger to carry important messages asking for reinforcements, seeking medical attention, or telling of enemy troop dispositions. In this picture, taken by a Coast Guard Combat Photographer, an American fighter and his dog seek shelter in a shallow fox hole before advancing further through the shambles of the Navy bombardment at Leyte.

MISSION OF MERCY, 1944. In the Pacific, where a ruthless and cruel foe refused to accept the meaning of the term "open city," the war inflicted almost as much injury upon helpless civilians—especially women and children—as it did upon the fighting men. But the American can and will take time out from repairing wounded fighting men to give aid to suffering civilians. That is why they were universally hailed as liberators. At a Naval Evacuation Center on the invasion beachhead, Leyte, a Filipino child is curious about the first aid being administered to his injured mother. In the background litter bearers can be seen bringing in more customers for the medical officers and pharmacist's mates, who have been trained to handle every sort of casualty.

THE BATTLE FOR
LEYTE GULF

By Admiral Thomas C. Kinkaid, USN and Admiral Marc A. Mitscher, USN

IT WAS between 23 and 26 October, 1944, that the Jap made his great challenge to our landings in the Philippines. During that period major naval and air actions occurred, actions that involved our carriers and battleships, cruisers and destroyers, submarines and PT boats.

There were three enemy forces to be dealt with. The first of these included 2 battleships, 1 heavy cruiser, and 4 destroyers. This force approached Leyte through Surigao Strait, and on the night of 24-25 October came into contact with units of our Seventh Fleet. In anticipation of the enemy's arrival, the Seventh Fleet was deployed in and at the mouth of the strait, so that when the Japanese had steamed into the trap they found themselves in the stem of a "T" crossed by

American cruisers and battleships, and flanked by light forces. In naval terminology, to be the stem of a "T" is to be caught in a hopeless position. Our heavy units pounded the dismayed Japs with big guns while destroyers launched fierce torpedo attacks. It was grim irony for the Japs. They were being sunk that night by our old battleships that they had "destroyed" at Pearl Harbor. The outcome of that encounter was decisive. Only one enemy destroyer escaped to meet defeat again. Only one of our ships, a destroyer, sustained damage.

While the enemy's Southern Force was being destroyed, the second force, to be known as the Central Force, was passing through San Bernardino Strait. Already it had been reduced in size, but still it came on.

On the 23rd two of our submarines had intercepted this force off Palawan when it consisted of 5 battleships, 10 heavy cruisers, 1 or 2 light cruisers, and about 15 destroyers. Our subs attacked and sank 2 heavy cruisers and seriously damaged another.

THE CENTRAL FORCE

ON THE 24th the Third Fleet carriers struck the Central Force as it passed through Mindoro Strait. Our carrier planes sent the Jap's new battleship *Musashi*, 1 cruiser, and 1 destroyer to the bottom. Other units were badly mauled. Yet despite these losses, the Japanese Central Force continued its drive for Leyte Gulf.

That same afternoon, carrier planes from our Third Fleet sighted the third, or Northern, enemy force north of Luzon. It was decided that our fast carrier task groups should intercept this force, and so, that night we steamed northward.

Dawn found the enemy's Central Force coming through San Bernardino Strait and down upon the 7th Fleet escort carriers and screens which were in three groups off Samar. An engagement followed with this enemy, at that time composed of 4 battleships, 5 cruisers, and 11 destroyers. Our lightly armed carriers retired, striking back at this formidable enemy with unexcelled courage. After more than two and one-half hours of struggle the enemy broke off the engagement, and withdrew in the direction of San Bernardino Strait.

Planes of the escort carriers and the Third Fleet struck the Central Force that afternoon, sinking 2 enemy heavy cruisers and 1 destroyer. Again on the 26th our planes attacked the depleted force and inflicted severe damage that resulted in several sinkings. Our losses in action with the Central Force amounted to one escort carrier and 2 destroyers sunk by surface fire, and approximately 105 planes.

That same morning to the north our Third Fleet commenced launching air attacks, and continued striking the Northern Force until 1800 that evening. By the end of the day this enemy force of 1 large carrier, 3 light carriers, 2 battleships with flight decks, 5 cruisers, and 6 destroyers was but a ghost. It was a "fleet out of being."

Forty of our planes went down in combat, and the light carrier *Princeton* was our only unit lost. The day was ours. The enemy fleet that had hoped to turn us back at Leyte had been cut to ribbons. Those enemy ships that were able to do so put on all possible steam for the homeland, and our reconquest of the Philippines went ahead.

T. C. Kinkaid

Marc A. Mitscher

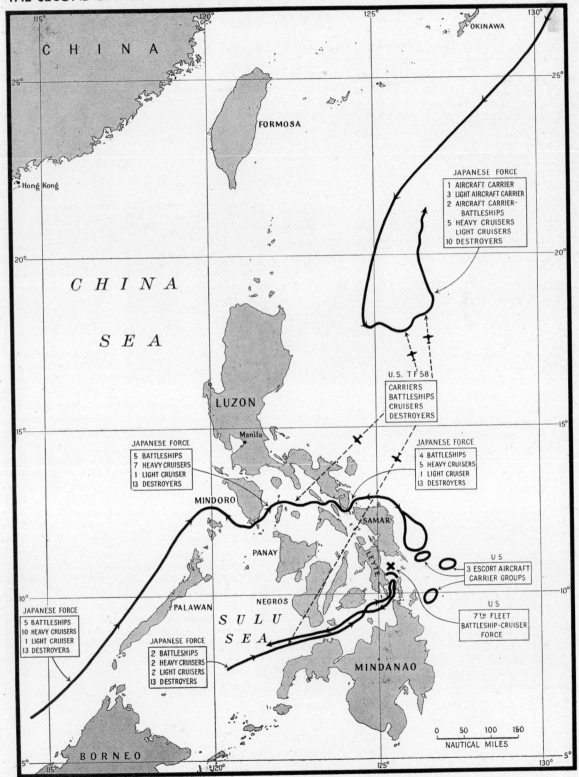

JAPANESE FORCE
1 AIRCRAFT CARRIER
3 LIGHT AIRCRAFT CARRIER
2 AIRCRAFT CARRIER-
  BATTLESHIPS
5 HEAVY CRUISERS
LIGHT CRUISERS
10 DESTROYERS

U.S. TF 58
CARRIERS
BATTLESHIPS
CRUISERS
DESTROYERS

JAPANESE FORCE
5 BATTLESHIPS
7 HEAVY CRUISERS
1 LIGHT CRUISER
13 DESTROYERS

JAPANESE FORCE
4 BATTLESHIPS
5 HEAVY CRUISERS
1 LIGHT CRUISER
13 DESTROYERS

US
3 ESCORT AIRCRAFT
CARRIER GROUPS

US
7TH FLEET
BATTLESHIP-CRUISER
FORCE

JAPANESE FORCE
5 BATTLESHIPS
10 HEAVY CRUISERS
1 LIGHT CRUISER
13 DESTROYERS

JAPANESE FORCE
2 BATTLESHIPS
2 HEAVY CRUISERS
2 LIGHT CRUISERS
13 DESTROYERS

CHINA

FORMOSA

Hong Kong

CHINA

SEA

LUZON

Manila

MINDORO

PANAY

SAMAR

LEYTE

NEGROS

PALAWAN

SULU

SEA

MINDANAO

OKINAWA

BORNEO

0   50   100   150
NAUTICAL MILES

Chart showing the Second Battle of the Philippine Sea, the Battle for Leyte Gulf.

WHEN JEEPS WISHED THEY WERE GNOMES. Presumably our carriers were safe because the Seventh Fleet had just annihilated a Japanese battle force trying to sneak around Leyte from the south. Task Force 38 supposedly had turned back a still greater enemy force descending on Leyte from the north; they then raced further north to intercept a Japanese carrier battle force. Suddenly the Japanese Central Force appeared in San Bernardino Strait and came charging at the jeep-carriers. Facing 4 Japanese battleships, 5 cruisers, and a dozen destroyers, our 16 baby flat-tops, 3 destroyers, and 4 destroyer escorts experienced a desperate time. The American escort carriers tried to get away in the thick smoke laid by the screen. The destroyers pressed torpedo attacks against impossible odds to save the carriers. RIGHT. The USS *Gambier Bay* takes cover. During the battle she, along with the valiant destroyers *Hoel* and *Johnston* and the destroyer escort *Roberts,* succumbed to the enemy fire. Intending to divert enemy fire from the carriers and turn the attack, Jeep-based planes, with open bomb bays and no ammunition, made dry-runs against the Japanese.

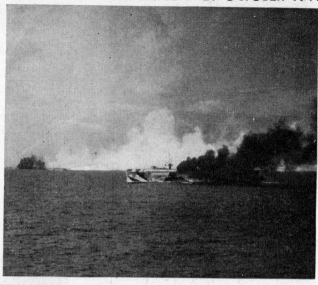

IN THE WAKE OF BATTLE. The Japs did not escape scot free. All the way west to Mindoro they were followed by vengeful U. S. carrier planes. They paid a price of 2 cruisers and 2 destroyers for the attack on the escort carriers during the morning of October 25, 1944.

LEFT. A large Japanese landing craft being bombed and sunk by carrier planes from the U. S. carrier *Hancock.* Fast carrier Task Force 38 was now in action, harrying the retiring Japanese forces and everything Japanese they sighted even far to the west of Leyte. Direct hits with 500 and 1,000 pound bombs have already been scored, and the Japanese craft is sinking amid clouds of smoke, steam and fire.

BELOW. Another Jap ship nearing its end. This is the large Jap carrier *Zuikaku* and escort ships under attack by the planes of Fast Carrier Task Force 38. It had been part of the Japanese tactics to sneak their carrier force down from around Luzon to the north to lure the Third Fleet up away from the Leyte beachhead while their Southern and Central Forces came in and wiped them off the map. But the Jap carriers had been spotted, and the planes from the 3 carrier groups that made up Task Force 38 drove in on them off Cape Engano on the northeast coast of Luzon. The Jap force consisted of 4 carriers, 2 battleships which had been made auxiliary carriers by replacing their after turrets with a flight deck, 5 cruisers, and 6 destroyers. Hit with bombs and torpedoes three of the Jap carriers were quickly sunk, and most of the other Japanese ships badly damaged. Later that day the remaining Jap carrier was sunk by our cruisers' gunfire, and one of our submarines picked off a crippled enemy cruiser.

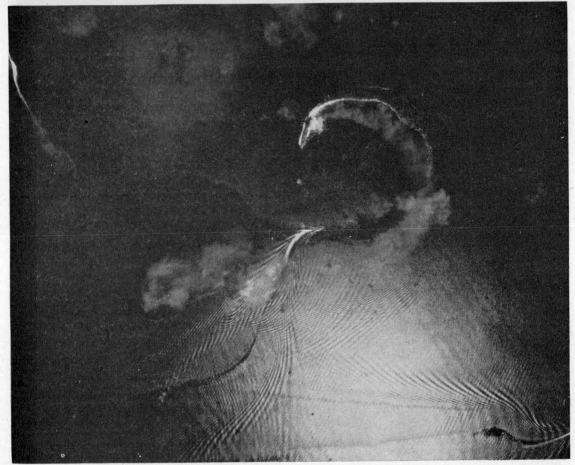

MISSION THWARTED. Out of a total of 7 Japanese battleships, 2 carrier-battleships, 4 carriers, 17 cruisers, and 23 destroyers which approached the Philippines in October, 1944, American Naval Forces sank 3 battleships, all 4 carriers, 10 cruisers and 5 destroyers in the Battle for Leyte Gulf. U. S. Navy losses amounted to 1 light carrier, 2 escort carriers, 2 destroyers and 1 PT boat. UPPER. Hard pressed by fliers of the United States Navy's Pacific Fleet this great Japanese battleship-aircraft carrier vainly tries to duck bomb and torpedo hits. Just a few hours before, the Japanese Southern Force, trying to sneak up on the Leyte landings via Surigao Strait, had been trapped by our Seventh Fleet, and only meager remnants of it got away.

LOWER. The wake of a fleeing Japanese ship etches a gigantic question mark in the waters of Tablas Strait as it vainly dodges the aerial attack of carrier planes from Admiral Halsey's Third Fleet.

"A HEADIN' FOR THE LAST ROUND-UP." UPPER. The large Jap carrier *Zuikaku* comes into the sights of a U. S. Navy carrier plane just before she heeled over on her side and sank. Here she puts on full steam in a last attempt to avoid the assault of U. S. Navy planes. This action took place east of Luzon in the Philippines, 24 October 1944. LOWER. The Japanese battleship *Nagato* evades bombs from American carrier planes in the Sibuyan Sea west of Leyte on October 24, during the first of the 3-day Battle for Leyte Gulf. The *Nagato* was part of the Central Force that received such a lacing in this action. Among the Jap ships sent to the bottom was the *Musashi*, super-battleship and much vaunted pride of the Japanese Navy.

RETURN TO THE PHILIPPINES. LANDINGS AT LIN-GAYEN GULF. Our carrier strikes at the Manila Bay area had led the Japanese to expect landings in that area. Instead, on January 9, 1944, we landed on the south and southeast coast of Lingayen Gulf, well north of Manila. The Luzon Attack Force was composed of Seventh Fleet units augmented by ships of the Pacific Fleet. All told there were more than 850 ships of all kinds, composing two attack forces, a reinforcement group, a fire support and bombardment group, and surface and air-covering groups. UPPER. A battleship of the fire support group lays a barrage while landing boats circle before hitting the beach at Lingayen. LOWER. Unloading supplies from an LCI (landing craft, infantry).

AIRCRAFT AND ANTI-AIRCRAFT AT LINGAYEN. The Third Fleet with its fast carrier task force covered and protected the operation at Lingayen by air strikes over Luzon, Formosa, and the Nansei Shoto. Complete surprise was attained in the attacks on Formosa and the southern Nansei Shoto. There was little airborne opposition, but unfavorable weather somewhat reduced the toll of enemy ships, planes, and facilities destroyed. Throughout the campaign there was little enemy air opposition. UPPER. An AA Gun emplacement on the shore of Lingayen Gulf. The crew is alert while the ships in the background are being unloaded. LOWER. Columns of smoke and debris heave skyward as the Marine light bombers pound objectives in Central Luzon.

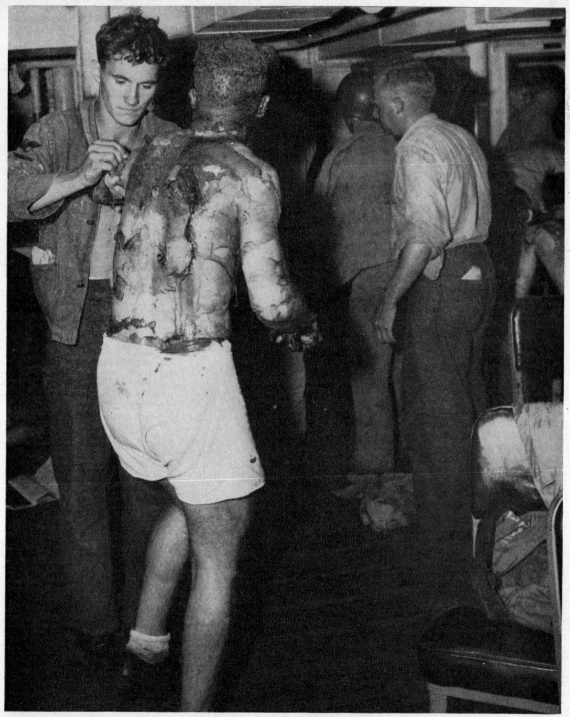

ORDEAL BY FIRE. Landings on Lingayen Gulf were scheduled for 9 January 1944. During the passage of the attack force to Lingayen there was no enemy surface opposition. One Japanese destroyer put out from Manila Bay, and was promptly sunk by our escorting destroyers. There was, however, intensive air attack during both the passage and the preliminary landing operations in Lingayen Gulf. As a result of these attacks the escort carrier *Ommaney Bay* and the minesweepers *Long, Hovey,* and *Palmer* were sunk.

ABOVE. His back badly burned, a U. S. Navy man submits to medical treatment on a warship in Lingayen Gulf. He is one of the crew of a sunken ship who was rescued from the blazing oil on the water. Expert medical care and immediate treatment will have this man in fighting trim within a few weeks. To the Medical research division of the Navy's Medical Corps goes the credit for the many miraculous cures for battle injuries during this war involving much research and development of new treatments.

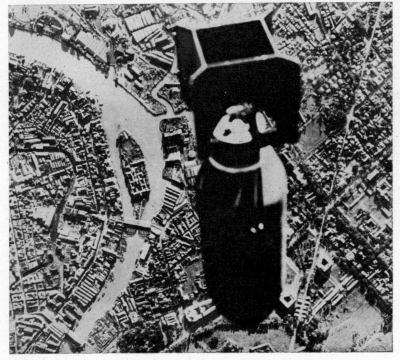

LUZON RECAPTURED. Shortly after the landings in the Lingayen Gulf area, additional landings were carried out in the Subic Bay area. On January 29, 1944, troops were landed northwest of Subic Bay. The landing was so unexpected that there was no opposition. On the following day, troops were landed on Grande Island in Subic Bay proper. By the 15th of January our forces had driven to the northern end of the Bataan peninsula, and on the same day another landing was made on the peninsula itself.

Throughout the Luzon campaign U. S. forces were aided by Philippine guerrillas, men of the Philippines who fought the Japanese from the day the enemy invaded their homeland until the last Japanese soldier in the islands had surrendered or was killed.

UPPER. A Marine Sergeant in the Philippines explains the use of a machine-gun cartridge magazine to a group of Filipino guerrillas. LOWER. A "calling card" from the U. S. Navy screams down on the docks and supply dumps in Manila Harbor.

LANDINGS ON MINDORO. On 15 December 1944, American forces landed on the southwest coast of Mindoro Island, 300 miles northwest of Leyte. The purpose of this landing was to establish air facilities on the island for support of the campaign on Luzon which was scheduled for early January. Enemy air activity on Luzon was particularly heavy at this time and our convoys suffered some damage from suicide planes while enroute to the Island. UPPER. The USS *Essex* takes a hit from a flaming Japanese suicide plane. LOWER. Unloading an LST (landing ship, tank) on Mindoro Island. The chain of officers and men, emphasizing the need for speed in unloading, is bringing anti-aircraft ammunition ashore. When action impends, everyone must turn to in preparation.

PANAY "INCIDENT" AVENGED IN THE PHILIPPINES. Seizing another strategic objective in the Philippines campaign, and in a sense "avenging" the Jap sinking of the Navy gunboat USS *Panay* in China in 1937, U. S. Troops invaded Panay Island on March 18, 1945. Within 60 hours—thanks to the co-operation of Filipino guerrillas—the Jap defenders of the island were overwhelmed.

UPPER. Symbolizing the invaluable assistance they have given U. S. forces of liberation, Filipino guerrillas help land an Army jeep. **LOWER.** PT boats were active not only in spotting and attacking Japanese Naval forces, but also in contacting and arming Filipino resistance troops. Here a PT boat is surrounded by native canoes loaded with men waiting to be armed.

U. S. NAVAL GROUP, CHINA

By Rear Admiral Milton E. Miles, USN

THE STORY of SACO, (Sino-American Cooperative Organization), dates back to the first few weeks after Pearl Harbor when the Navy and the National Military Council of China, laying immediate foundations for offensive action against Japan moved to establish a weather service in Asia, where the weather for the Pacific originates. After months of inspecting, planning, negotiating, and preparation, the first United States Naval personnel arrived in China and commenced setting up the organization with the Chinese.

Once in China it became apparent that to achieve our primary mission, that of establishing weather and intelligence units whose reports would be of value to American forces in the Pacific and Asia, it would be necessary to train and equip Chinese guerrillas and to set up and maintain the many and varied establishments that such an undertaking would require. It was a long, progressive task that improved until victory was finally realized.

By the end of 1942 our Weather Central near Chungking, with the cooperation of the Chinese Government, was sending regular weather reports from many occupied areas in the Far East to the U. S. Fleet. China assigned substantial undercover forces to protect American observers. Navy, Marine Corps, and Coast Guard personnel participated in the training and equipping of roughly 30,000 Chinese. 50,000 more were trained but due to lack of "hump" transportation allowances they could not be equipped. With American equipment and American participation in the raids they became the best organized and most effective of all Chinese guerrillas.

From the administrative offices of the India Unit in Calcutta all American personnel were flown into China. From early 1942 until the Stilwell road was completed, everything that went into the project, books, radio equipment, jeeps, guns, mines, gasoline, and other essentials had to come into China over the "Hump" by air as part of the monthly 150-ton allocation assigned to our project.

BEHIND THE LINES

WITH these materials SACO units set up weather, communications, and intelligence stations all the way from the border of Indo-China to the northern reaches of the Gobi Desert. Much of the concentration of activities was located along the China Coast behind the north-south Japanese lines. While it was sometimes possible to enter or depart from some portions of Jap-held territory by air, SACO Americans became adept at Chinese disguises and, guided by SACO Chinese, they slipped safely through enemy lines whenever and wherever they chose. Through months and years only 3 Americans from SACO were captured.

Chinese and American personnel lived, worked and fought side by side, knowing that they were the most important source of essential intelligence in China for the prowling U. S. Fleet and for our submarines just off the coast. Fleet operations in the Western Pacific made the most of SACO weather reports, especially in planning and executing hazardous carrier strikes despite the treacherous weather conditions prevailing near Formosa and the Japanese home islands.

ACCOMPLISHMENTS

THE 14th Air Force at all times benefited from SACO activity. Much of its intelligence emanated from the American Navy in China. Facts concerning Japanese troop movements, supply concentrations, airfield developments, bridges, and other strategic targets reached 14th Air Force Headquarters from SACO-manned stations, and the hard-hitting Army fliers used this information to great advantage. Directed by SACO forces, aerial mining of the China Coast and vital inland water routes was effected. A principal achievement of these mining operations combined with SACO coast watchers was to force Jap shipping far out to sea, where it fell into the ambushes of U. S. submarines.

The Chinese guerrillas trained in 12 SACO camps made a fine record in their offensive against Japanese units. Killing 3 Japs to every guerrilla lost, they are credited with wiping out more than 2,000 Japanese a month in 1945. Sabotage units developed and carried out extensive operations against Japanese establishments.

During the war SACO, working with our own Chinese rescue agencies, rescued 76 fliers forced down in China.

The success of our mission in China is attributable to the over 2,500 volunteers of the U. S. Navy, Marine Corps, and Coast Guard who served in SACO, and to the close relationship that existed there between U. S. Naval personnel and the Chinese.

AMERICA'S RICE PADDY NAVY. UPPER. Somewhere in China in 1944, the Stars and Stripes, flanked by the flags of free China, pass in review. This picture was taken at one of the several SACO camps where Chinese guerrillas received their training. The primary objective of this training was the protection of American groups engaged in aerology and intelligence work. Much of this weather work and the gathering of intelligence was carried on along the China Coast behind Japanese lines. Therefore, guerrilla fighters were essential in keeping the Japanese garrisons on their heels. **BELOW.** With "baker" waving on the hill, a chief petty officer and an officer of the U. S. Navy instruct Chinese guerrillas in the use of American automatic rifles.

SOCKO! American Navy men in China pronounced the title of their organization (SACO) "socko," a term well known in fighting circles. UPPER. A marksmanship class of Chinese guerrillas poses with its American instructors at one of the twelve SACO camps in China. These Chinese, equipped with American rifles and pistols, and at times led by American Naval and Marine Corps personnel, carried out many successful raids against Japanese garrisons in occupied China. LOWER. This railroad bridge was the object of SACO sabotage units. During the war SACO guerrillas destroyed 209 bridges, 84 locomotives, 141 ships and river craft, and 97 depots and warehouses. In this period they killed 23,540 Japs, wounded 9,166, and captured 291.

NAVAL TRANSPORT SERVICE, CHINA STYLE. To carry out their many jobs in China, American Navy personnel used various means of transportation. To cover the vast distances of China they used rafts, trucks, jeeps, carts, and airplanes. On the Gobi Desert, where personnel were engaged in aerology work, camels furnished a means of transportation. However, when no camels, jeeps or airplanes were available, U. S. Navy men were known to have walked 500 miles or more in one stretch. UPPER. A group of Chinese guerrillas, led by SACO Americans, cross the Huang Cheng River on a raft. These forces, trained in an American camp, now move out to strike at Japanese garrisons. LOWER. A Navy convoy in China crosses the Salween River Bridge.

INVESTMENT OF CORREGIDOR. In February, 1945, the mighty Rock of Corregidor, powerful bastion guarding Manila Bay, was battered by surface ships and aircraft, assaulted by amphibious forces and paratroopers, and once more the Stars and Stripes were hoisted from the spot where they had been lowered in May of 1942. During this bombardment the Navy had become so contemptuous of Jap opposition that, after a day of shelling, one cruiser speeded its run back to Subic so the quarterdeck could be rigged for nightly movies. Back in Honolulu the black-out was still in effect. UPPER. Seventh Fleet shells explode near under-surface mines, off Corregidor's shores. LOWER. Paratroopers descend in a deadly cloud on Corregidor to exterminate the Japs entrenched there.

CORREGIDOR ASSAULTED. U. S. Navy and Army units combined operations in a display of power to overwhelm Jap Corregidor defenses February 16.

UPPER. Gutted skeletons are all that remain after surface and aerial bombardment. White parachutes of airborne troops can be seen settling down on The Rock. One naval officer, observing the airborne invasion from the bridge of his ship, jocularly paid tribute to Army women by remarking as he saw the white 'chutes billow out, "The Wacs are coming in early."

LOWER. A raft from a Navy PT boat makes for the shore of Corregidor to pick up paratroopers who overshot the top of the Rock in the airborne assault. Paratroopers suffered heavy casualties int his operation. As long as Corregidor remained in Japanese possession, valuable cargo ships entering Manila bay with supplies for the invasion of the Jap homeland could be cut to pieces by enemy guns.

THE BOSS OF THE LANDINGS. When the strike is over and the flight returns to its home carrier, no man aboard is more important than the Landing Signal Officer. It is his job to guide the planes in for a perfect landing, indicating their way to the center of the runway. When the approach is faulty or a plane is crippled, he must quickly recognize the situation and coach the plane in for the best possible landing under adverse conditions.

NEARING THE HOME ISLANDS. UPPER. At Iwo Jima a U.S. tanker is hit by enemy action and goes up in flames as the battle rages ashore. LOWER. A Baka bomb which was captured intact on Okinawa. These tiny suicide planes were released from their parent plane and piloted in to hit their targets. Loaded with explosives they were certain death for their fanatical pilots, since they were either shot down or reached their objective.

THE PHILIPPINES RETAKEN. The sound of gunfire had scarcely passed on into the hills when Navy Seabees and Army engineers bent relentlessly to the task of transforming the Philippines into one vast base for future operations. Captured airfields were rebuilt. Manila harbor, like Naples, Cherbourg, and Marseilles before it, was the scene of devastation and ruin. Its resurrection was the most awesome salvage job Commodore Sullivan and his Seabees had yet undertaken. UPPER. A marksmen's-eye view of the ship-littered mouth of the Pasig River, where Jap troops are still fleeing across the water. LOWER. A Jap "Jill" plane shot down off the coast of Indo-China by a Navy plane.

THE BATTLE FOR
IWO JIMA

By Lieutenant General Harry Schmidt, USMC

ON FEBRUARY 19th, 1945, two Marine Divisions of the Fifth Amphibious Corps landed on the East beaches of Iwo Jima. Five miles long and two and one-half miles wide at its widest point, the island was less than seven hundred miles from Tokyo itself. It was a point on the bomber route from the Marianas to Japan, and was meticulously prepared for defense by the enemy.

Our heavy bombing program was suffering serious losses from the lack of a base between Japan and the hard-won airfields in the Marianas. Enemy bombers were being shuttled south through Iwo to bomb the B-29 bases. Iwo radar was making wide, gas consuming detours necessary for the raiding bombers. The planned assault on the Ryukyu islands could not be undertaken until Iwo Jima with its airfields was captured.

The Fifth Amphibious Corps, comprising the Fourth and Fifth Marine Divisions with the Third Division in reserve, was picked for the assault. While the Marianas were being built up after their capture in the summer of 1944 and while the Fifth Corps trained and rehearsed for the February landing, the enemy on Iwo was working night and day to perfect his installations. Through aerial photographs his progress was studied. The Army and Navy increased their air and surface ship bombardments of the island. Prior to D-Day the Army had flown bombing missions for seventy-two days against Iwo, and the air photos finally showed a terrain so pocked with bomb and shell craters that it resembled the surface of the moon. Three days of intensive naval gunfire immediately preceded the landing. But Lieutenant General Kuribayashi, the Japanese commander, knew his business. On the 19th he was ready and waiting for our assault troops.

THE LANDING

AT 0900 the first waves landed, the Fourth Division on the right half of the two mile landing beach, the Fifth Division on the left. Following closely our rolling barrage, the first waves landed minor opposition. But men and vehicles bogged down in the soft volcanic ash, the steep grade impeded progress, and the enemy opened up. Artillery, mortars, rockets, and coast defense guns, all cunningly concealed and emplaced in depth throughout the island, opened with a tremendous concentration on the beach. To the Marines coming ashore that day the beach was as the stage of a huge amphitheatre with the enemy looking down on them from all the seats.

It was a rough spot. Men and tanks labored in their frontal assault. Concentrated enemy fire, directed by observers on both flanks, took a serious toll of incoming boats and beached supplies. Boats were wrecked in the surf, blown up by direct hits, supply and ammunition dumps disappeared in shattering explosions. But the stream of supplies never stopped, and the assault troops moved steadily forward. By nightfall there were 30,000 men ashore, armed and supplied. Suribachi had been isolated from the rest of the island, and we were ready for a counterattack. But the enemy had learned a lot in three years and there would be no suicidal Banzai charges breaking themselves—and the backbone of the island defense—against the taut battleline of Marines.

The reserve—the Third Marine Division less one Regimental Combat Team—was committed on the third day of the battle. Suribachi was taken, the flag raised at its summit, on the fifth day. With the Fourth Division as a pivot, the Corps swung right to the north and advanced three divisions abreast.

Using every cave and crevice, taking skillful advantage of a year's preparation for just such an attack, the enemy forced the Fifth Amphibious Corps to fight a bitter and deadly frontal assault.

Not until March 16 was the island secured. In that time some 60,000 Marines had fought at Iwo, the greatest concentration of troops for the area involved in the history of modern warfare and the largest force of Marines ever to be committed in a single battle. In the words of Fleet Admiral Nimitz, Iwo Jima was the battle "where uncommon valor was a common virtue." Of the force engaged over 20,000 were killed or wounded, but before the end of the war over 3,000 B-29's had landed at Iwo. The bulk of them, with their ten man crews, would have been lost without the haven of Iwo.

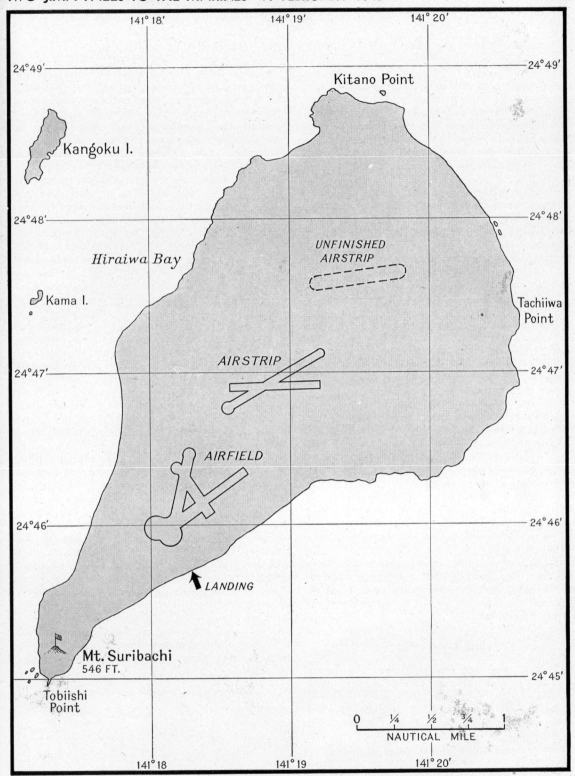

Map of the island of Iwo Jima, showing landing points.

SINEWS OF WAR. UPPER. Pouring men and material on the tiny Iwo Jima beachhead are LST's, LSM's, and LCI's. Just off the beach more landing craft await their chance at the unloading area, while small boats from the transports ply back and forth bringing assault troops and returning wounded. Farther out, the transports, APA's and AKA's, stand by to unload. Along the horizon, the protective screen of destroyers, destroyer escorts and cruisers can be discerned. On the island, Marine tanks can be spotted moving over the rough terrain toward the first airfield at left. LOWER. Fifth Division Marines swarm up the volcanic ash ridge from the beach of Iwo Jima.

D-DAY FINDS A SHAMBLE ON IWO JIMA'S BEACHES. UPPER. Amtracks from Coast Guard-manned LST's carrying Fourth Division Marines poke through the wreckage to crawl up on the blackened sands of Iwo Jima. At right is a shattered Jap transport, shelled to destruction by the terrific pre-invasion bombardment of U. S. Navy guns.

American equipment, bogged down in the volcanic ash sands, was caught in a cross-fire from hidden Jap positions. The "alligators," however, were able to creep forward through the destruction and consequently assumed a more important role than is usual in a beach head assault. The difficult terrain and the ferocity with which the Japanese fought from their entrenched positions contributed to make the battle of Iwo Jima one of the bloodiest assaults ever attempted by the Marines.

LOWER. From the U.S.S. *Yorktown*, Essex class carrier, these F6F's came to the assistance of Marine infantry men slugging their way across the island. In this mid-morning attack on D-Day plus 2, the airmen make a low level fighter bomber attack to soften up Jap positions immediately back of the assault lines. In the background may be seen part of the supporting fleet which brought the Marines to the battleground.

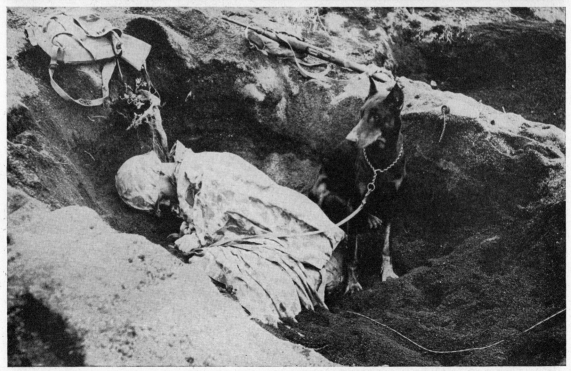

SHELTER IS FOUND IN HOLES. UPPER. Diving head first into the shallow hole in the foreground, a Marine seeks cover from a Jap shell as it whistles through the air. Behind him other Marines race for shelter. Seconds after the picture was taken the missile exploded in the area. During the battle the Marine learns to keep one ear always cocked for the whine of the bomb—and to move fast when he hears that whine. LOWER. "Butch," a Doberman Pinscher Marine War-Dog stands guard as his partner, of the Fifth Marine Division, grabs a little sleep in a volcanic ash fox hole in Iwo Jima. War Dogs were used for scouting and for messengers. Scouting teams like this eliminated many Jap snipers who played dead inside blasted pillboxes, but they could not fool the dogs.

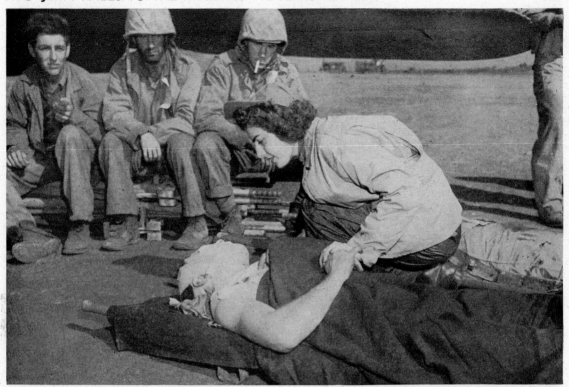

GOOD WORD, PRACTICAL HELP. UPPER. A Navy flightnurse checks a wounded U. S. Marine at a captured airstrip on Iwo Jima. Within a few minutes, the Marine will be transferred to a C-54 for transport to a hospital on Guam. Air ambulances were credited with saving the lives of thousands of badly injured men by carrying them swiftly from battle areas to stations where the best in modern surgical technique was available. LOWER. Even in the foxholes of Iwo Jima, where the postman never had to ring twice, mail was delivered whenever a lull in battle permitted. There is nothing like a letter from home to boost a fighting man's morale.

LETHAL WEAPONS. UPPER. Here is the first picture ever released of the U. S. Marine mobile rocketeer units at work. The photograph was taken on Iwo Jima. The value of this weapon is self-evident. Its projectiles soared over hills to blast the Japanese on the other side. Mobility was also a great asset. Before enemy artillery could find the range of rocketeers, the units were off to another sector. LOWER. This picture shows one of the many kinds of booby traps rigged up by the retreating Japanese troops. Sharp-eyed ordnancemen were not so easily fooled, though. Here we see a seasoned Marine jungle fighter exposing a fragmentation grenade hidden in a cabbage.

GERMAN BOGEY WEAP-ONS. German scientists, run-ning a losing race with time, completed their fantastic "re-venge" weapons, the V-1 and V-2, just before the Allied landings in Normandy. Had they been perfected earlier in the war, they might have spelled disaster for the Ameri-can and Allied forces staging in the British Isles. The two weapons were directed prin-cipally at targets in London and later Antwerp.

The U.S. Navy first felt the effect of these Nazi secret wea-pons when its base in South London was blasted by the V-1 "buzz-bomb." A Naval technical mission made a study of the V-1 and V-2 to deter-mine which German techniques could be incorporated into its guided missile program. The V-1 was a flying bomb, moti-vated by an oxygen-fed jet propulsion unit, and achieved a speed of upwards of 450 miles per hour.

The larger V-2 pictured here in launching position, was actually a rocket. At the peak of its trajectory it reached an altitude of 70 miles, and as it hurtled back to earth, attained a speed of over 3,000 miles per hour. Neither of these weapons could be aimed at specific targets, but were di-rected at large metropolitan areas as nuisance devices. German scientists were also working on other fantastic and deadly weapons, including an atomic bomb, all of which came under the purview of the Naval Technical Mission. The mission also made a thorough study of synthetic training devices.

EXOTIC CARGO. When King Ahdul Aziz Ibn Saud, monarch of Saudi Arabia, accompanied by nearly 50 retainers, boarded a U.S. Navy destroyer at Jidda Bay in his homeland to steam northward to meet President Franklin D. Roosevelt in Suez Canal, his entourage introduced notes which appeared strange to the destroyer's crew—exotic customs such as sleeping in rugs, slaughtering sheep, and cooking over charcoal braziers.

But the Navy took these oriental customs in stride, for strangers with strange customs are not new to the Navy. It is the Navy which through the years has carried the American flag and American prestige to far-away foreign lands.

UPPER. In strange contrast to modern efficiency of the destroyer, an Arabian servant slaughters a sheep in the old-age manner of his race on the ship's fantail. In the foreground, some of the sheep find thin "grazing" on the hard deck. LOWER. During the day the sleeping rugs are stowed near the rail of the destroyer by Arabian servants.

BIG BEN WOUNDED. Beginning in March, 1945, in the Western Pacific, and ending in May at the Brooklyn Navy Yard, the USS *Franklin,* affectionately known to her crew as "Big Ben," unfolded a saga which has scarcely been equaled in the annals of any Navy.

On March 19, while the *Franklin* was launching her aircraft for renewed assaults on Japan's Inland Sea, an enemy dive bomber came out of the clouds and scored hits with two five hundred pound armor-piercing bombs. Flames shot through the ship, and she was rocked by one terrific explosion after another as fuel and ammunition blew up. There were more than 1,000 casualties, as brave men fought to save lives and the ship. Chaplain Joseph Timothy O'Callahan was awarded the Medal of Honor for courageously leading a rescue party into a flaming compartment.

UPPER. Navy men fighting one of the many fires on the *Franklin.* LOWER. "Big Ben's" hangar deck engulfed in smoke and flames.

THE OKINAWA CAMPAIGN

By Lieutenant General Roy S. Geiger, USMC

ON APRIL 1, 1945, the First and Sixth Marine Divisions of the Third Amphibious Corps, and the XXIV Army Corps, which made up the newly organized Tenth Army, began landing on the western coast of Okinawa.

The Third Amphibious Corps was initially assigned the securing of the northern half of the island. Negligible opposition was encountered in the landings and the advance inland. By nightfall a beachhead eight miles wide and three miles deep had been established by the Tenth Army.

Enemy opposition stiffened as the advance progressed. The enemy's use of artillery was accelerated and counter-attacks at night were frequently employed. The final drive for the northern tip of the island was marked by savage fighting on Motobu Peninsula. Here it was mountain warfare of the most rugged sort. Infantry combat was at short ranges, and cave and pillbox positions demanded heavy employment of flamethrowers and demolitions. Final success was achieved only after execution of vigorous bayonet assaults.

By April 19th, the entire northern half of the island was secured, although patrol action continued in order to mop-up remnants of the enemy forces.

The XXIV Corps, which had fought its way south, was stopped by an elaborate defense line drawn across the island near its southern end from Naha, capital city of Okinawa, to Shuri, and then to Yonabaru.

The enemy plan of defense was based on the natural barriers afforded by the Asa River in the Naha sector, and the rugged and dominating terrain masses in the Shuri and Yonabaru areas.

At the end of April, the Third Amphibious Corps moved into the sector to the right or west of the XXIV Corps. The First Marine Division moved into the Machinato Airfield area just north of the Asa River on May 1. On May 9 the Sixth Marine Division moved into the lines above the Asa River on the extreme right flank.

COUNTERATTACK

DURING the period from May 3 to 5, the Japanese made a strong counterattack, using land, sea, and air forces. Several heavy attacks were made against our main line while strong raiding parties landed behind our positions on both coasts. Every enemy counterattack and infiltration attempt was repulsed.

The enemy defenses were so tough and deep that they were dubbed the "Pacific's Siegfried Line." Massed artillery protected their installation—log bunkers and concrete pillboxes and natural fortifications. The Japs were burrowed in caves with connecting tunnels far beneath the surface.

In the pre-dawn darkness of May 10 the Asa River was bridged at a point about a mile from Naha. The next day Marines were in the outskirts of the capital. Lashing out at night the Japs drove the Marines back 200 yards across a valley before the Marines rallied and smashed the assault. Grenades were tossed about like baseballs, and the dead were strewn on both sides of the valley. In furious fighting around "Sugar Loaf Hill," a strategic mound guarding the approaches to Naha, severe and heavy casualties were suffered by the Marines. This hill was assaulted 11 times before the Marines were able to make their way down the other side.

Meanwhile, after 11 days of rain had turned the terrain into a quagmire, hampering our supply problem, the Japs moved their troops to the east side of Shuri, in belief that the approaches to their positions were impenetrable. On May 29, the First Marine Division captured Shuri Castle. This permitted the Japanese to be outflanked and soon the entire Shuri position was wiped out.

In a quick amphibious maneuver below Naha, the Sixth Marine Division landed behind the Jap lines and fought their way to the airfield on June 6. Next day they overran the field, and struck southeastward toward a juncture with the First Marine Division.

LAST STAND

FOR their final desperate stand, the Japs consolidated the remnants of their force on Yaeju-Dake, an escarpment about 3,000 yards long and 600 feet high. A frontal assault against this was met with furious resistance. One by one the enemy's positions on vital ridges in the sector were outflanked and taken. The Eighth Regimental Combat Team of the Second Marine Division was brought into action and helped the final drive to the sea.

Organized resistance on Okinawa was at an end by June 21. From Okinawa flew all types of aircraft, driving the final wedge into the Japanese innermost defenses, and setting up the invasion which was fortunately proved unnecessary.

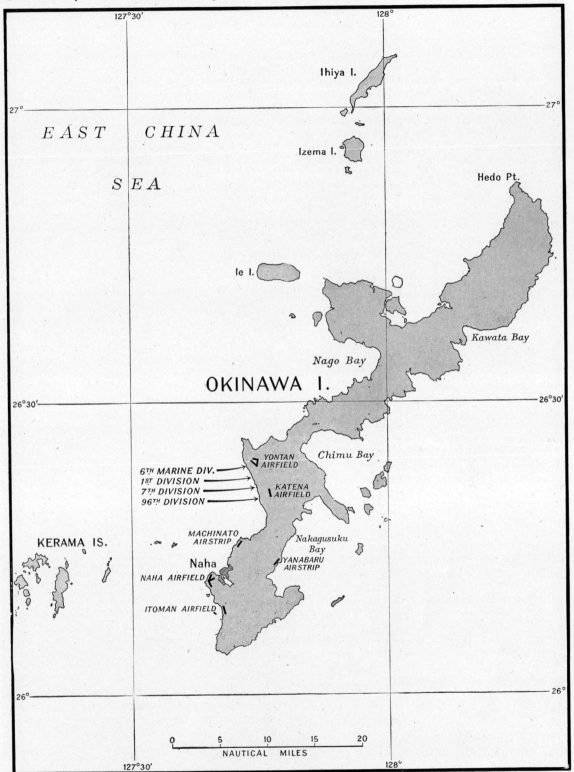

Map of Okinawa and adjacent islands, showing landing points.

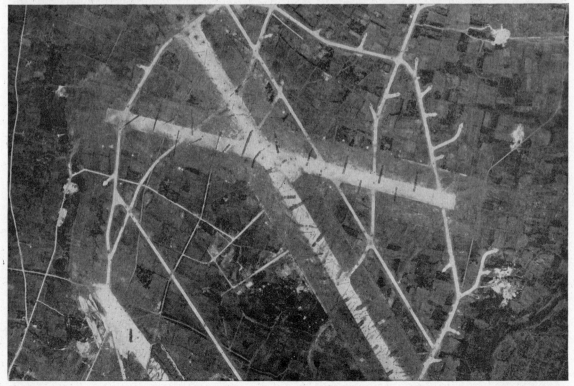

THE NAVY'S MIGHT. UPPER. The thundering voice of one of the Navy's most powerful weapons speaks in defiance to the enemy as a United States battleship hurls salvoes of destruction into the beach on Okinawa. Under the muzzles of its guns the amtracks can be seen as they carry their cargoes of troops toward the beach for the landing on April, 1945. LOWER. As seen from this aerial photograph, the Japs have torn up the runways of their airfield on the island of Ie Shima, final resting place of famed war correspondent Ernie Pyle, just west of Okinawa. All taxiways have been purposely put out of commission by digging ditches and blasting holes across them.

PACIFIC OFFENSIVE. UPPER. Not many men can truthfully say that they went in before the first-wave combat troops, but the Navy's demolition teams have done it and done it often. Here Underwater Demolition Squadron D-19 arrives on a beach in Ryukyu Retto in a rubber boat. These men had cleaned up some of the obstacles that remained after the landings were well under way.

LOWER. Naha falls to the Sixth Marine Division. Infantry and tanks of the Sixth Marine Division push their way across the fields of Okinawa into the island's battered capital, Naha. As they advance they concentrate their bombardment on a small Japanese house where a group of enemy soldiers are fiercely resisting. In the center, a large bridge has been blasted and few of the town's buildings remain undamaged. Note the Marines taking cover in gullies and behind hedges as they struggle forward.

The Okinawa operation was from many standpoints, the most difficult ever undertaken by U. S. forces in the Pacific. Okinawa was defended by 120,000 Japanese, and its proximity to the home islands of Japan presented the American forces with the problem of combatting a great part of Japan's airpower. Many of the Japanese planes materialized in the form of Kamikaze (suicide) attacks. The Jap fliers were known to men of the fleet as the Katzenjammer kids. It was the job of the U. S. carrier planes, fleet guns, and later, when airfields on Okinawa were secured, Marine land-based planes to intercept and destroy this formidable foe whose efforts to break up the American operation were fantastically fierce.

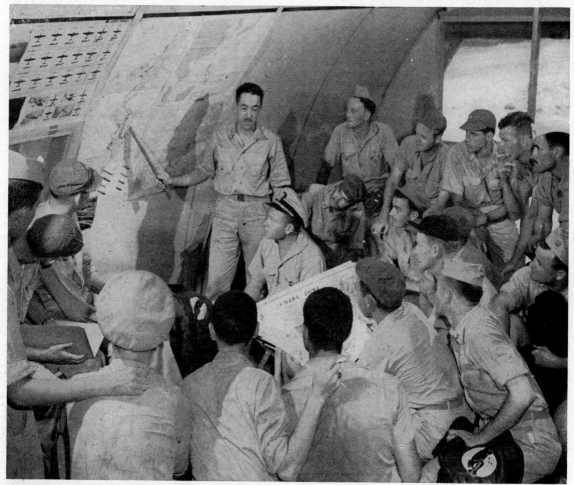

MARINE FLYERS BACK UP THE TROOPS. UPPER. A Marine Corsair fighter looses its rocket projectiles on a run against a Jap stronghold on Okinawa. Close air-ground support is a Marine specialty, and waves of these planes were used to soften up enemy positions as American land, sea, and air forces smashed forward in the bitter struggle to dislodge the enemy from the southern sector of the island. **LOWER.** The capture of Japanese headquarters in the honeycombed caves of Kushi-Yake mountain, long pounded by Marine planes, signified the final phase of the struggle for Okinawa. These pilots are being briefed before their take-off for patrol sweeps.

USS *BUNKER HILL.* UPPER. As smoke boils from the stern of the USS *Bunker Hill* where a Jap dive bomber crashed among planes preparing to take off for a strike on Okinawa, firefighters battle the explosion and gun crews man their battle stations to ward off any further attacks. LOWER. Army and Seabee camps provided the ingredients. A private first class from St. Louis, Missouri, cuts out doughnuts (left), a corporal from Plattsburg, Missouri, fries them (center), and a private first class from Syracuse, N. Y., applies icing made from candy and cocoa as three Marines of the Fourth Marine Regiment make chocolate covered doughnuts behind the lines on Okinawa.

JAP ROCKET AND LAUNCHER ON OKINAWA.
UPPER. In their drive in the south of Okinawa Shima,
Marines of the Sixth Division came upon this Jap rocket
and launcher. Although the rocket is inaccurate, it deto-
nates with tremendous force. The rocket has been called
"Bubbley-Wubbley" because of the sound it makes in
flight. LOWER. These two ships were part of the toll of
U. S. Navy vessels at Okinawa during its typhoon of
October 9. An ARB (Repair ship, battle damage) collided
with the SS Ocelet in Buckner Bay and this mass of wreckage resulted. The 140-mile an hour typhoon drove aground
more than 130 U. S. Navy ships.

RHINELAND FLEET. Rhineland maidens, those fabulous but beautiful traditions, probably scurried behind rocks and bushes when the U.S. Navy's strange amphibious craft began taking the armies of General Eisenhower across the great German river. Not since the 1860's, when U.S. warships cleared the Mississippi, had the Navy fought a war so far from the sea, but when General Eisenhower called upon Admiral Stark for a naval force to effect the amphibious crossing of the Rhine, sailors and small amphibious craft were trucked to the west bank, where they once again became water-borne.

With field artillery instead of the traditional guns of battleships and cruisers providing the fire cover and support, the small amphibious craft scurried back and forth, up and down German's historic waterway taking the conquering Allied forces into the heart of Nazi power.

UPPER. LCVP's (Landing Craft, Vehicle, Personnel) carrying an Army jeep across the Rhine past the famed Remagen railway bridge. LOWER. Another LCVP unloads an Army ambulance ashore.

THE U. S. NAVY ON THE RHINE. Nazi Germany planned a last stand on the far side of the Rhine. Her armies had been badly battered on the west bank, and she had only a thin line standing between the Allied Expeditionary Force and Berlin. The Remagen bridgehead was quickly followed up by the amphibious crossing of the Rhine by Generals Patton, Hodges, Simpson, and Field Marshall Montgomery, who sent column after column through the thin German line and delivered the final crushing blow to forces of Hitler. UPPER. Army tanks are placed aboard Navy LACM's for ferrying across the Rhine. LOWER. LCVP's holding section of Army treadway bridge in place on the Rhine near Remagen, while Army trucks cross to the other side.

NAVAL RESPECT FOR C-IN-C. The U. S. Navy's Union Jack flies at half mast from a destroyer while the bow sentry stands guard, wearing watchcap and the prescribed undress blues, scabbard, and cartridge belt, as respect was paid for the deceased President Roosevelt. For thirty days after the President's death on April 12, 1945, all U. S. ships flew their flags at half mast when in port. The U. S. Navy's Union Jack, is the blue flag with the white stars flown from the jack-staff when a ship is in port. Other usual naval regulations for mourning the passing of a President, such as the wearing of the mourning patch and firing of salvos, were dispensed with during the thirty-day mourning period because of the requirements of war and the impracticability.

NATION'S TRIBUTE. All the services were represented in the Pennsylvania Avenue funeral procession as the saddened nation paid its final tribute to the wartime President. For the Navy it was a special tribute, because President Roosevelt, early in his economic recovery program, earmarked emergency funds to begin the reconstruction of the Navy which had been allowed to wither in the backwash of World War I. UPPER. Enroute to the White House, where ceremonies were conducted in the historic East Room, an artillery caisson bearing the late President's body passes along Pennsylvania Avenue. LOWER. Officers and enlisted personnel of Waves escort the caisson.

ALL QUIET ON THE WESTERN FRONT. LEFT. Unconditional surrender terms were signed by German military leaders on May 4, 1945, ending the fighting in Holland and Northwestern Germany. Field Marshall Sir Bernard Montgomery (left) listens to peace overtures in his tent. **LOWER.** Representatives of German and Allied Nations in the War Room of SHAEF Headquarters at Reims Industrial School, May 7, 1945, prepare to sign the surrender documents which end the greatest of all European wars. Seated nearer the camera is the German delegation headed by Col. General Gustav Jodl (center). Across the table (left to right) are: Lt. General Frederick E. Morgan, Maj. General Francois Sevez, Admiral Sir Harold Burrough, Lt. General Walter Bedell Smith, Maj. General Ivan Suslaparoff, General Carl A. Spaatz, Air Marshall Sir James M. Robb. At foot of table, Col. Ivan Zenkovitch and Maj. General Harold R. Bull.

END OF THE WOLF PACK. UPPER. The U-858, first German submarine to surrender to the U.S. Navy in American waters, heads for Delaware Bay. The 740 ton U-boat gave up May 10, 1945 to two destroyer escorts of the Atlantic Fleet at a position 700 miles off the New England coast. At a rendezvous point off Cape May, a boarding party from the USS ATR-57 goes aboard the U-858, while a Navy blimp stands by. In the background is one of the destroyer escorts which chaperoned the sub 1,000 miles to the rendezvous. LOWER. A view of the submarine building ways, at Bremen, Germany, which, like its sister port at Bremerhaven, was taken under control by U.S. Naval Forces as the Nazi surrender document was being signed, to be used for Allied operations.

AMERICAN BLUEJACKETS IN BREMEN. Close on the heels of surrendering Nazi garrisons, U.S. Navy port parties moved into the two great German naval ports of Bremen and Bremerhaven on the Weser River. At Bremerhaven ships which the Germans dared not send to sea, including the 52,000 ton liner *Europa*, were either docked and in need of repairs or scuttled. At Bremen, half finished submarines, some of which had been destroyed by Allied bombs, lay on the building ways. Our Navy established bases at these former Nazi harbors and immediately set about demilitarizing the naval facilities there. Salvage crews cleaned up the harbor devastation and, within a few days, bases which had nurtured the wolf packs preying on Allied convoys served as ports for the sustenance of American troops in Germany.

ABOVE. Armed with carbines, two American shore-patrolmen stand guard on a German harbor control craft. Other bluejackets manned Nazi radio stations, naval vessels, port-control stations, and communication centers, as special Navy bomb disposal crews, equipped with demolition gear, methodically blew up all military installations which might have served in another war.

POTSDAM CONFERENCE. The sudden death of President Roosevelt, plus the surrender of Germany, made a "Big Three" meeting imperative, a meeting conducted at Potsdam, once the home of German rulers. Missouri-born President Truman selected the historic cruiser USS *Augusta*, to carry him from the United States to Antwerp. On this voyage the man from the midlands proved himself a salty sailing man, whose informal inspection tours and casual habit of dropping in for chow with the enlisted men endeared him to the bluejackets. UPPER. President Truman greeted by British ships upon his arrival in Europe. LOWER. The "The Big Three", Prime Minister Churchill, President Truman and Marshall Stalin, in front of the Prime Minister's quarters in Potsdam.

POTSDAM CONFERENCE. Germany's fate is decided at Potsdam by leaders of the victorious Allies. Other important decisions were made here also, including a declaration which paved the way for capitulation by Japan. UPPER. The conference opens in a room of the palace at Potsdam, Germany. LOWER. Wars and conferences on wars do not stop a democratic people from expressing their will at the ballot box, and a change of leaders does not disrupt an aroused people from prosecuting a common end. Death brought a new United States leader to the "Big Three;" and election gave Britain a new leader during the Potsdam conference. Here is shown the new "Big Three," Prime Minister Attlee, President Truman, and Marshall Stalin.

SEA-AIR POWER. Fast, modern carriers, teamed with fast, modern battleships, cruisers, and destroyers was the combination which gave the U. S. Pacific Fleet's task forces their mobility and striking power.

ABOVE. The famous carrier USS *Ticonderoga*, her planes spotted aft, steams into a far Pacific anchorage, followed by the battleships *Washington*, *North Carolina*, *South Dakota*, and a *Cleveland* class cruiser. The *Ticonderoga*, known to her crew as the big "T," had a record typical of the *Essex* class carrier, left a blistering trail of destruction during her first three months in the Pacific.

More than once the Japanese concentrated against the "TI," and finally succeeded in putting her out of action. On January 21, 1945, while operating off the coast of Formosa, the big "T" was hit by two suicide planes within half an hour. Tokyo announced another carrier "instantaneously sunk," but brave and courageous crew members put out the fires and saved the ship. She returned to a West Coast Navy Yard, where inspired workmen had her back with the Fleet before the end of the war.

Also shown in this picture, the *South Dakota* was known early in the war as Battleship X. It was her anti-aircraft guns which saved the famed *Enterprise* from Japanese air attack while escorting a convoy to Guadalcanal in October of 1942. This use of a battleship's anti-aircraft batteries to protect the vulnerable flat-tops was a new theory of naval deployment, but, proved in 1942, it was a theory which gave the great Task Force 58 its defensive strength.

A SMART JAP. Japanese Lieutenant Minoru Wade was a smart Jap. While many of his fellow country-men refused to be persuaded by the United States Marines until they had stepped in front of a flame thrower, or had been pierced by the rifle bullet from a Devil Dog sharpshooter, he was persuaded early that trying to stop a Marine was pretty futile business.

With the typical Japanese proclivity for imitation, he quickly applied the U. S. political axiom, "If you can't stop 'em, join 'em" to his own ends, and, while not joining the Marines, he worked with them, faithfully and well. His knowledge of Japanese positions, of Japanese camouflage methods, and of tactical deployment enabled him to make invaluable contributions to Marine air strikes. This was particularly true during the Philippine invasion, where Naval and Marine planes provided most of the air cover for General MacArthur's men.

During the early weeks, when the foot soldiers were slowly winning control of Leyte, there were no fields for Army shore-based aircraft, other than tactical aircraft, to operate from. Strategic bombing raids on other islands were conducted by carrier based aircraft and by Marine bombers, until such time as the infantry had won a foot-hold for the heavy bombers of the Far Eastern Air Force. ABOVE. In this picture, from the waist of a Marine Billy Mitchell bomber, Japanese Lieutenant Wade scans the terrain below, picking out landmarks and transmitting the date to the air strike co-ordinator in the nose of the ship.

WAKE REVISITED. Wake's strategic value lay in its position which enabled it to serve as a convenient air and naval base far out in the central Pacific. Originally developed as a trans-Pacific station by a commercial air line, it became, a couple of years before the war, a stop-over point for heavy Navy air transports. Along with Honolulu, Midway, and Guam, it helped form a series of stepping stones from the west coast of the United States to the Philippines and other Pacific areas.

But with the advent of greater air transports and seaplanes with long flying ranges its importance was lessened. An attempt to retake Wake after its capture by the Japanese, immediately following the attack on Pearl Harbor, was never made. Our forces, concentrating their full fighting fury on objectives of greater importance in the south Pacific, were supplied by well integrated systems of transport that had no need of this remote island. Wake was spared a direct onslaught by our forces. The Japanese, though, had visions of transforming isolated Wake into a major air base from which their aircraft could take off to harass American convoys. Their visions were never realized. Navy carrier-based planes, carrying out bombing expeditions at frequent intervals, wrecked enemy installations as soon as they were painstakingly erected.

ABOVE. Acrid billows of white smoke rise from fires kindled by a deluge of phosphorous bombs on one of the Navy bombing missions. Thus Wake, taken by the enemy at great cost, proved of little benefit to them.

THE LAST DAYS OF
THE JAPANESE FLEET

By Rear Admiral Robert B. Carney, USN

WITH the overwhelming defeat of the main Imperial Japanese Battle Fleet at the battles of the Philippine Sea and Leyte Gulf, the remnants of the Japanese forces sought the comparative safety of their home bases. The job of destroying or neutralizing the moderately powerful task force that remained from the once proud Japanese fleet was given to the United States Fleet's fast carrier forces.

On 14 March 1945, the carrier force proceeded toward Japan proper to seek out and destroy those Japanese units based on the home island of Kyushu. This was to be the first of many strikes at the home islands planned as a measure to divert attention, and naval and air strength, from the Okinawa invasion.

The first strike met with signal success. Besides the destruction of air fields and installations in the Kure-Kobe area, the carrier based planes heavily damaged the Japanese carrier *Ryuho*, tied up at Kure.

SUPPORT OF OKINAWA

WHEN the invasion of Okinawa began on 1 April, planes from the fast carriers began a series of almost continuous strikes and combat patrols in direct support of the operation. For the first few days enemy air activity was light, but on 6 April, the Japanese struck with full force. After beating off the savage enemy air attacks, the carrier force turned northward, and on 7 April, located a task force of the remaining Japanese fleet. In spite of heavy weather and violent anti-aircraft fire, carrier planes attacked and sank the Japanese super-battleship *Yamato*, the cruiser *Yahagi*, and four escorting destroyers. In thirty minutes of violent precision bombing and torpedo attacks, the suicidal sally of the Jap force had been broken at a cost to us of seven planes.

With the victorious end of the Okinawa operation, the Navy offensive against the Japanese homeland mounted in intensity. Combining deception and relentless pressure, the Third Fleet carrier and surface forces pounded the Empire.

On 24, 25, and 28 July, in a series of U. S. Navy carrier strikes unparalleled in modern history, the remainder of the Japanese fleet was sunk or severely damaged in raids on the Kure Naval Base. In these strikes the battleships *Haruna*, *Hyuga*, and *Ise*, all damaged in previous attacks, were sunk. Also sunk or heavily damaged were the carrier *Katsuragi*, the heavy cruisers *Aoba* and *Tone*, the light cruisers *Oyodo* and *Kitagami*, and a number of destroyers and minor combatant ships.

THE LAST OF THE JAPS

THIS strike completed the job of neutralizing the Japanese fleet and the job was the U. S. Navy's answer to Pearl Harbor. At the time of the surrender of the Japanese forces the only combatant ships of the Japanese fleet left afloat and undamaged were the cruiser *Sakawa* and a handful of destroyers and submarines.

Also afloat, but heavily damaged, were the battleship *Nagato*, three light cruisers, and three light or converted carriers.

Japanese losses during the war included 12 battleships, 15 carriers, 4 escort carriers, 15 heavy cruisers, 1 old heavy cruiser, 20 light cruisers, 126 destroyers, and 125 submarines.

But the Nip Navy was not the only target. Our surface groups bombarded the coast wherever good targets could be found; steel mills were demolished by 16" shells, car ferries and fishing fleets were sunk, locomotives were destroyed and industries wrecked. The bombardments brought home to millions of Japs the fact that they were powerless to stop us and were doomed.

No single factor contributed more than the bombardments in informing the Japanese people of the truth so long held from them—that the war was lost.

And mark you! Japan sued for peace before the atomic bomb hit Hiroshima and before Russia entered the Pacific war.

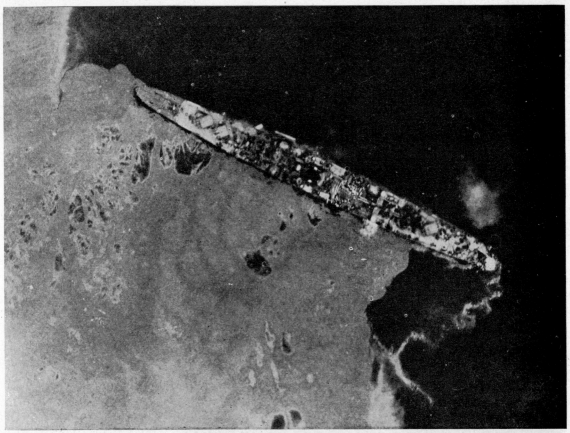

MORE HONORABLE JAPA-
NESE SHIPS JOIN HONOR-
ABLE ANCESTORS. With the
invasion of Okinawa April 1,
1945, planes from our fast carrier
task forces began making almost
continuous strikes and combat
patrols. Possibly the greatest
single encounter during the last
phases of the war was the strike on
Japanese fleet units in the East
China Sea area. On April 7,
1945, carrier task forces proceed-
ing north from Okinawa contacted and attacked strong enemy
naval forces off Kyushu. Despite
heavy weather, our pilots sank the
enemy super-battleship *Yamato*,
two cruisers, and three destroyers.

UPPER. With an oil slick
spreading from her torn sides, an
Agano class Japanese light cruiser
lies dead in the water, helpless
prey for co-ordinated carrier
based dive bomber and torpedo
plane attack.

LOWER. A direct hit! A bomb
from an American carrier-based
dive bomber explodes on the
stern of a Japanese light cruiser.
This ship was later sunk by a torpedo attack. The split-second
timing and perfect co-ordination
of the attack so confused Japanese
gunners that their anti-aircraft fire,
while heavy, was entirely ineffectual.

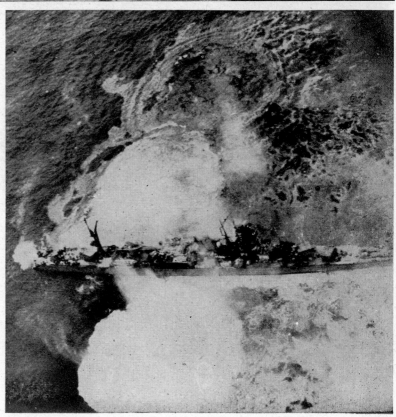

PRACTICE SALVO. One of the tensest moments in the shakedown of a new ship is when she first fires her guns. The stresses arising from the terrific concussion often do slight structural damage which must be rectified before the ship is ready to join the fleet and participate in action. But modern ship designers are able to allow for all but the most minor effect. ABOVE. The USS Missouri fires a round of 16-inch shells during her shakedown cruise. The shells which have just left the guns can be seen in the air in the upper right.

UTTER DESOLATION. Somehow seeming even more terrible against the green hills surrounding it, the city of Nagasaki presents a scene of complete destruction in these two photographs taken after the atomic bomb hit had wiped out the city. Only a twisted mass of rubble, now unrecognizable, remains of what was a prosperous city. When the Americans occupied Japan, they made detailed studies of the results of the bomb hits here and in Hiroshima.

"PARDON ME, YOUR SHIP IS SHOWING!" The Army's B-29's, joining with the Navy's carrier based aircraft, struck again and again at the last Japanese stronghold, the home islands themselves. In strikes at Kure Naval Arsenal, a large Japanese naval base, two-ton bombs blasted installations and ships in the harbor.

UPPER. A Japanese battleship, bracketed and blasted. A direct hit on the stern has just been registered. This battleship was sunk in a later attack by dive bombers and torpedo planes from U. S. carriers. Noticeable in the picture is the absence of flak; the Japanese were caught off guard.

LOWER. Its camouflaged deception pierced, a Japanese cruiser of the *Tone* class, Nippon's most modern 8-inch gun class, rocks under the hammer blows of carrier based aircraft. Completely hidden by geysers caused by near misses in the center is another ship. In a period of less than three months U. S. carrier based planes had destroyed 2,336 enemy planes and sunk or damaged 2 battleships, 1 carrier, 2 heavy cruisers, 2 light cruisers, and a number of destroyers and smaller combatant craft.

AN INGLORIOUS END FOR THE IMPERIAL JAPAN-ESE NAVY. On July 10, 1945 the planes of the Third Fleet's carriers, at a point 170 miles from Kyushu, Japan, were sent aloft to strike at targets in the Kure-Kobe area. These strikes were carried off with little enemy opposition. On the 17th of July, our forces were joined by units of the British Fleet and struck at the Japanese naval units in Yokosuka naval base near Tokyo. UPPER. The Japanese battleship *Hyuga* rests on the bottom of the Inland Sea near Nasake Shima. She was sunk by planes of the Third Fleet. LOWER. The battleship *Haruna* is heavily bombed by Allied planes as she lies at anchor in Kure harbor. The *Haruna* was a floating hulk when the Allies took over Japan.

". . . THE SOUND AND THE FURY . . ." When the Third Fleet moved north toward the islands of Japan, it had a specific task ahead of it, the systematic destruction of anything that floated and was Japanese. It was also to bomb and bombard the coastline at various points and destroy certain strategic objectives. The Third Fleet carried out its job with a thoroughness that left Japan completely shaken. UPPER. Obscured by smoke and geysers of water, a Japanese ore ship, caught as it leaves the inlet at the top left of the page, is destroyed by planes from the Third Fleet. LOWER. The battleship *Haruna* fares no better than the ore ship. Planes from American and British carriers damaged her beyond repair in a series of violent raids on the naval base at Kure.

YANKS CHEER RUSSIA AS ALLY. When Admiral Nimitz's forces became firmly intrenched in Okinawa, Japan knew she was defeated. Her fleet was sunk or resting in repair docks in the Inland Sea. Her merchant fleet was down to a few straggling ships, slipping at night from inlet to inlet along the coast of China, trying to run the blockade with vital oil and foodstuffs. Japan's leaders had long since been convinced that the war was lost for them. They only looked for a good excuse to get out of it, an incident which would permit face saving.

What additional convincing of this fact was required was provided by the U. S. Third Fleet, which appeared off the Japanese Coast line, steaming from one end to the other. Carrier aircraft struck here, there, and everywhere. Japanese ships holed up in the Naval Bases were sunk at anchorage or smashed, together with the dry docks in which they were berthed. U. S. surface ships came close ashore to pump shells into steel plants and other important industries. Inland railroad trestles, car ferries, bridges were blown up by dive bombers. Japan urgently required an excuse.

Early in August she was provided two excuses. The atom bomb was delivered to Hiroshima in a roar of destruction. Almost simultaneously mighty Russia declared war and her victorious armies marched into Manchuria. Sailors, Marines and doughboys knew this was the event signalling the early end of the war. ABOVE. This picture shows how GI's in Manila reacted to the news. The scene was reenacted all over the Pacific, wherever American fighting men gathered.

PRESIDENT ANNOUNCES VICTORY. Tuesday, August 14, 1945, dawned clear and warm in Washington. Official and unofficial Washington spent a nervous day, listening, watching, waiting. When the marble columned office buildings were emptied, the streets filled rapidly; suburban gardens went untended; eating places filled beyond their normal capacity. Crowds began an early vigil in Lafayette Square, opposite the White House. News and radio correspondents were summoned at 6:45 to a White House Press Conference. At seven o'clock the President greeted reporters. In his hands was a message from the Swiss Legation; its contents were the Japanese diplomatic words accepting the terms of the Potsdam Declaration. War was over. Peace had come at last.

THE SURRENDER OF JAPAN

By Admiral of the Fleet William F. Halsey, USN

BY JULY, 1945, the United States Fleet had brought to bear in the Pacific tremendous sea-air power. Our carrier planes were blasting air fields, navy yards, industries, and storage facilities throughout the "home islands" of the Japanese Empire. Our battleships, cruisers, and destroyers bombarded the "sacred soil" of Nippon almost at will. Our submarines had ventured into the innermost parts of the Inland Sea and the Sea of Japan and had made those waters as unsafe for Japanese shipping as the waters of the Southwest Pacific and the China Sea.

As a prelude to the main and final objective, the invasion of Japan, the preliminary bombings and bombardments were stepped up. Our secret weapon, the atomic bomb, was used, first against the military targets and industries at Hiroshima, later against the munitions plants and repair yards at Nagasaki. Our ally Russia entered the war in Manchuria; China, armed with lend-lease supplies, began new drives against the enemy.

THE JAPS ACCEPT SURRENDER

WHEN the Japanese delivered their message of acceptance of the Potsdam Ultimatum on 14 August, the Third Fleet was ready with plans for occupation, and the unprecedented operation was executed smoothly. The official instrument of surrender was presented to the Japanese representatives by General of the Army MacArthur at Manila on 19 August. This instrument provided for the capitulation of the Imperial General Staff, and the surrender of all ground, sea, and air commanders of the Islands of Japan, the Philippine Islands, and the Southern parts of Korea to the Commander-in-Chief, United States Army Forces, Pacific; the surrender of all land, sea, air, and auxiliary force commanders in the Japanese mandated islands was to be made to the Commander-in-Chief, United States Pacific Fleet.

The first units of the United States Third Fleet, after being delayed for two days by a typhoon, moved into Sagami Bay, southwest of Tokyo Bay, on 27 August in the first step of the occupation.

On 29 August, Fleet Admiral Nimitz arrived from Guam and boarded his flagship, the battleship *South Dakota*. Admiral Halsey, Commander of the Third Fleet, entered Tokyo Bay and anchored off Yokosuka Naval Base in the forenoon of that day. On 30 August, 10,000 Marines and Naval personnel landed on this base and the surrounding fortress islands. The naval base at Tateyama, across the bay from Yokosuka, was occupied on 1 September by Marine forces as the occupation control progressed smoothly and rapidly.

The formal surrender of the Imperial Japanese Government was made aboard the United States battleship *Missouri* in Tokyo Bay at 0908 on 2 September 1945. General of the Army MacArthur signed as Supreme Commander for the Allied Powers, and Fleet Admiral Nimitz as representative for the United States.

THE ISLANDS SURRENDER

EVEN before the formal surrender of the Japanese government, the enemy commanders of Marcus Island and of Mille atoll in the Marshall Islands had capitulated to American forces. The largest scale island surrender came shortly after the beginning of the occupation of the main Japanese Islands. The commander of the 31st Japanese Army committed the islands of Truk, Wake, the Palaus, Mortlock, Mille, Ponape, Kusaie, Jaluit, Maleolap, Wotje, Enderby, Mereyon, Rota, and Pagan to the United States. On Truk alone the surrender involved 130,000 Japanese military personnel.

While the naval and air forces of Japan were either destroyed or rendered impotent by our sea-air blockade, her army was still more than 4 million strong and better trained, and larger than at the time of the initial attack at Pearl Harbor.

Never before in the history of warfare has there been a more convincing example of the effectiveness of sea power than when, despite this undefeated, well armed, and highly efficient army, Japan surrendered her homeland unconditionally to the enemy without even a token resistance.

The devastation wrought by past bombings plus the destruction of the atomic bombs spelled nothing less than extinction for Japan. The bases from which these attacks were launched—Saipan, Iwo Jima, and Okinawa—were to have been the spring boards for the mightiest sea-borne invasion yet conceived by man. The "fighting fleets" of the United States which had made possible every invasion victory for America and her allies were ready and waiting. The Japanese had two alternatives; to fight and face destruction, or to surrender. The Imperial Japanese Empire chose to surrender.

W.F. Halsey

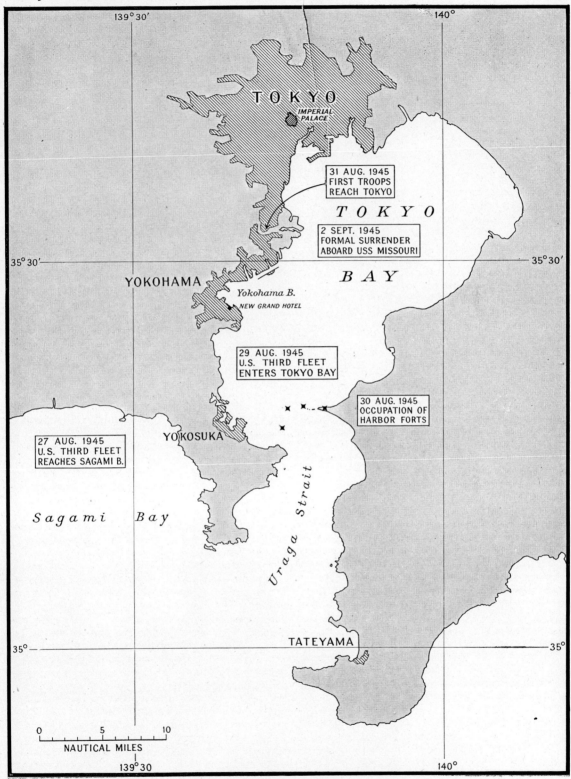

TOKYO

IMPERIAL PALACE

31 AUG. 1945
FIRST TROOPS
REACH TOKYO

T O K Y O

2 SEPT. 1945
FORMAL SURRENDER
ABOARD USS MISSOURI

YOKOHAMA

Yokohama B.
NEW GRAND HOTEL

B A Y

29 AUG. 1945
U.S. THIRD FLEET
ENTERS TOKYO BAY

30 AUG. 1945
OCCUPATION OF
HARBOR FORTS

27 AUG. 1945
U.S. THIRD FLEET
REACHES SAGAMI B.

YOKOSUKA

Sagami   Bay

Uraga   Strait

TATEYAMA

0   5   10
NAUTICAL MILES

Chart showing steps in the surrender of Japan and
the American occupation.

U. S. NAVY RETURNS TO TOKYO. Commodore Perry first opened up Japan to the outside world in the mid-19th century; and almost 100 years later the Navy again opened Japan to the outside world. The scenes on this page show the return of the Navy, and by contrast depict accurately how that return was effected.

UPPER. Part of the great Third Fleet commanded by Admiral William F. Halsey, Jr., who engineered the first and last naval offensive blows against Japan, is seen in Sagami Wan (Bay). This picture was taken from the USS *Shangri-La,* an *Essex*-class carrier, named for the mythical place from which the first Tokyo air raiders took off. Actually the raiders took off from the old USS *Hornet.*

LOWER. In contrast to the power of the Third Fleet is the antiquated tug which bore the Japanese admiral in command of Yokosuka Naval Base out to make arrangements for surrender of the base. The Japanese admiral probably would have preferred a more pretentious ship, but such vessels were resting on the bottom, or were unseaworthy.

INSTRUMENT OF SURRENDER

Signed at TOKYO BAY, JAPAN at 09 04 I
on the _____ SECOND _____ day of _____ SEPTEMBER _____ , 1945.

By Command and in behalf of the Emperor of Japan
and the Japanese Government.

By Command and in behalf of the Japanese
Imperial General Headquarters.

Accepted at TOKYO BAY, JAPAN at 0908 I
on the _____ SECOND _____ day of _____ SEPTEMBER _____ , 1945,
for the United States, Republic of China, United Kingdom and the
Union of Soviet Socialist Republics, and in the interests of the other
United Nations at war with Japan.

Supreme Commander for the Allied Powers

United States Representative

Republic of China Representative

United Kingdom Representative

Union of Soviet Socialist Republics
Representative

Commonwealth of Australia Representative

Dominion of Canada Representative

Provisional Government of the French
Republic Representative

Kingdom of the Netherlands Representative

Dominion of New Zealand Representative

We, acting by command of and in behalf of the Emperor of Japan, the Japanese Government and the Japanese Imperial General Headquarters, hereby accept the provisions set forth in the declaration issued by the heads of the Governments of the United States, China and Great Britain on 26 July 1945, at Potsdam, and subsequently adhered to by the Union of Soviet Socialist Republics, which four powers are hereafter referred to as the Allied Powers.

We hereby proclaim the unconditional surrender to the Allied Powers of the Japanese Imperial General Headquarters and of all Japanese armed forces and all armed forces under Japanese control wherever situated

We hereby command all Japanese forces wherever situated and the Japanese people to cease hostilities forthwith, to preserve and save from damage all ships, aircraft, and military and civil property and to comply with all requirements which may be imposed by the Supreme Commander for the Allied Powers or by agencies of the Japanese Government at his direction

We hereby command the Japanese Imperial General Headquarters to issue at once orders to the Commanders of all Japanese forces and all forces under Japanese control wherever situated to surrender unconditionally themselves and all forces under their control

We hereby command all civil, military and naval officials to obey and enforce all proclamations, orders and directives deemed by the Supreme Commander for the Allied Powers to be proper to effectuate this surrender and issued by him or under his authority and we direct all such officials to remain at their posts and to continue to perform their non-combatant duties unless specifically relieved by him or under his authority.

We hereby undertake for the Emperor, the Japanese Government and their successors to carry out the provisions of the Potsdam Declaration in good faith, and to issue whatever orders and take whatever action may be required by the Supreme Commander for the Allied Powers or by any other designated representative of the Allied Powers for the purpose of giving effect to that Declaration

We hereby command the Japanese Imperial Government and the Japanese Imperial General Headquarters at once to liberate all allied prisoners of war and civilian internees now under Japanese control and to provide for their protection, care, maintenance and immediate transportation to places as directed.

The authority of the Emperor and the Japanese Government to rule the state shall be subject to the Supreme Commander for the Allied Powers who will take such steps as he deems proper to effectuate these terms of surrender

INSTRUMENT OF SURRENDER. The above document, the instrument of surrender, was signed on September 2, 1945, aboard the USS *Missouri*, in one of the strangest and most unusual ceremonies in the annals of history.

The Japanese Empire, after four years of undeclared warfare against China, formally declared war on United States and Great Britain on December 7, 1941. By the first of September 1945, her armies were actually larger than they were in 1941. Her air force was larger. Her main armies had never been defeated. Outlying garrisons had been smashed on many islands; other garrisons had been by-passed. One of her armies in the Philippines had been cut to pieces. But the bulk of her forces had never tasted battle. Yet she was cut off from many of her troops, and the troops remaining in the homeland were cut off, isolated from vital supplies. Her Navy had been completely defeated, and coincidentally with that defeat, her merchant shipping had been sunk. Japan's life line had been severed. Because of superior sea power, frock-coated little men, representing the emperor, climbed aboard the USS *Missouri*, bowed low, apologized sibilantly, and carefully, meticulously, signed the instrument of surrender, shown with the signatures of the Japanese and Allied representatives.

Never before had a once great nation, with its military strength still almost intact, quit so quickly and completely. It was clear-cut, convincing and emphatic evidence of what an independent Navy can do when pitted against a Navy which is used primarily as an auxiliary to an Army

TWO VICTORY FACTORS. On this page are pictures illustrating two of the important reasons why Japan was forced to quit: radar and amphibious warfare.

UPPER. Tokyo appears on the Plan Positional Indicator, which visualized what the radar signals pick up. When war came, the Navy had already highly developed this strategic weapon, and under the impetus of the war many more advances were made.

LOWER. Lt. Commdr. Hugh D. Scott, Jr., USNR, a former member of Congress from Philadelphia, but during the war an intelligence officer with the Third Amphibious Force, talks with Japanese officers as the Navy occupies Tateyama Seaplane Base. Amphibious warfare was the type of warfare which seized strategic island after strategic island as the United States forces marched across the Central Pacific to Tokyo.

Although both these techniques were developed separately by the Navy, amphibious warfare used and depended heavily upon radar, and many of the new developments of radar were designed specifically for the needs and requirements of amphibious warfare. Freedom to conduct independent research, either in the field of cold science, such as radar and electronics, or in the field of technique, such as amphibious warfare, is credited with providing the United States with the greatest and most fluid fighting machine in history.

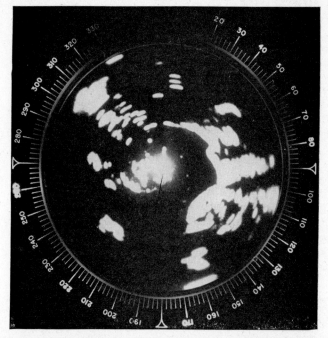

JAP CONQUERORS. Three of the reasons why Japan was forced to capitulate are seen here at Yokosuka Naval Base. They are, left to right, Rear Admiral O. F. Badger, Fleet Admiral Chester W. Nimitz, and Admiral William F. Halsey, Jr. Admiral Halsey has since been elevated to the rank of fleet admiral.

When the Japs struck at Pearl Harbor, Nimitz was a rear admiral and Chief of the old Bureau of Navigation, now known as the Bureau of Personnel, of the Navy Department. He was named Commander-in-Chief, U. S. Pacific Fleet (CinCPac) and traveled to San Francisco in civilian clothes, his movements shrouded in greatest secrecy. Arriving at Pearl Harbor he found not only the material Navy in shambles, but morale was shattered. He quickly restored morale and set to work to build up the physical

equipment for the long haul against the Japanese. He turned to Admiral Halsey, who set out with a carrier task force and delivered the first offensive blows of the war, a hit and run raid on the Marshalls and Gilberts.

As the war progressed Admiral Nimitz used Admiral Halsey and Admiral Raymond A. Spruance as his one-two punch. While Halsey operated, Spruance and the Fifth Fleet planned; and while Spruance operated, Halsey and the Third Fleet planned.

Rear Admiral Badger was a commander under Halsey in the Third Fleet when the war closed. The system of alternating the two fleet commanders enabled Admiral Nimitz to maintain continuous pressure against the Japs, never once letting up, never giving the enemy a chance to regain his balance from one blow before the next one fell.

TWO KINDS OF DESTRUCTION. UPPER. Very few signs of life had been restored in Hiroshima on October 30, 1945, when that city was inspected by Army and Navy officers. **LOWER.** Vital military warehouses, destroyed by carrier based aircraft in pin-point bombing attacks at Yokosuka Naval Base, greeted a Coast Guard manned LCVP as it brought occupation forces to the once great shipyard. This landing fittingly terminated the long history of Coast Guard aided invasions across the Bloody Pacific, and the peaceful, silent shores were something new to invasion-weary Coast Guardsmen. The warehouse was raked by bombs before the occupation.

PEACE AND WAR. UPPER. This view of the palace gates, in Tokyo, seems incongruous in a land which unleashed the horrors of war over Asia and the Pacific. LOWER. Here are nearly 100 5-man submarines in various stages of completion, construction delayed by lack of vital materials which could not easily run the U. S. Navy's blockade, and further delayed as workmen at this Kure shipyard scurried for cover from repeated attacks by carrier planes. These midget submarines were at the other end of the pole from the vast plane-carrying submarines which the Japs also constructed, but Japanese submarine warfare was ineffectual, since the underseas craft were used to supply outlying Army garrisons rather than to prey upon enemy shipping.

CONGRESSIONAL MEDAL OF HONOR

Officers and Enlisted Men of the Navy, Marine Corps and Coast Guard Who Have Been Awarded the Medal of Honor from 7 December 1941 to 15 March 1946. Recommendations for others are still pending.

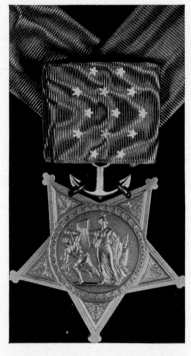

AGERHOLM, Harold C. (Deceased), Pfc, USMCR, 2nd Division. Marine Corps. Medal won at Tarawa, 20-24. November 1943.

ANDERSON, Richard B. (Deceased), Pfc, USMC, 4th Division Marine Corps. Medal won at Kwajalein, 1 February 1944.

BAILEY, Kenneth Dillon (Deceased), Major, USMC, Marine Raiders. Marine Corps. Medal won at Guadalcanal, 12-13 September 1943.

BASILONE, John (Deceased), Gunnery Sergeant, USMC, 7th Division Marine Corps. Medal won at Guadalcanal, 24-25 October 1942.

BAUER, Harold W. (Deceased), Lt. Col., USMC Air Corps (Fighter). Medal won at Guadalcanal

BAUSELL, Lewis K. (Deceased), Corp., USMC. Medal won at Guam.

BENNION, Mervyn Sharp (Deceased), Capt., USN. USS *West Virginia*. Medal won at Pearl Harbor.

BORDELON, William James (Deceased), Staff Sgt., USMC. Marine Corps. Medal won at Tarawa.

BIGELOW, Elmer Charles (Deceased), Water Tender 2/c, USNR. (DD) USS *Fletcher*. Medal won at Philippines (Corregidor)

BOYINGTON, Gregory, Lt. Col., USMC, Air Corps. Medal won at South Pacific—Solomons area

BULKELEY, John Duncan, Commander, USN. PT Boats. Medal won at Philippines

BUSH, Richard E., Corp., USMCR. Medal won at Okinawa

BUSH, Robert Eugene, Ex-Hospital Apprentice 1/c, USNR. USN Hospital Corps, Marines. Medal won at Okinawa

CALLAGHAN, Daniel Judson (Deceased), Rear Admiral, USN. USS *San Francisco*. Medal won at Savo Island.

CANNON, George H. (Deceased), First Lieut., USMC. Medal won at Sand Island, Midway Islands.

DAMATO, Anthony J. (Deceased), Corp., USMC. Medal won at Eniwotok.

DAVID, Albert LeRoy (Deceased), Lieut., USN. USS *Pillsbury*. Medal won at South Atlantic

DAVIS, George Fleming (Deceased), Commander, USN. USS *Walke*. Medal won at Lingayen Gulf

DEALEY, Samuel David (Deceased), Commander, USN. Submarine, USS *Harder*. Medal won in Pacific

DUNLAP, Robert Hugo, Captain, USMCR. Medal won at Iwo Jima

DYESS, Aquilla J. (Deceased), Lt. Col., USMCR. Marine Corps. Medal won at Kwajalein, Marshalls, 2 February 1944.

EDSON, Merritt A., Brigadier General, USMC. Medal won at Solomon Islands

EPPERSON, Harold G. (Deceased), Pfc, USMC. Medal won at Tarawa.

EVANS, Ernest E. (Deceased), Commander, USN. (DD) USS *Johnston*. Medal won at Samar Island

FINN, John William, Lieut., USN. Naval Air Station. Medal won at Honolulu

FLAHERTY, Francis Charles (Deceased), Ensign, USNR. USS *Oklahoma*. Medal won at Pearl Harbor.

FLEMING, Richard E. (Deceased), Captain, USMC. Air Corps. Medal won at Battle of Midway.

FLUCKEY, Eugene B., Commander, USN. Submarine Service. USS *Barb*. Medal won in Pacific, Coast of China

FOSS, Joseph Jacob, Major, USMC Air Corps (Fighter). Medal won in South Pacific—Solomons area

FUQUA, Samuel Glenn, Captain, USN. USS *Arizona*. Medal won at Pearl Harbor

GALER, Robert Edward, Lt. Col. USMC. Air Corps (Fighter). Medal won over Guadalcanal—Solomons area

GARY, Donald Arthur, Lieut., USN. USS *Franklin*. Medal won off Japan

GILMORE, Howard Walter (Deceased), Commander, USN. Submarine Service. Medal won in Southwest Pacific

GORDON, Nathan Green, Ex-Lt., USNR. Air Corps (pilot). Medal won at Kavieng Harbor, 15 February 1944

GURKE, Henry (Deceased), Pfc, USMC. Marine Corps. Medal won at Empress Augusta Bay.

HALL, William Edward, Ex-Lieut. Commander, USNR. Air Corps. Medal won at Coral Sea

HANSON, Robert M. (Deceased), First Lieut., USMCR. Fighter pilot, Marine Corps. Medal won near Rabaul, 3 February 1944.

HARRELL, William G., Sgt., USMC. Medal won at Iwo Jima

HAWKINS, William Deane (Deceased), First Lieut., USMC. Marine Corps. Medal won at Tarawa.

HERRING, Rufus G., Lieut. (jr. grade), USNR. LCI. Medal won at Iwo Jima

HILL, Edwin Joseph (Deceased), Chief Boatswain, USN. USS *Nevada*. Medal won at Pearl Harbor.

HUTCHINS, Johnnie David (Deceased), Seaman 1/c, USNR. LST-473. Medal won at Lae, New Guinea.

JACKSON, Arthur J., Second Lieut., USMCR. (Pfc when received medal). Medal won at Peleliu

JACOBSON, Douglas T., Ex-Cor., USMCR. Marine Corps. Medal won at Iwo Jima

JONES, Herbert Charpiot (Deceased), Ensign, USNR. Medal won at Pearl Harbor.

JULIAN, Joseph R. (Deceased), Platoon Sergeant, USMCR. Marine Corps. Medal won at Iwo Jima

KEPPLER, Reinhardt J. (Deceased), Boatswain's Mate 1/c, USN. USS *San Francisco*. Medal won at Savo Island.

KIDD, Isaac Campbell (Deceased), Rear Admiral, USN. USS *Arizona*. Medal won at Pearl Harbor.

KRAUS, Richard E. (Deceased), Pfc., USMCR. Marine Corps. Medal won at Peleliu.

LUCAS, Jacklyn H., Pfc., USMCR. Marine Corps. Medal won at Iwo Jima

McCAMPBELL, David, Commander, USN. Air Corps (Fighter). Medal won at Philippines

McCANDLESS, Bruce, Commander, USN. USS *San Francisco*. Medal won at Savo Island

McCARD, Robert H. (Deceased), Gunnery Sgt., USMC. Medal won at Saipan.

McCARTHY, Joseph J., Ex-Captain, USMCR. Marine Corps. Medal won at Iwo Jima

McCOOL, Richard Miles, Jr., Lieut., USN. LCS-122. Medal won at Okinawa

MASON, Leonard F. (Deceased), Pfc., USMC. Marine Corps. Medal won at Guam.

MUNRO, Douglas Albert (Deceased), Signalman 1/c, USCG. Amphibious. Medal won at Guadalcanal.

NEW, John Drury (Deceased), Pfc., USMC. Marine Corps. Medal won at Peleliu.

O'CALLAHAN, Joseph Timothy, Commander (ChC), USNR. USS *Franklin*. Medal won off Japan

O'HARE, Edward Henry (Deceased), Lt. Comdr., USN. Air Corps. Medal won at Bougainville.

OWENS, Robert A. (Deceased), Sgt., USMC. Marine Corps. Medal won at Bougainville

OZBOURN, Joseph W. (Deceased), Private, USMC. Marine Corps. Medal won at Tinian.

PAIGE, Mitchell, First Lieut., USMC. Marine Corps. Medal won at Solomons Islands

PARLE, John Joseph (Deceased), Ensign, USNR. LST-375. Medal won at Sicily.

PETERSON, Oscar Verner (Deceased), Chief Watertender, USN. USS *Neosho*. Medal won in Japanese Waters.

POPE, Everett, Major, USMC. Marine Corps. Medal won at Peleliu

POWER, John V. (Deceased), First Lieut., USMCR. Marine Corps. Medal won at Namur Island— Marshalls, February 1944.

POWERS, John James (Deceased), Lieut., USN. Air Corps (Dive-bomber). Medal won in the Pacific.

RAMAGE, Lawson Paterson, Commander, USN. Submarine Service. Medal won in the Pacific

REEVES, Thomas James (Deceased), Radio Electrician, USN. USS *California*. Medal won at Pearl Harbor.

RICKETTS, Milton Ernest (Deceased), Lieut., USN. USS *Yorktown*. Medal won at Coral Sea.

ROAN, Charles H. (Deceased), Captain, USMC. Marine Corps. Medal won at Peleliu.

ROOKS, Albert Harold (Deceased), Captain, USN. USS *Houston*. Medal won in South Pacific.

ROSS, Donald K., Lieut., USN. USS *Nevada*. Medal won at Pearl Harbor

ROUH, Carlton R., First Lieut., USMCR. Marine Corps. Medal won at Peleliu

SCHONLAND, Herbert E., Captain, USN. USS *San Francisco*. Medal won at Savo Island

SCOTT, Norman (Deceased), Rear Admiral, USN. USS *Atlanta*. Medal won at Cape Esperance & Guadalcanal.

SCOTT, Robert R. (Deceased), Machinist's Mate 1/c, USN. USS *California*. Medal won at Pearl Harbor.

SHOUP, David M., Colonel, USMC. Marine Corps. Medal won at Tarawa

SIGLER, Franklin E., Private, USMCR. Medal won at Iwo Jima

SKAGGS, Luther, Jr., Pfc, USMCR. Medal won at Guam

SMITH, John Lucian, Lt. Col., USMC. Air Corps (Fighter). Medal won at Solomon Islands

SORENSON, Richard K., Sergeant, USMCR. Marine Corps. Medal won at Kwajalein

STREET, George Levick, III, Commander, USN. USS *Tirante*. Medal won at Korea

SWEET, James E., Ex-Major, USMCR. Air Corps (Fighter). Medal won at Guadalcanal

THOMAS, Herbert J. (Deceased), Sgt., USMC. Marine Corps. Medal won at Bougainville, 7 November 1943.

THOMASON, Clyde (Deceased), Sgt., USMC. Marine Corps. Medal won at Makin.

TIMMERMAN, Grant F. (Deceased), Sgt., USMC. Marine Tanks. Medal won at Saipan

TONICH (TOMICH), Peter (Deceased), Chief Water Tender, USN. USS *Utah*. Medal won at Pearl Harbor.

VANDEGRIFT, Alexander A., General, USMC. Marine Corps. Medal won at Guadalcanal

VAN VALKENBURGH, Franklin (Deceased), Captain, USN. USS *Arizona*. Medal won at Pearl Harbor.

WAHLEN, George Edward, Ex-Pharmacist's Mate 2/c, USNR. USN Hospital Corps. Medal won at Iwo Jima

WALSH, Kenneth Ambrose, Captain, USMC. Air Corps. Medal won in Solomons area

WALSH, William G. (Deceased), Gunnery Sgt., USMC. Marine Corps. Medal won at Iwo Jima

WARD, James Richard (Deceased), Seaman 1/c, USN. USS *Oklahoma*. Medal won at Pearl Harbor.

WATSON, Wilson D., Ex-Private, USMCR. Medal won at Iwo Jima

WILLIAMS, Hershel W., ex-Corp., USMCR. Medal won at Iwo Jima

WILLIAMS, Jack (Deceased), Pharmacist's Mate 3/c, USNR. Hospital Corps. Medal won at Iwo Jima

WILLIS, John Harlan (Deceased), Pharmacist's Mate 1/c, USN. Hospital Corps, USMC. Medal won at Iwo Jima

WILSON, Louis H., Jr., Major, USMC. Marine Corps. Medal won at Guam

WILSON, Robert L. (Deceased), Pfc., USMC. Marine Corps. Medal won at Tinian.

WITEK, Frank P. (Deceased), Pfc, USMCR. Medal won at Guam.

YOUNG, Cassin (Deceased), Captain, USN. USS *Vestal*. Medal won at Pearl Harbor.

STATISTICS
GERMAN NAVAL LOSSES
1939–1945

KEY TO SYMBOLS: A—Accident; Air—Airplane; AO—Amphibious Operations; Cap—Captured; Col—Collision; EO—Enemy Occupation; Ex—Exercises; Exp—Explosion; Gdg—Grounding; Gun—Gunfire; OD—Overdue; S—Scuttled; SC—Surface Craft; Unkn—Unknown; W—Weather.

BATTLESHIPS
Bismarck—N Atlantic—27 May '41—SC
Gneisenau—Gdynia—28 Mar '45—S
Scharnhorst—N Cape—26 Dec '43—SC
Schle Holstein—Gdynia—Dec '44—Air
Schlesein—Swinemunde—May '45—Air
Tirpitz—Tromso—12 Nov '44—Air

AIRCRAFT CARRIERS
Graf Zeppelin—Stettin—May '45—S

HEAVY CRUISERS
Admiral Graf Spee—Montevideo—17 Dec '39—S
Admiral Hipper—Kiel—3 May '45—Air
Admiral Scheer—Kiel—9 Apr '45—Air
Bluecher—Oslo—9 Apr '40—Gun
Leutzow—Swinemunde—16 Apr '45—Air
Seydlitz—Konigsberg—10 Apr '45—S

LIGHT CRUISERS
Emden—Kiel—Mar '45—Air

Karlsruhe—Kristiansand—9 Apr '40—Sub
Koeln—Wilhelmshaven—30 Mar '45—Air
Koenigsberg—Bergen—10 Apr '40—Air

DESTROYERS
Albatros—Oslo—10 Apr '40—SC
Anton Schmidt—Narvik—10 Apr '40—SC
Bernard Arnim—Narvik—13 Apr '40—SC
Bruno Heineman—Eng Channel—Jan '42—Mine
Diether Roeder—Narvik—13 Apr '40—SC
Erich Giese—Narvik—13 Apr '40—SC
Erich Koellner—Narvik—13 Apr '40—SC
Falke—LeHavre—14 Jun '44—Air
Fried Eckholdt—Bear Is—31 Dec '42—SC
Georg Thiele—Narvik—13 Apr '40—SC
Greif—Seine—24 May '44—Air
Hans Ludemann—Narvik—13 Apr '40—SC
Hermann Kunne—Narvik—13 Apr '40—SC

Herman Schoman—Arctic—2 May '42—SC
Hermes—Tunis—7 May '43—Air & S
Iltis—Boulogne—12 May '42—SC
Jaguar—LeHavre—14 Jun '44—Air
Kondor—LeHavre—28 Jun '44—Air
Leberecht Maas—N Sea—22 Feb '40—Mine
Leopard—N Sea—30 Apr '40—Col
Luchs—N Sea—26 Jul '40—Sub
Max Schultz—Trondheim—22 Feb '40—Mine
Moewe—LeHavre—14 Jun '44—Air
Seeadler—Boulogne—12 May '42—SC
Tiger—Unkn—'40—SC
Wilhm Heidkamp—Narvik—10 Apr '40—SC
Wolfgang Zenkr—Narvik—13 Apr '40—SC
Wolf—Dunkirk—8 Jan '41—Mine
T22—Finland—18 Aug '44—Air
T24—Biscay—24 Aug '44—Air
T25—Biscay—28 Dec '43—SC
T26—Biscay—28 Dec '43—SC
T27—Brittany—29 Apr '44—SC
T29—France—26 Apr '44—SC
T30—Finland—18 Aug '44—Mine
T31—Finland—20 Jun '44—Mine

T32—Finland—18 Aug '44—Mine
T34—Baltic—20 Nov '44—Mine
T36—Baltic—4 May '45—Mine
TA9—Toulon—23 Aug '44—A'r
TA10—Rhodes—26 Sep '43—SC
L'Agile—Nantes—16 Sep '43—Air
Z23—LaPallice—21 Aug '44—S
Z24—LeVerdon—25 Aug '44—Air
Z26—Arctic—29 Mar '42—SC
Z27—Biscay—28 Dec '43—SC
Z28—Sassnitz—6 Mar '45—Air
Z32—Ushant—9 Jun '44—SC
Z35—Finland—12 Dec '44—Mine
Z36—Finland—12 Dec '44—Mine
Z37—Bordeaux—24 Aug '44—S
Z43—Geltinger—3 May '45—S
ZH1—Brittany—9 Jun '44—SC

SUBMARINES

Total	Cause	Time
354	Air	War
246	SC	War
217	S	After V-E
49	SC & Air	War
30	Mine	War
28	Unkn	War
21	Sub	War
49	Other Causes	War

VESSELS SURRENDERED
Cruisers: Leipzig, Nurenberg, Prinz Eugen
Destroyers: Beitzen, Galster, Ihn, Jacobi, Lody, Riedel, Seerose, Steinbrinck, T23, T28, T33, T35, T38, T39, Z25, Z29, Z30, Z38, Z39, Z31
Submarines: 3, 11, 59, 92, 101, 143, 145, 149, 150, 155, 170, 181, 190, 195, 218, 219, 228, 234, 244, 245, 249, 255, 256, 262, 276, 278, ,281, 291, 293, 294, 295, 298, 299, 310, 312, 313, 315, 318, 324, 328, 363, 368, 369, 427, 437, 481, 483, 485, 510, 511, 516, 530, 532, 539, 541, 555, 622, 637, 668, 680, 712, 716, 720, 739, 758, 760, 764, 773, 775, 776, 778, 779, 802, 805, 806, 825, 826, 858, 861, 862, 868, 873, 874, 875, 883, 889, 901, 907, 926, 928, 930, 953, 956, 968, 977, 978, 985, 991, 993, 994, 995, 997, 1002, 1004, 1005, 1009, 1010, 1019, 1022, 1023, 1052, 1054, 1057, 1058, 1061, 1064, 1102, 1103, 1104, 1105, 1108, 1109, 1110, 1163, 1165, 1171, 1194, 1197, 1198, 1201, 1202, 1203, 1228, 1230, 1231, 1232, 1233, 1271, 1272, 1301, 1305, 1307, 2321, 2322, 2324, 2325, 2326, 2328, 2329, 2334, 2335, 2336, 2337, 2341, 2345, 2348, 2350, 2351, 2353, 2354, 2355, 2356, 2361, 2363, 2502, 2506, 2511, 2512, 2513, 2518, 2529, 2550, 3008, 3017, 3035, 3036, 3041, 3514, 3515, 975, 992.

ITALIAN NAVAL LOSSES
1939–1945

BATTLESHIPS
Cavour—Trieste—20 Feb '45—Air
Impero—Trieste—'45—S
Roma—Bonifacio St—9 Sep '43—Air

AIRCRAFT CARRIER ESCORTS
Aquila—Genoa—24 Apr '45—S
Caio Mario—LaSpezia—Unkn—S
Cornelio Silla—Genoa—30 Sep '44—S
Giul Germanico—DiStabia—17 Sep '43—S
Ottav—Ancona—1 Nov '43—Air
Sparviero—Genoa—9 Sep '44—S
Ulpio Traiano—Palermo—1 Mar '43—Air

HEAVY CRUISERS
Bolzano—LaSpezia—22 Jun '44—Human torpedo
Fiume—C Matapan—28 Mar '41—SC
Pola—C Matapan—28 Mar '41—SC
San Giorgio—Tobruk—22 Jan '41—Air
Trento—Malta—15 Jun '42—Air & Sub
Trieste—La Naddalena—10 Apr '43—Air
Zara—C Matapan—28 Mar '41—SC

LIGHT CRUISERS
Attendolo—Naples—4 Dec '42—Air
Augusto—Ancona—1 Nov '43—Air
Bande Nere—Stromboli—1 Apr '42—Sub
Barbiano—C Bon—13 Dec '41—SC
Bari—Livorno—28 Jun '43—Air

Colleoni—Crete—19 Jul '41—SC
Diaz—Sfax—25 Feb '41—Sub
Germanico—Castellamare Stabial—18 Sep '43—S
Giussano—C Bon—13 Dec '41—SC
Quarto—Livorno—Nov '43—S
Taranto—LaSpezia—23 Sep '44—S

DESTROYERS
Alfieri—C Matapan—28 Mar '41—SC
Alpino—LaSpeza—19 Apr '43—Air
Aquilone—Benghazi—17 Sep '40—Mine
Artigliere I—Sicily—12 Oct '40—SC
Ascari—Zembretta Is—25 Mar '43—Mine
Aviere—38-00N, 10-05E—17 Dec '42—Sub
Baleno—Tunisia—15 Apr '41—SC
Battisti—Massaua—4 Apr '41—SC
Bersagliere—Palermo—7 Jan '43—Air
Bombardiere—Marettimo—17 Jan '43—Sub
Borea—Benghasi—17 Sep '40—Air
Carducci—C Matapan—28 Mar '41—SC
Carrista—Livorno—Jul '43—Air
Corizziere—Genoa—9 Sep '43—SC
Corsaro I—Bizerte—9 Jan '43—Mine
Corsaro II—Genoa—4 Sep '44—Air
Crispi—Crete—8 Mar '44—Air
Da Mosto—Tripoli—1 Dec '41—SC

Da Noli—Bonifacio St—9 Sep '43—Mine
Dardo—Genoa—24 Apr '45—S
Espero—Sicily—28 Jun '40—SC
Euro—Leros—1 Oct '43—Air
Folgore—37-40N, 11-16E—2 Dec '42—SC
FR21—LaSpezia—8 Sep '43—S
FR22—LaSpezia—8 Sep '43—S
FR24—Genoa—24 Apr '45—S
FR32—Genoa—28 Oct '44—S
Freccia—Genoa—19 Aug '43—Air
Fulmine—Calabria—9 Nov '41—SC.
Geniere—Palermo—1 Mar '43—Air
Gioberti—LaSpezia—9 Aug '43—Sub
Lampo—Ras Mustafa—30 Apr '43—Air
Lanciere—Unkn—23 Mar '42—Foundered
Leone—Massaua—1 Apr '41—S
Libeccio—Calabria—9 Nov '41—SC
Ljubljana—C Bon—1 Apr '43—Air
Maestrale—Genoa—9 Sep '43—S
Malocello—C Bon—24 Mar '43—Mine
Manin—Massaua—13 Apr '41—Air
Mirabello—Cape Dukato—21 May '41—Mine
Nembo—Tobruk—20 Jul '40—Air
Nullo—Red Sea—21 Oct '40—SC
Ostro—Tobruk—20 Jul '40—Air
Pancaldo—LaGoulette—30 Apr '43—Air
Pantera—Jedda—3 Apr '41—S
Pessagno—Benghazi—29 May '42—Sub

Pigafetta—Trieste—17 Feb '45—Air
Premuda—Genoa—24 Apr '45—S
Saetta—Tunis—3 Feb '43—Mine
Sauro—Massaua—4 Apr '41—Air
Scirocco—Ionian S—23 Mar '42—Foundered
Sebenico—Trieste—3 May '45—S
Sella—Venice—18 Sep '43—SC
Strale—Sidi Daoud—6 Jun '42—Air
Tarigo—Mediterranean—15 Apr '41—SC
Tigre—Red S—3 Apr '41—S
Turbine—Piraeus—15 Sep '44—Air
Usodimare—C Bon—8 Aug '42—Sub
Verazzano—Lampedusa—19 Oct '42—Sub
Vivaldi—Bonifacio St—9 Sep '43—Sub
Zeffiro—Tobruk—5 Jul '40—Air
Zeno—LaSpezia—9 Sep '43—S

SUBMARINES

Total	Cause	Time
32	SC	War
24	Air	War
19	Sub	War
17	S	After Sur.
4	S	Before Sur.
4	SC & Air	War
4	A	War
4	Cap	War
2	Col	War
2	Mine	War
3	Unkn	War
1	Grounded	War

VESSELS SURRENDERED
Battleships: Cesare, Doria, Duilio, Italia, Veneto
Cruisers: Abruzzi, Africano, Cadorna, D'Aosta, Etna, Garibaldi, Gorizia, Magno, Montecuccoli, Regolo, Savoia, Vesuvio
Destroyers: Artiglieri, Carabiniere, Da Recco, Fuciliere, Granatiere, Grecale, Legionario, Mitragliere, Orani, Riboty, Velite
Submarines: Alagi, Atropo, Brin, Cagni, Da Procida, Dandolo, Diaspro, Galatea, Giada, H-1, Jalea, Mameli, Maria, Nichelia, Onice, Otari, Platino, Speri, Terchese, Vortice, Zoea

JAPANESE NAVAL LOSSES
1941–1945

Note: Where no year appears, the year next preceding should be understood.

BATTLESHIPS
Hiyei—Savo—13 Nov '42—Air
Kirishima—Savo—15 Nov '42—SC
Matsu—Hiroshima—8 Jun '43—Exp
Yamashiro—Surigao—25 Oct—SC
Fuso—Surigao—25 Oct '44—SC
Musashi—Sibuyan—25 Oct '44—Air
Kongo—Foochow—21 Nov—Sub
Yamato—Kyushu—7 Apr '45—Air
Nagato—Yokosuka—18 Jul—Air
Haruna—Kure—28 Jul '45—Air
Hyuga—Kure—28 Jul '45—Air
Ise—Kure—28 Jul '45—Air

AIRCRAFT CARRIERS
Hosho—Japan Area—Unkn—Unkn
Shoho—Coral Sea—7 May '42—Air
Akagi—Midway—4 Jun '42—Air
Kaga—Midway—4 Jun '42—Air
Soryu—Midway—4 Jun '42—Air
Hiryu—Midway—5 Jun '42—Air
Ryujo—Solomons—24 Aug '42—Air
Shokaku—Yap—19 Jun '44—Sub
Taiho—Yap—19 Jun '44—Sub
Hitaka—Philippine S—20 Jun—Air
Chitose—Luzon—25 Oct '44—Air
Chiyoda—Luzon—25 Oct '44—Air
Zuiho—Luzon—25 Oct '44—Air
Zuikaku—Luzon—25 Oct '44—Air
Shinano—Japan—29 Nov '44—Sub
Hayataka—Japan—9 Dec '44—Air
Unryu—China—19 Dec '44—Sub
Ryuho—Kure—19 Mar '45—Air
Amagi—Kure—24-8 Jul '45—Air
Katsuragi—Kure—24-8 Jul '45—Air

ESCORT AIRCRAFT CARRIERS
Chuyo—Honshu—4 Dec '43—Sub
Otaka—Luzon—18 Aug '44—Sub
Unyo—China—16 Sep '44—Sub
Jinyo—China—17 Nov '44—Sub
Kaiyo—Japan—24 Jul '45—Air

HEAVY CRUISERS
Mikuma—Midway—6 Jun '42—Air
Kako—Bismarcks—10 Aug—Sub
Kurutka—Savo—11 Oct '42—SC
Kinugasa—Savo—14 Nov '42—Air
Atago—Palawan—23 Oct '44—Sub
Maya—Palawan—23 Oct '44—Sub
Takao—Palawan—23 Oct '44—Sub
Chokai—Sibuyan—24 Oct '44—Air
Chikuma—Samar—25 Oct '44—Air
Mogami—Mindanao—25 Oct—Air
Suzuya—Samar I.—25 Oct '44—Air
Nachi—Manila—5 Nov '44—Air
Kumano—Luzon—25 Nov '44—Air
Myoko—Saigon—13 Dec '44—Sub
Haguro—Penang—16 May '45—SC
Ashigara—Singapore—8 Jun '45—Brit Sub
Aoba—Kure—28 Jul '45—Air
Tone—Kure—28 Jul '45—SC

LIGHT CRUISERS
Yura—Solomons—25 Oct '42—Air
Tenryu—Bismarcks—18 Dec—Sub
Jintsu—Solomons—13 Jul '43—Sub
Sendai—Solomons—2 Nov '43—SC
Kuma—Penang—11 Jan '44—Sub
Agano—Truk—16 Feb '44—Sub
Naka—Truk—17 Feb '44—Air
Tatsuta—Japan—14 Mar '44—Sub
Yubari—Palau—1—27 Apr '44—Sub
Oi—S. China Sea—19 Jul '44—Sub
Nagara—Kyushu—7 Aug '44—Sub
Natori—Samar—18 Aug '44—Sub
Tama—Luzon—25 Oct '44—Sub
Abukuma—Negros I.—26 Oct '44—Air & SC
Kinu—Masbate I.—26 Oct '44—Air
Noshiro—Panay—26 Oct '44—Air
Kiso—Manila—13 Nov '44—Air
Isuzu—Soembaya—7 Apr '45—Sub
Yahagi—Kyushu—7 Apr '45—Air
Kitagami—Kure—24-8 Jul '45—Air
Oyodo—Kure—28 Jul '45—Air

TRAINING CRUISERS
Katori—Truk—17 Feb '44—Air
Kashii—China—12 Jan '45—Air

DESTROYERS
Isonami—Celebes—9 Dec '41—Sub
Hayate—Wake—11 Dec '41—Gun
Kisaragi—Wake—11 Dec '41—Gun
Shinome—Borneo—18 Dec '41—Mine
Sagiri—Borneo—24 Dec '41—Sub
Natsushio—Makassar—8 Feb—Sub
Kikutsuki—Solomons—4 May—Air
Yamakaze—Japan—25 Jun—Sub
Nenohi—Aleutians—4 Jul '42—Sub
Arare—Kiska—5 Jul '42—Sub
Arashi—N. Georgia—6 Aug—SC
Obero—Honshu—12 Aug '42—Sub
Mutsuki—Solomons—25 Aug '42—Air
Asagiri—Solomons—28 Aug '42—Air
Yayoi—Normanby I.—11 Sep '42—Air
Fubuki—Savo I.—11 Oct '42—SC
Natsugumo—Savo I.—11 Oct—SC
Murakumo—N. Georgia—12 Oct '42—Air
Akatsuki—Savo—13 Nov '42—SC
Yudachi—Savo—13 Nov '42—SC
Ayanami—Savo—15 Nov '42—SC
Hayashio—New Guinea—24 Nov '42—Air
Takanami—Savo—30 Nov '42—SC
Terutsuki—N. Georgia—12 Dec—SC
Ckikaze—Honshu—10 Jan '43—Sub
Hakaze—Bismarcks—23 Jan—Sub
Makigumo — Guadacanal — 1 Feb '43—Mine
Oshio—Admiralties—20 Feb '43—Sub
Arashio—N. Guinea—3 Mar—Air
Asashio—N. Guinea—3 Mar—Air
Shirayuki—N. Guinea—3 Mar—Air
Tokitsukaze—New Guinea—3 Mar '43—Air
Kagero—New Georgia—8 May '43—Air & Mine
Kuroshio—New Georgia—8 May '43—Mine
Oyashio—N. Georgia—8 May—Air
Nagatsuki—N. Georgia—6 Jul—SC
Niizuki—N. Georgia—6 Jul—SC
Hatsuyuki—Solomons—17 Jul—Air
Kiyonami—N. Georgia—20 Jul—Air
Yugure—N. Georgia—20 Jul—Air
Ariake—N. Britain—28 Jul—Air
Mikatsuki—N. Britain—28 Jul—Air
Hagikaze—N. Georgia—6 Aug—SC
Kawakaze—N. Georgia—6 Aug—SC
Yugumo—Solomons—6 Oct—SC
Mochizuki—N. Britain—24 Oct—Air
Hatsukaze—Solomons—2 Nov—SC
Suzunami—Rabaul—11 Nov—Air
Senae—Celebes Sea—18 Nov—Sub
Makinami—Solomons—25 Nov—SC
Onami—Buka I.—25 Nov '43—SC
Yugiri—Solomons—25 Nov '43—Air
Numakaze—China—18 Dec—Sub
Fuyo—Manila—20 Dec '43—Sub
Sazanami—Yap I.—14 Jan '44—Sub
Suzukaze—Ponape—26 Jan '44—Sub
Umikaze—Truk—1 Feb '44—Sub
Minekaze—Formosa—10 Feb '44—Sub
Fumitsuki—Truk—17 Feb '44—Air
Maikaze—Truk—17 Feb '44—Air
Tachikaze—Truk—17 Feb '44—Air
Oite—Truk—18 Feb '44—Air
Shirakumo—Japan—Mar '44—Sub
Wakatake—Palau—Mar '44—Air
Akigumo—Mindanao—11 Apr—Sub
Ikazuchi—Guam — 13 Apr '44—Sub
Amagiri—Makassar—23 Apr—Mine
Karukaya—Manila—10 May—Sub
Inazuma—Philippines—May—Sub
Asanagi—Bonin—22 May—Sub
Minazuki—Philippines—6 Jun—Sub
Hayanami—Philippines—Jun—Sub
Harusame—N. Guinea—8 Jun—Air
Kazagumo—Mindanao—Jun—Sub
Matsukaze—Bonin I.—9 Jun—Sub
Tanikaze—Philippines—9 Jun—Sub
Urakaze—Philippines—9 Jun—Sub
Shiratsuyu—Philippines—Jun—Air
Hokaze—Celebes—6 Jul—Sub
Tamanami—Manila—7 Jul—Sub
Usugumo—Okhotsk—7 Jul—Sub
Matsu—Bonin Is.—4 Aug—SC
Asakaze—Luzon—23 Aug '44—Sub
Yunagi—Luzon—25 Aug '44—Sub
Samidare—Palau I.—26 Aug '44—Air & Sub
Namikaze—Kuriles—8 Sep—Air
Shikinami—China—12 Sep—Sub
Satsuki—Manila—21 Sep '44—Air
Wakaba—Mindoro—24 Oct—Air
Asagumo—Surigao—25 Oct—SC
Michishio—Surigao—25 Oct—SC
Nowake—Surigao—25 Oct—SC
Yamagumo—Surigao—25 Oct—SC
Hayashimo—Mindoro—26 Oct—Air
Uranami—Philippines—26 Oct—Air
Fujinami—Mindoro—27 Oct—Air
Shiranuhi—Philippines—Oct—Air
Arikaze—China—3 Nov—Sub
Hamanami—Ormoc—11 Nov—Air
Naganami—Ormoc—11 Nov—Air
Shimakaze—Ormoc—11 Nov—Air
Wakatsuki—Ormoc—11 Nov—Air
Akebono—Manila—13 Nov—Air
Akishimo—Manila—13 Nov—Air
Hatsuharu—Manila—13 Nov—Air
Okinami—Manila—13 Nov—Air
Ushio—Manila—14 Nov '44—Air
Kishinami—Luzon—20 Nov—Sub
Hatsuzuki—Manila—25 Nov—Sub
Shimotsuki—Borneo—25 Nov—Air
Kuwa—Ormoc Bay—3 Dec—SC
Iwanami—China—4 Dec—Sub
Maki—Mejima Is.—9 Dec—Air
Uzuki—Leyte—12 Dec '44—SC
Kiri—Leyte—12 Dec '44—Air
Yuzuki—Leyte—13 Dec '44—Air
Akitsuki—Honshu—22 Dec—Sub
Kiyoshimo—Mindoro—26 Dec—Air
Kaya—Mindoro—27 Dec—Air
Kuretake—Luzon—30 Dec—Sub
Fuyutsuki—Moji—Unkn—Mine
Hagi—Japan—Unkn—Unkn
Hanatsuki—Japan—Unkn—Unkn
Yakaze — Japan — '45 Converted to target ship
Yukaze — Japan — '45 Converted to target ship
Hinoki—Manila—5 Jan '45—Air
Momi—Manila—5 Jan '45—Air
Hatakaze—Takao—15 Jan '45—Air
Tsuga—Pescadores—15 Jan—Air
Hasu—Hongkong—16 Jan '45—Air
Harukaze—Bako—21 Jan—Unkn
Kashi—Takao—21 Jan '45—Unkn
Sugi—Takao—21 Jan '45—Unkn
Shigure—Borneo—24 Jan—Sub
Kaede—Formosa—31 Jan—Unkn
Shiokaze—Formosa—31 Jan—Unkn
Ume—Takao—31 Jan '45—Air
Nokaze—Saigon—20 Feb '45—Sub
Hibiki—Himejima—29 Mar—Unkn
Amatsukaze—Amoy—6 Apr—Air
Asashimo—Kyushu—7 Apr—Air
Hamakaze—Kyushu—7 Apr—Air
Isakaze—Kyushu—7 Apr '45—Air
Kasumi—Kyushu—7 Apr '45—Air
Suzutsuki—Kyushu—7 Apr '45—Air
Yoitsuki—Himejima—2 Jun—Unkn
Natsuzuki—Matsure—16 Jun—Unkn
Nire—Kure—22 Jun '45—Air
Nara—Shimonoseki—30 Jun—Unkn
Sakura—Osaka—11 Jul '45—Unkn
Tachibana—Ominato—15 Jul—SC
Yanagi—Ominato—15 Jul '45—SC
Shigezakura—Japan—18 Jul—Air
Enoki—Maizuru—24 Jul '45—Unkn
Kaba—Inland Sea—24 Jul—Unkn
Tsubaki—Okayama—24 Jul—Air
Nashi—Kure—28 Jul '45—Unkn
Hatsushimo—Miyazu—30 Jul—Unkn
Yukikaze—Miyazu—30 Jul—Unkn
Asagao—Moji—22 Aug '45—Unkn

SUBMARINES
I-170—Pearl H.—10 Dec '41—Air
RO-66—Wake I.—17 Dec '41—Col
RO-60—Kwajalein—29 Dec—Gdg
I-160 (60)—Sunda Straits—17 Jan '42—Brit. SC
I-124—P. Darwin—20 Jan '42—SC
I-173 (73)—Midway—27 Jan '42—Sub
RO-30—W. Pacific—Apr '42—Air
RO-32—W. Pacific—Apr '42—Air
I-23—Johnston—26 Apr—Sub
I-28—Truk—17 May '42—Sub
I-164—Kyushu—17 May '42—Sub
I-30—W. Pacific—Jun '42—Air
I-33—W. Pacific—Jun '42—Gdg
I-123—Guadalcanal—29 Aug—SC
RO-33—N. Guinea—29 Aug—SC
RO-61—Aleutians—31 Aug '42—Air & SC
RO-65—Kiska—28 Sep '42—Air
I-15—S. Pacific—Nov '42—Air
I-172—S. Pacific—Nov '42—Air
I-22—San Cristobal—19 Nov—SC
I-3—Guadalcanal—9 Dec '42—SC
I-4—Rabaul—21 Dec '42—Sub
I-18—N. Guinea—25 Dec '42—SC
I-1—Guadalcanal—29 Jan '43—SC
RO-102—Santa Isabel I.—4 Apr '43—SC
RO-34—San Cristobal I.—7 Apr '43—SC
RO-103—N. Hebrides—29 May—SC
I-178—Pacific—Jun '43—Air
RO-107—Pacific—Jun '43—Air
I-9—Attu—10 Jun '43—SC
I-31—Kiska—13 Jun '43—SC
I-7—Kiska—22 Jun '43—SC
RO-101—Solomons—1 Jul '43—SC
I-24—New Hanover—27 Jul '43—SC
I-17—New Caledonia—19 Aug '43—Air & SC
I-168—New Hebrides—3 Sep '43—SC
I-182—Surigao—9 Sep—'43—Sub
RO-35—Solomons—Oct '43—Air
I-20—Solomons—1 Oct '43—SC
I-25—Pacific—Nov '43—Air
I-34—Malacca—13 Nov '43—Sub
I-35—Tarawa—23 Nov '43—SC
RO-100—Bougainville—Nov—SC
I-19—Makin Is.—26 Nov '43—SC
I-39—Guadalcanal—24 Dec—SC
I-181—Bismarcks—16 Jan '44—Air
RO-37—Solomons—22 Jan '44—SC
I-179—Pacific—Feb '44—Air
I-171—Buka—1 Feb '44—SC
RO-39—Marshalls—3 Feb '44—SC
I-21—Marshalls—5 Feb '44—SC
RO-110—India—11 Feb '44—SC
I-27—Maldive I.—12 Feb—SC
I-43—Truk—15 Feb '44—Sub
I-11—Marshalls—17 Feb '44—SC
RO-38—Pacific—Mar '44—Air
RO-40—Pacific—Mar '44—Air
I-42—Palau I.—23 Mar '44—Sub
I-32—Marshalls—24 Mar '44—SC
I-40—Pacific—Apr '44—Air
I-169—Truk—4 Apr '44—Air
I-2—Admiralties—7 Apr '44—SC
I-174—Truk—12 Apr '44—Air
RO-45—Saipan—20 Apr '44—Sub
I-180—Kodiak—26 Apr '44—SC
I-183—Japan—29 Apr '44—Sub
I-175—Truk—30 Apr '44—SC
RO-501—Atlantic—13 May '44—SC
I-176—Buka—17 May '44—SC
I-16—Solomons—19 May '44—SC
RO-106—Bismarck I.—22 May—SC
RO-104—Bismarck I.—23 May—SC
RO-116—Bismarck I.—24 May—SC
RO-108—Bismarck I.—26 May—SC
RO-105—Bismarck I.—31 May—SC
I-5—Bismarck I.—10 Jun '44—SC
RO-42—Kwajalein—10 Jun—SC
RO-36—Saipan—13 Jun '44—SC
RO-44—Eniwetok—16 Jun '44—SC
RO-111—Truk—16 Jun '44—Air
RO-114—Guam—16 Jun '44—SC
I-185—Guam—17 Jun '44—SC
RO-117—Truk—17 Jun '44—Air
I-184—Saipan—21 Jun '44—SC
I-52—Atlantic—24 Jun '44—Air
I-6—Saipan—4 Jul '44—SC
RO-48—Saipan—14 Jul '44—SC
I-166—Penang—17 Jul '44—SC
I-10—Truk—18 Jul '44—SC
I-29—Luzon—26 Jul '44—Sub
I-55—Saipan—27 Jul '44—SC
I-41—Honshu—16 Sep '44—Sub
I-364—S. Pacific—Oct '44—SC
I-26—Leyte Gulf—25 Oct '44—SC
I-54—Leyte Gulf—28 Oct '44—SC
I-45—Dinegat I.—29 Oct '44—SC
I-177—Pacific—Nov '44—Air
I-38—Oahu—13 Nov '44—SC
I-37—Samar—18 Nov '44—Air
I-362—Camotes Sea—27 Nov—SC

I-365—Tokyo Bay—29 Nov—Sub
I-46—Pacific—Dec '44—Air
I-371—Truk—Jan '45—Air
I-48—Carolines—23 Jan '45—SC
RO-115—Luzon—10 Feb '45—Sub
RO-112—Luzon—11 Feb '45—Sub
RO-113—Luzon—13 Feb '45—Sub
RO-43—Luzon—14 Feb '45—Sub
RO-55—Luzon—14 Feb '45—Sub

RO-49—Japan—24 Feb '45—Sub
I-368—Iwo Jima—26 Feb '45—SC
I-370—Iwo Jima—26 Feb '45—Air
RO-47—Philippine S.—23 Mar—SC
I-53—Japan Area—30 Mar '45—Air
I-8—Okinawa—31 Mar '45—SC
RO-41—Okinawa—31 Mar '45—SC

RO-67—Japan—4 Apr—Mine
I-56—Okinawa—5 Apr '45—SC
RO-46—Okinawa—9 Apr '45—SC
I-44—Okinawa—18 Apr '45—SC
RO-109—Okinawa—29 Apr—SC
I-12—Pacific—May '45—Air
RO-56—Kuriles—May '45—Air
RO-64—Hiroshima—May '45—Air

I-361—Japan—30 May '45—Air
I-122—Japan—10 Jun '45—Sub
I-351—Borneo—15 Jul '45—Sub
I-13—Honshu—16 Jul '45—Air
I-372—Yokosuka—18 Jul '45—Air
I-373—China Sea—14 Aug—Sub
I-14—Pacific—27 Aug '45 Cap—
I-400—Pacific—27 Aug '45—Cap
I-401—Pacific—29 Aug '45—Cap

LOSSES OF U. S. NAVAL VESSELS FROM ALL CAUSES
7 December 1941—1 October 1945

Note: Where no year appears, the year next preceding should be understood.

BATTLESHIPS
Arizona—Pearl Harbor—7 Dec '41—Air
Oklahoma—Pearl Harbor—7 Dec '41—Air

AIRCRAFT CARRIERS
Lexington—Coral Sea—8 May '42—Air
Yorktown—Midway—7 Jun '42—Sub
Wasp—Solomons—15 Sep '42—Sub
Hornet—Santa Cruz—26 Oct '42—Air
Princeton—Luzon—24 Oct '44—Air

ESCORT AIRCRAFT CARRIERS
Liscome Bay—Makin I.—24 Nov '43—Sub
Block Island—Canary Is.—29 May '44—Sub
Gambier Bay—Samar I.—25 Oct '44—SC
Saint Lo—Samar I.—25 Oct '44—Air
Ommaney Bay—Panay I.—4 Jan '45—Air
Bismarck Sea—Iwo Jima—21 Feb '45—Air

HEAVY CRUISERS
Houston—Java Sea—1 Mar '42—SC
Astoria—Savo I.—9 Aug '42—SC
Quincy—Savo I.—9 Aug '42—SC
Vincennes—Savo I.—9 Aug '42—SC
Northampton—Savo I.—30 Nov '42—SC
Chicago—Rennell I.—30 Jan '43—Air
Indianapolis—Leyte—29 Jul '45—Sub

LIGHT CRUISERS
Atlanta—San Cristobal I.—13 Nov '42—SC
Juneau—San Cristobal I.—13 Nov '42—Sub
Helena—Kula Gulf—6 Jul '43—SC

DESTROYERS
Reuben James—Atlantic—31 Oct '41—Sub
Truxtun—Newfoundland—18 Feb '42—Gdg
Peary—Port Darwin—19 Feb '42—Air
Jacob Jones—Cape May—28 Feb '42—Sub
Edsall—Java—1 Mar '42—Air
Pillsbury—Bali Strait—1 Mar '42—SC
Pope—Java Sea—1 Mar '42—SC
Stewart—Java—2 Mar '42—Cap
Sturtevant—Key West—26 Apr '42—Mine
Sims—Coral Sea—7 May '42—Air
Hammann—Midway—6 Jun '42—Sub
Tucker—Espiritu Santo—4 Aug '42—Mine
Jarvis—Guadalcanal—9 Aug '42—Air
Ingraham—Nova Scotia—22 Aug '42—Col
O'Brien—San Cristobal I.—15 Sep '42—Sub
Duncan—Savo I.—12 Oct '42—SC
Meredith I.—San Cristobal I. 15 Oct '42—Air
Porter—Santa Cruz I.—26 Oct '42—Sub
Barton—Guadalcanal—13 Nov '42—SC
Cushing—Savo I.—13 Nov '42—SC
Laffey—Savo I.—13 Nov '42—SC
Monssen—Savo I.—13 Nov '42—SC
Benham—Savo I.—15 Nov '42—SC
Preston—Savo I.—15 Nov '42—SC
Walke—Savo I.—15 Nov '42—SC
Worden—Aleutians—12 Jan '43—Gdg
De Haven—Savo I.—1 Feb '43—Air
Aaron Ward—Savo I.—7 Apr '43—Air
Strong—Kula Gulf—5 Jul '43—Sub
Maddox—Sicily—10 Jul '43—Air
Gwin—Vella Lavella—13 Jul '43—SC
Blue—Savo I.—22 Aug '43—SC
Rowan—Salerno—11 Sep '43—SC
Henley—Huon Gulf—3 Oct '43—Sub
Chevalier—Vella Lavella—6 Oct '43—SC
Buck—Salerno—9 Oct '43—Sub
Bristol—Algeria—13 Oct '43—Sub
Borie—Azores—1 Nov '43—Rammed enemy submarine
Beatty—Algeria—6 Nov '43—Air
Perkins—New Guinea—29 Nov '43 Col
Leary—Atlantic—24 Dec '43—Sub
Brownson—New Britain—26 Dec '43—Air
Turner—Ambrose Light—3 Jan '44—Ex
Lansdale—Algeria—20 Apr '44—Air
Parrott—Norfolk, Va.—2 May '44—Col
Corry — Cherbourg — 6 Jun '44—Mine
Glennon—I. of Wight—8 Jun '44—Mine
Meredith II.—Cherbourg—8 Jun '44—Mine
Warrington — Bahamas — 13 Sep '44—W
Hoel—Samar—25 Oct '44—SC
Johnson—Samar—25 Oct '44—SC
Abner Read—Leyte—1 Nov '44—Air
Cooper—Ormoc Bay—3 Dec '44—Sub
Mahan—Ormoc Bay—7 Dec '44—Air
Reid—Ormoc Bay—11 Dec '44—Air
Hull—Philippine Sea—18 Dec '44—W
Monaghan — Philippine Sea — 18 Dec '44—W
Spence—Philippine Sea—18 Dec '44—W
Halligan—Okinawa—26 Mar '45—Mine
Bush—Okinawa—6 Apr '45—Air
Calhoun—Okinawa—6 Apr '45—Air
Mannert L. Abele—Okinawa—12 Apr '45—Air
Pringle—Okinawa—16 Apr '45—Air
Little—Okinawa—3 May '45—Air
Luce—Okinawa—4 May '45—Air
Morrison—Okinawa—4 May '45—Air
Longshaw—Okinawa—18 May '45—Gdg
Drexler—Okinawa—28 May '45—Air
William D. Porter—Okinawa—10 Jun '45—Air
Twiggs—Okinawa—16 Jun '45—Air
Callaghan—Okinawa—28 Jul '45—Air

DESTROYER ESCORTS
Leopold—Atlantic—9 Mar '44—Sub
Holder — Mediterranean — 11 Apr '44—Air
Fechteler—Gibraltar—4 May '44—Sub
Rich—Cherbourg—8 Jun '44—Mine
Fiske—Atlantic—2 Aug '44—Sub
Shelton—Morotai I.—3 Oct '44—Sub
Samuel B. Roberts — Samar — 25 Oct '44—SC
Eversole—Mindanao—28 Oct '44—Sub
Frederick C. Davis—Atlantic—24 Apr '45—Sub
Oberrender—Okinawa—9 May '45—Air
Underhill—Philippine Sea—24 Jul '45—Sub

SUBMARINES
Sealion—Cavite—10 Dec '41—Air
S-27—Aleutians—19 Jan '42—Gdg
S-36—Makassar Strait—20 Jan '42—Gdg
S-26—Gulf of Panama—24 Jan '42—Col
Shark I.—Molucca Sea—Feb '42—OD
Perch—Java Sea—3 May '42—SC
Grunion—Aleutians—Jul '42—OD
S-39—Russell I.—14 Aug '42—Gdg
Argonaut—New Britain—10 Jan '43—SC
Amberjack—New Britain—Feb '43—OD
Grampus—New Britain—Feb '43—OD
Triton—Admiralties—Mar '43—OD
Grenadier—Malaya—Apr '43—OD
Pickerel—Japan—May '43—OD
Runner—Japan—Jun '43—OD
R-12—Key West—12 Jun '43—Ex
Grayling—Philippines—Aug '43—OD
Pompano—Japan—Sep '43—OD
Cisco—Pacific—Oct '43—OD
Dorado—Canal Zone—Oct '43—OD
S-44—Kuriles—Oct '43—OD
Wahoo—Japan—Oct '43—OD
Corvina—Marshalls—Nov '43—OD
Capelin—Celebes Sea—Dec '43—OD
Sculpin—Gilberts—Dec '43—OD
Scorpion—E. China Sea—Jan '44—OD
Grayback—Ryukyus—Feb '44—OD
Trout—Ryukyus—Feb '44—OD
Tullibee—Palau I. —Apr '44—OD
Gudgeon—Marianas—May '44—OD
Herring—Kuriles—May '44—OD
Golet—Japan—Jun '44—OD
Robalo—Borneo—Jul '44—OD
S-28—Oahu—4 Jul '44—Ex
Flier—Borneo—Aug '44—OD
Harder—Philippines—Aug '44—OD
Escolar—Japan—Oct '44—OD
Seawolf—Morotai I.—Oct '44—OD
Shark II—Hong Kong—Oct '44—OD
Tang—Formosa—Oct '44—OD
Dartar—Palawan—24 Oct '44—Gdg
Albacore—Japan—Nov '44—OD
Growler—Philippines—Nov '44—OD
Scamp—Japan—Nov '44—OD
Swordfish—Ryukyus—Jan '45—OD
Barbel—Borneo—Feb '45—OD
Kete—Ryukyus—Mar '45—OD
Trigger—Ryukyus—Mar '45—OD
Snook—Hainan I.—Apr '45—OD
Bonefish—Japan—May '45—OD
Lagarto—S. China Sea—Jun '45—OD
Bullhead—Java Sea—Aug '45—OD

MINELAYERS
Miantonomah—LeHavre—25 Sep '44—Mine
Montgomery—S. Pacific—17 Oct '44—Mine
Gamble—Iwo Jima—18 Feb '45—Air

MINESWEEPERS
Penguin—Guam—8 Dec '41—Air
Bittern—Cavite—10 Dec '41—Air
Hornbill—San Francisco Bay—30 Jan '42—Col
Finch—Corregidor—10 Apr '42—Air
Tanager—Corregidor—4 May '42—SC
Quail—Corregidor—5 May '42—Gun
Bunting—San Francisco Bay—3 Jun '42—Col
Wasmuth—Aleutians—29 Dec '42—W
Sentinel—Sicily—13 Jul '43—Air
Crow—Puget Sound—3 Sep '43—A
Skill—Salerno Gulf—25 Sep '43—Sub
Osprey—English Channel—5 Jan '44—Mine
Portent—Anzio—22 Jan '44—Mine
Tide—Cherbourg—7 Jun '44—Mine
Valor—Nantucket—29 Jun '44—Col
Swerve—Anzio—9 Jul '44—Mine
Perry—Palau—13 Sep '44—Mine
Hovey—Lingayen Gulf—6 Jan '45—Air
Long—Lingayen Gulf—6 Jan '45—Air
Palmer—Lingayen Gulf—7 Jan '45—Air
Skylark—Okinawa—28 Mar '45—Mine
Emmons—Okinawa—6 Apr '45—Air
Swallow—Okinawa—22 Apr '45—Air
Salute—Borneo—8 Jun '45—Mine

SUBMARINE CHASERS
SC 709 Cape Breton—21 Jan '43—Gdg
SC 1024 Cape Hatteras—2 Mar '43—Col
PC 496—Portugal—4 Jun '43—Mine
SC 740—Coral Sea—17 Jun '43—Gdg
SC 751—Australia—22 Jun '43—Gdg
SC 694 Palermo—23 Aug '43—Air
SC 696 Palermo—23 Aug '43—Air
SC 1067 Attu—19 Nov '43—W
SC 700—Vella Lavella—10 Mar '44—Fire
SC 984—New Hebrides—9 Apr '44—Gdg

PC 558—Sicily—9 May '44—Sub
PC 1261—France—6 Jun '44—Gun
SC 744—Tacloban Bay—27 Nov '44—Air
SC 1059—Bahamas—12 Dec '44—Gdg
PC 1129—Luzon—31 Jan '45—SC
SC 1019—Cuba—22 Apr '45—Gdg
PC 1603—Okinawa—21 May '45—Air
SC 521—San Cristobal I.—10 Jul '45—W

GUNBOATS
Wake—Shanghai—8 Dec '41—Cap
Asheville—Java—3 Mar '42—SC
Mindanao—Corregidor—2 May '42—Air
Oahu—Corregidor—4 May '42—SC
Luzon—Corregidor—5 May '42—Cap
Erie—Curacao I.—12 Nov '42—Sub
Plymouth—Norfolk, Va.—5 Aug '43—Sub
St. Augustine—Delaware Bay—6 Jan '44—Col
PGM 7—Bismarck Sea—18 Jul '44—Col
PGM 18—Okinawa—8 Apr '45—Mine
PE 56—Portland, Me.—23 Apr '45—Exp
PGM 17—Okinawa— 4 May '45—Gdg

COAST GUARD VESSELS
Alexander Hamilton—Iceland—29 Jan '42—Sub
Acacia—Caribbean—15 Mar '42—Sub
Natsek—Belle I.—17 Dec '42—W
Catamount — Ambrose Light — 27 Mar '43—Exp
CG 58012—Cape Cod—2 May '43—Fire
Escanaba—Greenland—13 Jun '43—Sub
CG 83421—Bahamas—30 Jun '43—Col
Wilcox—Cape Hatteras—30 Sep '43—W
Dow—Caribbean—15 Oct '43—W
Bodega—Gulf of Mexico—20 Dec '43—Gdg
CG 83415—France—21 Jun '44—W
CG 83471—France—21 Jun '44—W
Bedloe—Cape Hatteras—14 Sep '44—W
Jackson—Atlantic—14 Sep '44—W
Vineyard Sound—Vineyard Sound —14 Sep '44—W

SEAPLANE TENDERS
Langley—Java—27 Feb '42—Air
Gannet—Bermuda—7 Jun '42—Sub
Thornton—Okinawa—5 Apr '45—Col

MOTOR TORPEDO BOATS
PT 33—Pt. Santiago—15 Dec '41—Gdg
PT 31—Subic Bay—20 Jan '42—Gdg
PT 32—Sulu Sea—13 Mar '42—S
PT 34—Cavit I.—9 Apr '42—Air
PT 35—Cebu I.—12 Apr '42—Demolished
PT 41—Mindanao—15 Apr '42—S

PT 32—Sulu Sea—13 Mar '42—S
PT 44—Pacific—12 Dec '42—SC
PT 43—Guadalcanal—10 Jan '43—SC
PT 112—Guadalcanal—10 Jan '43—SC
PT 28—Alaska—12 Jan '43—Gdg
PT 37—Guadalcanal—1 Feb '43—SC
PT 111—Guadalcanal—1 Feb '43—SC
PT 123—Guadalcanal—1 Feb '43—Air
PT 67—New Guinea—17 Mar '43—Exp
PT 119—New Guinea—17 Mar '43—Exp
PT 165—New Caledonia—23 May '43—Sub
PT 173—New Caledonia—23 May '43—Sub
PT 22—Pacific—11 Jun '43—W
PT 153—Solomons—4 Jul '43—Gdg
PT 158—Solomons—5 Jul '43—Gdg
PT 166—Solomons—20 Jul '43—Air
PT 117—Rendova—1 Aug '43—Air
PT 164—Rendova—1 Aug '43—Air
PT 109—Blackett Straits—2 Aug '43—SC
PT 113—New Guinea—8 Aug '43—Gdg
PT 219—Attu—Sep '43—W
PT 118—Vella Lavella—7 Sep '43—Gdg
PT 172—Vella Lavella—7 Sep '43—Gdg
PT 136—New Guinea—17 Sep '43—Gdg
PT 68—New Guinea—1 Oct '43—Gdg
PT 147—New Guinea—19 Nov '43—Gdg
PT 322—New Guinea—23 Nov '43—Gdg
PT 239—Solomons—14 Dec '43—Fire
PT 145—New Guinea—4 Jan '44—Gdg
PT 110—New Guinea—26 Jan '44—Col
PT 279—Bougainville—11 Feb '44—Col
PT 200—Rhode Island—22 Feb '44—Col
PT 251—Bougainville—26 Feb '44—Gun
PT 337—New Guinea—7 Mar '44—Gun
PT 283—Bougainville—17 Mar '44—Gun
PT 121—New Britain—27 Mar '44—Air
PT 353—New Britain—27 Mar '44—Air
PT 135—New Britain—12 Apr '44—Gdg
PT 346—New Britain—29 Apr '44—Air
PT 347—New Britain—29 Apr '44—Air
PT 247—Bougainville—5 May '44—Gun
PT 339—New Guinea—27 May '44—Gdg

PT 63—New Ireland—18 Jun '44—Exp
PT 107—New Ireland—18 Jun '44—Exp
PT 193—New Guinea—25 Jun '44—Gdg
PT 133—New Guinea—15 Jul '44—Sub
PT 509—English Channel—9 Aug '44—SC
PT 202—France—16 Aug '44—Mine
PT 218—France—16 Aug '44—Mine
PT 555—Mediterranean—23 Aug '44—Mine
PT 371 — Molukka Passage — 19 Sep '44—Gdg
PT 368—Halmahera, N. E. I.—11 Oct '44—Gdg
PT 493—Surigao Strait, P. I.—25 Oct '44—SC
PT 320—Leyte—5 Nov '44—Air
PT 301—New Guinea—7 Nov '44—Exp
PT 321—San Isadoro Bay—11 Nov '44—Gdg
PT 311 — Corsica — 18 Nov '44—Mine
PT 363—Halmahera—25 Nov '44—Gun
PT 323—Leyte—10 Dec '44—Air
PT 300—Mindoro I., P. I.—18 Dec '44—Air
PT 73—Philippines—15 Jan '45—Gdg
PT 338—Mindoro I., P. I.—28 Jan '45—Gdg
PT 77—Luzon—1 Feb '45—SC
PT 79—Luzon—1 Feb '45—SC

TUGS
Napa—Bataan—8 Apr '42—S
Genesee—Corregidor—5 May '42—S
Seminole—Tulagi—25 Oct '42—SC
Grebe—Pacific—2 Jan '43—Gdg
Nauset—Naples—9 Sep '43—Air
Navajo—New Hebrides—11 Sep '43—Exp
ATR 98—Atlantic—12 Apr '44—Col
Patridge—France—11 Jun '44—SC
ATR 15—LeHavre—19 Jun '44—Sub
Sonoma—Leyte—24 Oct '44—Air

TANKERS
Neches—Oahu—23 Jan '42—Sub
Pecos—Java—1 Mar '42—Air
Neosho—Coral Sea—7 May '42—Air
Kanawha — Guadalcanal — 7 Apr '43—Air
Mississinewa—Carolines—20 Nov '44—Sub
Sheepscot—Iwo Jima—6 Jun '45—Gdg

TROOP TRANSPORTS
George F. Elliott—Guadalcanal—8 Aug '42—Air
Colhoun — Guadalcanal — 30 Aug '42—Air
Gregory—Guadalcanal—5 Sep '42—SC
Little—Solomons—5 Sep '42—SC
Thomas Stone—Spain—7 Nov '42—Air
Leedstown—Algiers—9 Nov '42—Sub

Joseph Hewes—Morocco—11 Nov '42—Sub
Edward Rutledge — Morocco — 12 Nov '42—Sub
Hugh L. Scott—Morocco—12 Nov '42—Sub
Tasker H. Bliss—Morocco—12 Nov '42—Sub
McCawley—New Georgia—30 Jun '43—SC
John Penn—Guadalcanal—13 Aug '43—Air
APC 35—New Georgia—22 Sep '43—Gdg
McKean — Bougainville — 17 Nov '43—Air
APC 21—New Britain—17 Dec '43—Air
Susan B. Anthony—LeHavre—7 Jun '44—Mine
Noa—Peleliu—12 Sep '44—Col
Ward—Leyte—7 Dec '44—Air
Dickerson—Okinawa—2 Apr '45—Air
Barry—Okinawa—25 May '45—Air
Bates—Okinawa—25 May '45—Air

CARGO VESSELS
Pollux — Newfoundland — 18 Feb '42—Gdg
Aludra—Solomons—23 Jun '43—Sub
Deimos—Solomons—23 Jun '43—Sub
Serpens—Guadalcanal—29 Jan '45—Exp

MISCELLANEOUS AUXILIARIES
Utah—Pearl Harbor—7 Dec '41—Air
Robert Barnes—Guam—13 Dec '41—EO
DCH 1—Pearl Harbor—28 Dec '41—S
Canopus—Bataan—10 Apr '42—S
Cythera—Atlantic—May '42—OD
Pigeon—Corregidor—3 May '42—Air
ex-Fisheries—Corregidor—5 May '42—S
ex-Maryann—Corregidor—5 May '42—S
ex-Perry—Corregidor—5 May '42—S
Muskeget—Atlantic—10 Oct '42—OD
Rescuer—Aleutians—1 Jan '43—Gdg
Niagara—Solomons—23 May '43—Air
Ronaki—Australia—18 Jun '43—Gdg
Redwing—Tunisia—28 Jun '43—Mine
Moonstone—Delaware Capes—16 Oct '43—Col
Macaw — Midway — 12 Feb '44—Gdg
Ailanthus—Aleutians—26 Feb '44—Gdg
Asphalt — Saipan — 6 Oct '44—Gdg
Mount Hood—Manus—10 Nov '44—Exp
Porcupine—Mindoro—28 Dec '44—Air
Extractor—Marianas—1 Jan '45—Sub
Pontiac—Halifax—30 Jan '45—W

KEY TO SYMBOLS: A—Accident; Air—Airplane; AO—Amphibious Operations; Cap—Captured; Col—Collision; EO—Enemy Occupation; Ex—Exercises; Exp—Explosion; Gdg—Grounding; Gun—Gunfire; OD—Overdue; S—Scuttled; SC—Surface Craft; Unkn—Unknown; W—Weather.

THE POST WAR NAVY

By Admiral of the Fleet Chester W. Nimitz, USN

ON THE day Japan surrendered, September 2, 1945, the United States Navy represented the greatest sea power the world has ever known. Its personnel included over 300,000 officers and 3,000,000 men, of which total over 750,000 were in the Naval Flying Forces alone. The U. S. Marine Corps, an integral part of the Navy, had attained a strength of 484,000; and the U. S. Coast Guard, operating as a war-time component of the U. S. Naval Forces, had a personnel exceeding 170,000.

In ships and equipment the United States Navy exceeded the total of the world's remaining navies combined. We had 23 battleships, 20 large aircraft carriers, 8 smaller aircraft carriers, 70 escort aircraft carriers, 2 large cruisers, 22 heavy cruisers, 48 light cruisers, 373 destroyers, 365 destroyer escorts, 240 submarines, and a vast number of auxiliary and small ships, such as tenders, mine and patrol craft, and landing craft. In sheer numbers alone our Navy possessed more than 100,000 craft of various types and 40,000 planes.

With the surrender of Japan our Navy immediately began to demobilize, both in ships and men. As a peacetime personnel, however, the Navy hopes to retain a force of about 500,000 men and 58,000 officers, plus an additional Marine Corps strength of 100,000 men and officers.

Of our ships and weapons, the world's finest at the end of the war, we plan to retain all the best part, either in active combat condition or in a state of reserve.

THE PEACETIME NAVY

OUR ACTIVE peacetime fleet will consist of 4 battleships, 13 carriers (including three 45,000 ton carriers), 13 escort carriers, 8 heavy cruisers, 20 light cruisers, 139 destroyers, 40 destroyer escorts, 90 submarines, and the necessary auxiliary craft such as tenders, repair ships, dry-docks, mine, patrol and amphibious craft, and approximately 8,000 planes.

Our reserve peacetime fleet will consist of 6 battleships, 5 carriers, 9 heavy cruisers, 9 light cruisers, 36 destroyers, and a number of mine and patrol craft. These ships will have partial crews and be kept materially equal to those in the active fleet, requiring only additional personnel to rejoin the active fleet.

More than twice the total number of active and reserve ships will be kept in inactive status with caretaker crews, but in such excellent shape that they can be put back into full fighting condition within a few days or weeks at most. Their preservation in such excellent shape will be due to new processes developed by Naval research laboratories. Instead of being preserved with oil or paint, the process by which we tried to preserve our equipment after World War I, our new reserve fleet for the most part will be hermetically sealed. Machinery, even of the most delicate sort, can now be covered airtight by a sprayed-on shield of plastic coatings. The air inside this plastic coating will be dehumidified, and kept dehumidified electrically. Even entire ship's hulls and gun turrets can thus be sealed and dehumidified.

However, as important as keeping this equipment in unimpaired state may seem, it is the least important aspect of our Post-War Navy. Too many people think of the Navy in terms of *equipment*—of battleships and aircraft carriers and submarines. The Navy is *not* ships and equipment! The Navy is an organization—the men and minds that conceive, develop, and then operate those ships and that equipment!

If another war comes, we may not use even the latest and best of the ships and weapons we are so carefully preserving today. The ships and weapons of our Navy ten, or even five, years from now may be very different from our ships and weapons of today.

LOOKING BACKWARD

PERHAPS the best way to get a vision of our future Navy is to look back over our Navy of the past. We might take the famous old frigate *Constitution* as a starting point.

The main reason why the *Constitution* won her victories and her fame is not only because she was so well fought by her splendid officers and crew, but because in her the U. S. Navy had produced a frigate far ahead of her times—a frigate superior by perhaps fifty percent to any frigate possessed by any other nation in the world at that time! Fifty years later, in the ironclads *Merrimac* and *Monitor*, the U. S. Navy again outdistanced the other navies of the world—so far outdistanced them that the wooden sailing ships of other navies were outmoded from that day on. I say that the U. S. Navy did this, because while the Southern Confederacy built the *Merrimac*, her Southern constructors were practically all ex-U. S. Navy men themselves.

Coming to more modern days, the U. S. Navy can be given the entire credit for developing the aircraft carrier. On the first such occasions in history, in November, 1910, an airplane took off from the deck of a ship—the USS *Birmingham*—and a month later an airplane landed on the deck of a ship—the USS *Pennsylvania*. From these successful experiments the aircraft carrier was born. And during the occupation of Vera Cruz in 1914, the U. S. Navy first made use of an airplane for scouting over enemy lines.

As far back as 1916, the U. S. Navy took the lead among the armed forces of the world in the matter of regularly planned scientific research and development by creating the U. S. Naval Research Laboratory. From that beginning has grown the present Office of Research and Inventions, which includes not only the original Naval Research Laboratory, but also the Special Devices Division of the Bureau of Aeronautics of the Navy, and the Office of Patents and Inventions.

It is this combination of the Navy's men, ideas, and knowledge working with the top scientists and laboratories of the nation that is an example of what I mean when I say that the Navy is not only equipment, but also an organization of men and minds.

SCIENTIFIC DEVELOPMENTS

FROM this combination of Navy and Science have emerged in recent years such marvelous discoveries and weapons in the field of war that they might have come directly out of the Arabian Nights. As far back as 1925 the Naval Research Laboratory was developing radio controlled craft, including target aircraft (drones) and target ships. In 1939 the Naval Research Laboratory was leading the world in government research on atomic energy. In its search for a revolutionary method for propulsion of warships, the Naval Research Laboratory developed a liquid thermal process for the separation of uranium isotopes. The Laboratory's discoveries were turned over to the Army and later used in one of the Oak Ridge plants manufacturing the atomic bomb.

Beginning its study of radar as far back as 1920, the Naval Research Laboratory had developed the first effective American radar even before the war. Subsequent research developed radar into one of the foremost American weapons of the war.

In addition U. S. naval research perfected the sono-buoy and other sonar devices by which enemy submarines, even though submerged, could be detected and accurately located even at great distances, and then quickly hunted down and exterminated.

As far back as 1940 the U. S. Navy had developed a successful pilotless aircraft which, radio controlled and television directed, made a practice torpedo hit on a maneuvering destroyer ten miles away from the controlling plane. A distantly controlled dive bomber was made to plunge accurately into a moving target. Other developments were glider bombs, directed by radio and television; jet-propelled bomb-carrying missiles directed into their targets either by radio or automatic target-seeking devices; and proximity fuses which would explode their missiles when they even came near the enemy target. Another recent development, but already surpassed by later discoveries, was the "Bat" bomb, a robot guided missile containing a radar which sent out radar impulses and then automatically followed the radar echoes home to the target, constantly seeking its enemy regardless of the desperate escape maneuvers of its target. To the long list of developments made by our naval research groups may be added rocket missiles, jet-assisted take-off devices, sonic depth finders, and mechanical firefoam.

TRAINING MEN

BUT ALL these were weapons, equipment. Equally important was "human engineering"—the training of the men to operate our weapons and equipment. Such was the objective of the Navy's Special Devices division. As a result more than 500 devices for synthetic training were in use in our Navy before V-J Day. Typical of these was the patrol bomber operational trainer by which, without leaving the ground, men are made masters of all the intricate operations necessary in flying and operating the bomber. In this fantastic device wind directions and forces can be changed, ice or other weather conditions reproduced on order, engine trouble created—almost every condition reproduced artificially that could occur under actual fighting conditions high in the air.

An equally marvelous device, the Link Celestial Navigation Trainer, was developed to do for the navigator what the operational trainer did for the pilot and the bombardier. In it artificial stars are created against an artificial sky, changing landscapes are seen below, ground speed and wind drifts are varied at will, and even the stars blotted out by artificial mist.

This is what I mean when I say again that the Navy is an organization—an organization of men and minds and material—and not just a collection of ships and guns. It is an organization which intends to insure the nation's security by the creation and operation of whatever weapon or defense the best minds in science can conceive.

THE FUTURE

THE atomic bomb has been invented, the atomic age is here. We know that the atomic bomb is capable of deadly damage to a degree as yet unmeasured. We intend to experiment and ascertain just what the atomic bomb is capable of doing when used by ourselves—and to devise the best possible defense for ourselves against such bombs when used by enemy powers. The Navy is staging these atomic tests, not for the purpose of substantiating any pre-conceived theory, but for the purpose of learning everything possible that can be learned about the atomic bomb, both offensively and de'ensively. The Navy is even holding up completion of its mightiest battleship so that all possible discoveries about the atomic bomb can be incorporated into the weapons and defenses of the finished ship.

What the future Navy will be like, we cannot say as yet. It may include battleships powered by an atomic plant, protected by unbelievedly stout new materials, and firing jet-powered atomic missiles instead of sixteen-inch shells. It may include carriers launching radar and target-directed jet missiles instead of man-piloted airplanes. It may even include submarines of very high speed both surface and submerged, making long voyages far beneath the sea to surface suddenly again off some distant enemy shore to launch their missiles, and then hiding themselves again in the ocean depths against retaliation.

But whatever it is like, there will still be a Navy. Until infinitely greater advances are made in air transport than have as yet been envisioned, the world's commerce must still be carried by ocean-going ships, and so too must its armed forces be transported with all their weapons and equipment for the final occupation that must inevitably be made to force a final peace upon an enemy. And neither commerce nor armed forces can be transported over the seas except under the protection of a Navy.

Yes, there will still be a Navy. Not necessarily a Navy of battleships, or submarines, or carriers, but a Navy in the sense of what the word Navy truly means—a mobile organization using the ocean highways, carrying its own defenses against any weapon directed against it by the enemy, and launching from its mobile platform whatever missiles—rockets, planes, atomic bombs, or anything else—that the Navy as an organization of men and minds has been able to conceive out of the limitless possibilities of science, research, and endeavor.

THE SIXTEENTH FLEET FORMS. The ships of the U. S. Fleet which are being maintained for future use are being assigned to the Sixteenth Fleet, the inactive fleet. UPPER. Two light cruisers, the *Brooklyn* and the *Phoenix,* are shown moored in the reserve basin at the Philadelphia Naval Base. They are the first major combatant ships to be completely preserved. At the right of the cruisers is the HMS *Stockham,* a destroyer escort that was lend-leased to England. In the foreground are U. S. submarines, stripped of armament and ready for scrapping. LOWER. One of the new principles to be used in maintaining the fleet in an inactive status is the dehumidification of the air in the ship. With the holds made airtight, this machine, an electrodrier dehumifier, regulates the humidity of the air in the ship by replacing humid air with dry air. An automatic control measures the humidity within the ship and starts the machine when necessary. It will be a simple operation to remove the seals and place the machinery in working order when the time comes.

PRESERVING. This blue-jacket is preserving, but not in the same sense that his mother may have preserved fruit, although the principle is similar. After World War I much material was lost because it became ruined by weather and corrosion.

Navy scientists have now devised a method for preserving ships and the guns, machinery, and other vital organs on ships. Ships are dehumidified, while equipment is sealed in an airtight package. This blue jacket is shown spraying a plastic covering on an MK 49 Gun Director. The gun director has been covered over with a fine mesh netting, which looks very much like a giant spider web. Using an ordinary spray gun, electrically powered, the sailor is spraying a liquid plastic which quickly cools and solidifies.

Before he began to package the director, it was cleaned, greased, and oiled. When he has completely covered the webbing, air will be sucked from the package and the gun director will be impervious to weather or the elements. This plastic material had wide wartime uses in packaging material for shipment to the forward areas.

PACKAGED GUNS. LOWER. Shown here are packaged 5"/38 complete mounts in outside storage at Naval Ordnance Plant, South Charleston, West Virginia. They have been given the treatment shown being applied in the upper picture on this page. Note the "window" which has been set in the plastic package, through which a periodical inspection of the equipment inside may be made. The plastic covering is easily removable. When the time comes, a hole will be cut and the covering peeled off. The equipment will be wiped dry, inspected and tested and it is then ready for use, in as good condition as it was the day it was packaged. This packaging material was developed jointly by Navy scientists and the plastic industry illustrating once again the cooperation of civilian organizations.

WEAPONS OF THE FUTURE. Naval research answers the challenge of modern warfare. UPPER. Largest member of the trio of "Glomb, Gorgon, and Gargoyle" is the "glomb," or glider-bomber. Model shown here is the television-controlled aircraft which will stand 300 miles an hour in a dive. LOWER. Known as "Little Joe," this radio controlled power bomb was being developed at the war's end as an answer to the Jap baka bomb. Launched from shipboard, it carries its 100-pound general purpose bomb straight up to 10,000 feet at 400 miles an hour, to intercept and destroy enemy bakas. The bomb is detonated by a proximity fuse which is activated by any alien presence within its range. "Little Joe" is powered by jet-assisted take-off and rockets.

NAVY "GUIDED MISSILE." The Navy was in the fore-front of research into and use of guided missiles, and before the war was over had perfected a radar-guided bomb, used widely by our searchplanes in attacks on enemy shipping in the far Pacific. Launched beyond range of ack-ack and guided by radar, the "Bat" destroyed many tons of Jap shipping during the last year of the war. Operating on a principle similar to that used by live bats, the robot was guided by radar echoes from targets. The Navy has embarked on an extensive research program which has already evolved weapons far in advance of the "Bat." UPPER. Privateer "Bat"-carrier in flight. LOWER. Close-up of "Bat" attached to Privateer's wings. The next development was a television camera to photograph the target.

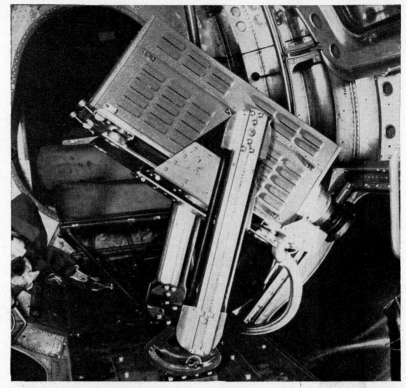

"RING" AND "BLOC." The latest aid to scientific warfare is airborne television equipment which instantaneously transmits battle action back to central headquarters where commanding officers have a photographic picture of the action as it progresses. Hitherto they have relied upon the word description of observers.

"Ring" television is the most powerful of airborne equipment, having a range of over 200 miles at an altitude of 1500 feet. It is mounted in a Martin JM-1.

"Bloc" television is a lighter, short-range version fixed in the nose of a Beechcraft JRB. It has a range of 15 to 20 miles. In actual use it has been installed in the nose of remotely controlled missiles, which are then guided by following their progress on a television screen mounted beside the control operator in the plane. Two Japanese vessels were sunk off Bougainville in the initial use of this adaption.

UPPER. A "Bloc" television camera is fixed in the nose of the plane and coordinated to the controls. LOWER. A photograph of the receiving screen showing the image received during a test flight.

NEW CARRIER AIRCRAFT. Although the war records proved that Naval aircraft were the best all-around carrier planes in the world, the U. S. Navy was and is constantly seeking improved models. UPPER. With her dive brakes open, the Martin Mauler, a new dive-torpedo-bomber, designed for operation from Midway-class 45,000 ton carriers, rests on a runway. This multi-purpose plane has a level flight speed of more than 350 miles per hour, a maximum range of over 1,700 miles. LOWER. New Douglas dive-bomber, designed for operation from Essex class carriers, shown in flight. This plane, whose maximum speed is at least 50 miles an hour faster than wartime dive bombers, combines dive bomber and torpedo attack functions thus doing away with the need for two types of planes.

JET PROPELLED FIGHTER. The Navy has developed a fighter powered exclusively by jet engines, designed for carrier operations. Known as the Phantom, the FD-1 has a service ceiling of more than seven miles, has attained a speed of more than 500 miles per hour, has an extremely high rate of climb, and a range of approximately 1,000 miles. Power for the Phantom is furnished by twin axial-flow Westinghouse turbo-jet engines built into wing roots.

UPPER. Streaking down the runway, the Phantom takes off with breath-taking suddenness during a test flight at St. Louis, Missouri, where it was built by the McDonnell Aircraft Corporation.

LOWER. This jet aircraft engine packs the propulsive punch of a piston engine nearly four times its weight. It is capable of producing plane speeds beyond the reach of usual engine-propellor combinations. So small it can fit entirely within the wing of a Navy fighter, it chops engine air resistance virtually to zero. Navy development of jet propulsion for its carrier based planes is typical of the way a tradition-steeped organization adopts modern science to its needs.

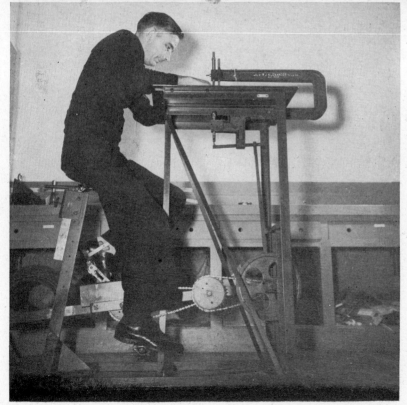

THE NAVY HEALS. Naval research goes far beyond engines of destruction. It has conducted vast research into new methods of healing torn and twisted bodies and of controlling strange and fatal maladies.

UPPER. Medical research is centered and directed from the Naval Medical Center, Bethesda, Maryland. This modern, new hospital and research center was completed and dedicated shortly before the war began. Here throughout the war came the battle casualties, the sick and the tired, many by plane directly from Pacific islands, for cure. Staffed by the Navy's ablest doctors, equipped with the finest and most extensive machinery of rehabilitation, Bethesda returned many a fighting man to duty in good trim.

LOWER. Occupational therapy was found by Navy doctors to be one of the most efficient means of restoring life to atrophied muscles as fighting men began to build themselves up to pre-wounded efficiency. Here a blue-jacket adjusts the therapeutic bicycle saw for height before removing the brace from his mending right foot and beginning to cut wood in the occupational therapy department of Bethesda.

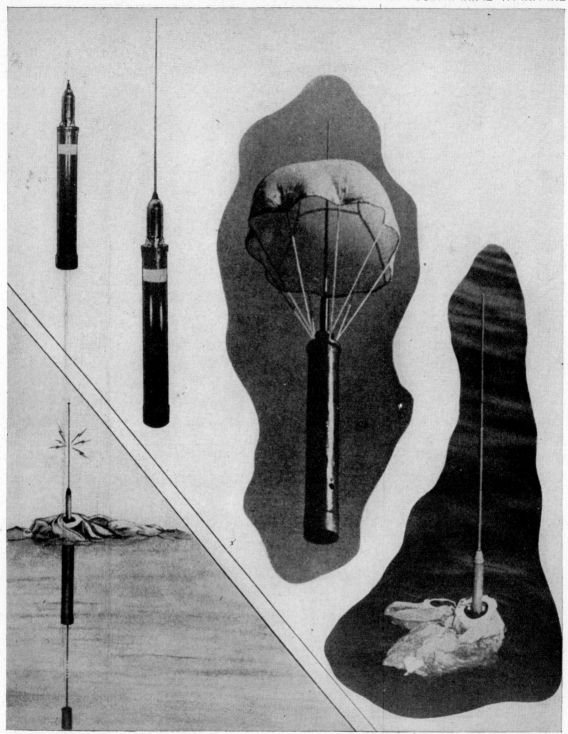

THE EXPENDABLE RADIO SONO-BUOY. One of the devices used successfully in anti-submarine warfare, the sono-buoy transmits the sounds made by the U-boat to patrolling planes. The figure at top left shows the bouy with antenna withdrawn, the figure second from the left shows the antenna extended. In the third figure the bouy floats to the water by parachute after being released from a plane. In the bottom right figure, it floats on the water with antenna aloft. The diagram at bottom left illustrates how the bottom compartment, containing a hydrophone, separates and sinks to a depth of 24 feet. The hydrophone picks up the sounds, relays them by cable up to a radio transmitter in the top compartment which broadcasts them via its antenna to planes in the vicinity.

NEW UNIFORMS FOR SAILORS. There has long been a feeling that enlisted men's uniforms—the "bell-bottom trousers" and jumper—were out of date and should be replaced by something more dignified. With the end of the war, new designs for both dress and working uniforms were prepared, and it was decided to test them out under actual conditions. LEFT. The "test" winter dress uniform consists of an unlined fly-front jacket and melton trousers worn with white shirt, black tie, and overseas cap. The present overcoat, the "pea coat," will be retained. RIGHT. The "test" summer dress uniform consists of a white shirt, conventional white trousers, black tie, and old-style white hat. The working uniform consists of shirt and conventional trousers worn with a cap similar to a jockey's cap.

ANNAPOLIS ON THE SEVERN. Although post war plans consider the possible necessity of expanding the officer-training facilities of the regular Navy, Annapolis will always be The Academy. UPPER. In this aerial photograph Bancroft Hall is the largest group in the center, Dahlgren is in the upper left, and MacDonough and Luce are below Bancroft. LOWER. Midshipmen march from chapel. Today's midshipmen wear almost the same uniform as in 1893. Two rows of nine brass buttons are retained on the jacket which remains practically unchanged in cut. Trousers are not quite so baggy and the cap is slightly different in shape, but in other respects the uniform is still one of the traditions of the Naval Service with which the Academy seeks to imbue its future Admirals.

USS *NEW JERSEY*. The USS *New Jersey*, a ship of the *Iowa* Class, is the largest type battleship in the U. S. Fleet. She has a standard displacement of 45,000 tons, but when carrying a full load this increases to 52,000 tons. The ship's overall length is 887 feet, 3 inches, with 108-foot beam. Maximum speed is better than 30 knots. The dreadnaught mounts a battery of nine 16-inch guns of 50 calibre in groups of three, and twenty 5-inch, 38 calibre anti-aircraft guns grouped in twos. The crew numbers 2,700 officers and men. Built at the Philadelphia Navy Yard, the *New Jersey* was launched on December 7, 1942, and commissioned on May 23, 1943.

USS *MIDWAY*. The USS *Midway* is one of the three longest and heaviest ships in the U. S. Fleet. The other two are its sister carriers, the *Franklin D. Roosevelt* and *Coral Sea*. The *Midway's* displacement is 45,000 tons standard, and 55,000 tons when carrying a full load. Her overall length is 986 feet, with a 113-foot beam. These dimensions enable the ship to carry more than 100 aircraft. To protect herself the carrier has a main battery of eighteen 5-inch, 54 calibre anti-aircraft guns, and she can do better than 33 knots. The *Midway* carries a crew in excess of 3,000. She was launched on March 20, 1945, and commissioned on September 10, 1945.

USS BUNKER HILL. The USS *Bunker Hill* is an *Essex* Class aircraft carrier, second in size to those of the *Midway* Class. She has a standard displacement of 27,100 tons which increases to 33,000 tons under a full load. With a beam of 93 feet, the *Bunker Hill's* overall length measures 855 feet, 10 inches. She supports over 80 aircraft, carries a main battery of twelve 5-inch, 38 calibre anti-aircraft guns, and has a speed of over 30 knots. To man the carrier a crew of more than 2,500 is needed. The *Bunker Hill* was launched on December 7, 1942, and commissioned on May 24, 1943.

USS VELLA GULF. The USS *Vella Gulf*, a *Commencement Bay* Class escort carrier, exemplifies the largest of this type ship in the U. S. Fleet. With a 75-foot beam and an overall length of 553 feet, she has a standard displacement of 12,000 tons. Under a full load, the ship's displacement measures 23,875 tons. Conceived to provide air cover for ocean convoys, the escort carrier is considerably less pretentious than the aircraft carrier in speed, armament, aircraft, and crew. The *Vella Gulf* does 18 knots, mounts a main battery of two 5-inch, 38 calibre anti-aircraft guns, carries over 21 aircraft and a 1,000-man crew. She was commissioned on April 9, 1945.

USS *ALASKA.* The USS *Alaska* is an example of the U. S. Fleet's large cruisers. Her standard displacement is 27,500 tons. Full load displacement equals 32,000 tons. The ship's beam is 89 feet, 6 inches, with an overall length of 808 feet 6 inches. She mounts a main battery of nine 12-inch, 50 calibre guns plus twelve 5-inch, 38 calibre anti-aircraft guns. With a speed of 30 knots plus, the *Alaska* is as fast as the *New Jersey.* It takes a crew of over 1,500 men to man her. Launched on August 15, 1943, the *Alaska* was commissioned on June 17, 1944.

USS *WICHITA.* The USS *Wichita* is a heavy cruiser of 10,000 tons standard displacement. With her full load, she displaces 13,400 tons. Her overall length covers 614 feet, with a beam of 61 feet, 9 inches. Not quite as heavily armed as a large cruiser, the *Wichita* is equipped with a main battery of nine 8-inch guns of 55 calibre, and eight 5-inch 38 calibre anti-aircraft guns. Faster than the *Alaska,* this heavy cruiser can reach 32.5 knots. Her crew comprises over 1,200 men. The *Wichita* was launched on November 16, 1937, and commissioned on February 16, 1939.

USS OAKLAND. The USS *Oakland* is a light cruiser of 6,000-ton standard and 7,500 tons full load displacement. With her lean destroyer lines, she rates tactically as an anti-aircraft cruiser. For this purpose the *Oakland* mounts a main battery of twelve 5-inch, 38 calibre guns in six twin turrets, plus numerous 40 and 20 millimeter anti-aircraft guns. Her overall length measures 541 feet with a beam of 52 feet 10 inches. Very fast, she can attain a speed of 33 knots, and carries a crew of 700. The *Oakland* was launched on October 23, 1942, and commissioned on July 17, 1943.

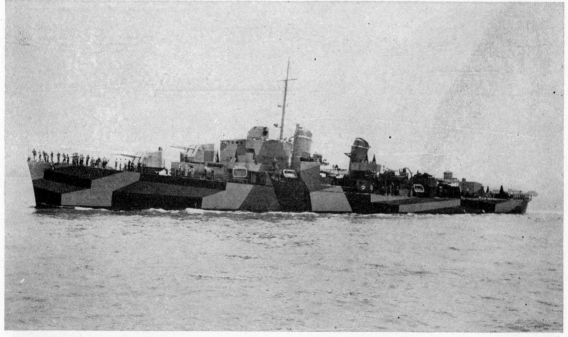

USS ALLEN M. SUMNER. The USS *Allen M. Sumner* is the second largest type destroyer in the U. S. Fleet. She has a standard 2,200-ton displacement. Her beam is 40 feet, 10 inches, and her overall length 376 feet, 6 inches. In armament, the *Allen M. Sumner* rates, with the *Gearing* Class, as best in the destroyer category. She mounts a main battery of six 5-inch, 38 calibre guns, coupled with ten 21-inch torpedo tubes. Not quite as fast as the speediest destroyers in the Fleet which reach 37 knots, she travels at 35 plus. Her crew is over 350 men; she was commissioned in 1944.

USS *EVERSOLE*. The USS *Eversole* was a destroyer escort of the WGT type, naval nomenclature for those which have a geared turbine drive and 5-inch guns. Characteristic of her type, the *Eversole* had a displacement of 1,275 tons and was manned by a crew of 220 men. Her overall length was 306 feet with a beam of 36 feet, 10 inches. She mounted a main battery of two 5-inch, 38 calibre guns, plus three 21-inch torpedo tubes. The *Eversole* was lost in the Philippines Area on October 28, 1944 during the Second Battle of the Philippine Sea.

USS LANDING SHIP-TANK (LST). The above are two of the 1,152 LST's ordered by the Navy since November 1941. They are unloading their war cargoes on Rendova Island in the Central Solomons. With an overall length of 327 feet and diesel engines driving twin screws, an LST is an ocean going ship. She carries smaller craft topside, plus numerous tanks, vehicles, guns, or cargo within her tunnel-like hold. Mass produced on both coasts and by many inland yards, the LST's formed the backbones of the invasion fleets. An additional asset of these ships is that they are readily converted to a variety of fleet auxiliaries to fulfill various functions.

USS *TREPANG*. The *Trepang*, SS 412, is one of the *Balao* class of 1941-42. Exceeded only by the *Corsair* class of 1943 on which information is still restricted, the *Trepang* has an overall length of 311 feet. Her surface displacement is 1,525 tons, and her surface speed better than 20 knots. She mounts one 5″/25 gun, although the armament may vary among her sister ships. All have ten 21″ torpedo tubes and carry a crew of 85 men. Constructed under the Second War Program, the *Trepang* was commissioned and saw duty in 1944.

USS *GRAYBACK*. The *Grayback*, SS 208, was one of the "G" type of 1939-40, of which there were twelve in her class, of which seven have been war casualties. Their overall length is 307 feet and surface displacement is 1,475 tons; surface speed is better than 20 knots. She mounted one 3″/50 gun, and was equipped with ten 21″ torpedo tubes. Her crew was 85 men. The *Grayback* was lost in the Ryukyus in February of 1944 and was awarded a Naval Unit Citation for her exploits. Three of her sister ships won similar citations.

PT BOATS. The motor torpedo boat (PT) above is known as a weapon of opportunity. Complementing daytime aircraft operations, her greatest effectiveness is at night, or when visibility is low. The primary mission of a PT is to attack surface vessels with torpedoes, rockets, or guns. Operating from advanced bases and numerous PT tenders, she is additionally employed to lay mines and smoke screens, rescue and escort, and to engage in commando or intelligence raids. PT's vary in length from 70 to 80 feet, mount two to four torpedo racks, and carry a crew of from twelve to fourteen men. Their standard tonnage ranges between 35 and 45 tons, and their best service speed is 40 knots.

LANDING CRAFT, SUPPORT (LCS). The Landing Craft, Support is a modified LCI-L armed with guns and rockets. They are 157 feet in length with a 23-foot beam. Their full load is 380 tons. The mission of the LCS is to move close inshore during Amphibious operations, blasting gun positions and enemy personnel with their self-propelled missiles.

USS LANDING SHIP-MEDIUM (LSM). Not as large as an LST, the LSM is faster and more maneuverable. Skillfully designed, she quarters her crew and operating equipment in side housings, thus leaving the major displacement for her cargoes of men and war materials. With an overall length of 203 feet, an LSM carries a dozen tanks, vehicles, or equivalent cargo. Latest variation of the LSM is the LSM (R) which is fitted with rocket gear.

USS LANDING CRAFT-INFANTRY (LCI). The above LCI's are gunboats with a length of 157 feet. They are modifications of the standard LCI (L)—Landing Craft, Infantry, Large. LCI's operate between beachheads and transports well off shore, or from advanced bases. They can carry over 200 infantrymen. Upon reaching the beach, the ramps of an LCI lower from catwalks forward. To further assist the landing, an LCI provides considerable supporting firepower. Other variations of the LCI include the LCI (R)-Rocket; and LC (FF)-Flotilla Flagship.

LANDING CRAFT-MECHANIZED (LCM). The above LCM is loaded with Marines headed for Tarawa from the Transport *William P. Biddle*. The date of the action was November 1943. With a length of 50 feet, LCM's rate as the largest landing craft normally attached to, and indentified with combat-loaded transports and cargo ships. Lowered overside empty, LCM's can transport 120 men, one medium tank or 30 tons of cargo. They bear their parent ship's identification on their bows. Capable of reaching 10 knots, LCM's are driven by three 225-h.p. diesels. After depositing their cargoes they are worked off the beach by means of windlasses and stern anchors.

"FLOATING REPAIR SHOP." This strange looking vessel demonstrates the autonomous nature of an amphibious force. Known as a repair barge, it plows up the beach like any other amphibious craft, but is equipped to set up shop on the battlefront and make necessary repairs under enemy fire.

BIOGRAPHICAL NOTES

REAR ADMIRAL ROBERT BOST-WICK CARNEY, USN. Born California 1895. Annapolis Class of 1916. Progressed to Rear Admiral, 1942. First command, USS *Laub*, 1919. Served as Gunnery Officer aboard USS *Cincinnati*, 1930-3. Commanded USS's *Buchanan*, 1935; *Reid*, 1936, *Sirius*, 1937. Assigned Executive Officer, USS *California*, 1940-1. As Chief of Staff to Comdr., Support Force, Atlantic Fleet, 1941-2; awarded DSM. Commanded USS *Denver*, 1942-3; won Legion of Merit, Bronze Star Medal. While Chief of Staff to Comdr., South Pacific Force, 1943-4; won second DSM. Awarded Navy Cross, third DSM as Chief of Staff to Comdr., Third Fleet, Pacific Fleet, 1944-5. Has been decorated by Norway. Designated Ass't Chief of Naval Operations (Logistics), 1946.

VICE ADMIRAL RICHARD LANSING CONOLLY, USN. Born Illinois 1892. Annapolis Class of 1914. Progressed to Vice Admiral, 1945. Won Navy Cross, 1918. Commanded USS's *Case* and *DuPont*, 1930; DD Squadron 6, 1941-2. Latter participated in initial Gilbert-Marshalls attack, and escorted *Hornet* in first Tokyo bombing. As Comdr., Landing Craft and Bases, NW African Waters, 1943, was awarded 2 Legions of Merit for services in Sicily and Italy Invasions. Appointed Comdr., Group 3, Amphibious Force, Pacific Fleet, 1944, won 3 DSM's for services in Kwajalein, Guam and Leyte Operations. Commanded landing of occupation troops on Hokkaido, Japan, 1945; later designated Deputy Chief of Naval Operations (Adm.). Has been decorated by Great Britain.

CAPTAIN SUE S. DAUSER, SUPERINTENDENT, NURSE CORPS, USN, Retired. Born California 1888. Calif. Sch. of Nurses, Class of 1914. Entered service, 1917. Appointed Chief Nurse, USN, 1918. In World War I, served at Naval Base Hospital, 3, Scotland. Duty in Guam and Philippines, 1926-8. Served as principal Chief Nurse, Naval Hospital, San Diego, 1928-31; Naval Dispensary, Long Beach, Calif. 1935-9. Appointed Sup't., Nurse Corps, 1939. Expanded her branch from strength of 436 to peak of 11,500 on V-J Day. Received permanent relative rank of Lt. Comdr., July 1942; Captain, Dec. 1942; first woman to wear the four gold stripes. In Feb. 1944, relative rank changed to actual for duration. Retired Nov. 9, 1945; awarded DSM for services.

VICE ADMIRAL LOUIS EMIL DENFELD, USN. Born Massachusetts 1891. Annapolis Class of 1912. Progressed to Vice Admiral, 1945. Served on USS *Ammen*, 1916-8. First Command, USS *McCall*, 1919. Com-

manded USS *S-24*, 1923-4; USS *Brooks*, 1926-9. Served as Aide to the Commander-in-Chief, U. S. Fleet, 1932-3. Commanded DD Division 11, 1935-7; DD Division 18, 1940. Assigned as Chief of Staff to Comdr., Support Force, Atlantic Fleet, in 1941; awarded Legion of Merit. As Assistant Chief of Naval Personnel, 1942-5, won a second Legion of Merit. In 1945, commanded Battleship Division 9, which participated in the Okinawa, Hokkaido and Honshu attacks. Won third Legion of Merit. Appointed Chief of Naval Personnel, 1945. Holds numerous decorations.

JAMES V. FORRESTAL

REAR ADMIRAL CALVIN THORNTON DURGIN, USN. Born New Jersey 1893. Annapolis Class of 1916. Progressed to Rear Admiral, 1943. In 1927, commanded Observation Squadron 1, Aviation Unit, USS *West Virginia*. Served aboard USS *Saratoga*, 1932-4; and as Executive Officer, USS *Wright*, 1938. Commanded latter, 1939. As Comdr., USS *Ranger*, 1942-3, was awarded Commendation Ribbon. Won Legion of Merit as Comdr., Fleet Air, Quonset Pt., R. I., 1943-4. Assumed command of a Task Force, Atlantic Fleet, June, 1944; awarded second Legion of Merit for services. In Dec. 1944, designated Comdr., Escort Carrier Group; won third Legion of Merit. Holds numerous other awards. Assigned Chief of Naval Air Adv. Training, Naval Air Station, Jacksonville, 1946.

VICE ADMIRAL AUBREY FITCH, USN. Born Michigan 1883. Annapolis Class of 1906. Progressed to Vice Admiral, 1942. First command USS *Terry*, 1914. Served as Aide to the Commander-in-Chief, Atlantic

Fleet, 1914-7; with Brazilian Navy, 1922-7. Commanded USS *Arctic*, 1927-9; Naval Air Station, Norfolk, 1932-5. Served as Chief of Staff to Comdr., Aircraft, Battle Force, 1935. Commanded USS *Lexington*, 1936; Carrier Division 1, 1940. As Comdr., Task Force, Pacific Fleet, 1942, awarded DSM for services in Coral Sea Battle. Commanded Aircraft, South Pacific Fleet; won DFC, second DSM, 1942-4. As Deputy Chief of Naval Operations (Air), 1944, awarded Legion of Merit. Assigned Sup't, Annapolis, 1945. Holds many foreign Decorations.

JAMES VINCENT FORRESTAL, SECRETARY OF THE NAVY. Born New York 1892. Princeton Class of 1915. Reporter in early youth. Bond salesman, Dillon, Read and Co., 1916. Enlisted in Naval Reserve, 1917, as Seaman, 2/c. Later commissioned Ensign with duty in Naval Operations' Office. Promoted Lt. (jg), 1918. Resigned from Service, 1919, with rank of Lt. Vice-Pres., Dillon, Read and Co., 1926; Pres., 1937. Administration Ass't to Pres. Roosevelt, June 1940; specialized in Latin-American Affairs. Appointed Under Sec't of the Navy, Aug. 1940. Charged principally with procurement as Service grew from 200,000 to over 3,000,000 men; from a one to a seven-ocean Navy. Succeeded Sec't Knox, May 1944; 48th to hold Office.

VICE ADMIRAL FRANK JACK FLETCHER, USN. Born Iowa 1885. Annapolis Class of 1906. Progressed to Vice Admiral, 1942. First command, USS *Dale*, 1912. Awarded Medal of Honor for services at Vera Cruz, 1914. Won Navy Cross, 1918, while Comdr., USS *Benham*. Served as Executive Officer, USS *Colorado*, 1927-9; Chief of Staff to the Commander-in-Chief, Asiatic Fleet, 1931-3. Commanded Cruiser Divisions 3 and 6, 1939-41; Cruisers, Pacific Fleet, 1942. As Senior Task Force Comdr., at Midway, 1942, won DSM for services. Designated Comdr., Alaskan Sea Frontier, 1944. Commanded Task Force which initially penetrated the Kuriles. In Nov. 1945, assigned to General Board, Navy Dep't. Holds numerous foreign Decorations.

REAR ADMIRAL WILLIAM REA FURLONG, USN. Born Pennsylvania 1881. Annapolis Class of 1905. Progressed to Rear Admiral, 1937. Served as Aide to the Commander-in-Chief, Atlantic Fleet, 1914-6. During 1923-6, duty in the Chief of Naval Operations' Office. Commanded DD Division 36, 1927; USS *Marblehead*, 1931. From 1934 to 1936, served as Inspector of Ordnance, Naval Proving Ground, Dahlgren, Va. Commanded USS *West Virginia*, 1936-7. As Rear Admiral, was Chief of the Bureau of

Ordnance, Navy Dep't, 1937-41. In Dec. 1941, assumed duty as Commandant, Navy Yard, Pearl Harbor. For services in this gigantic salvage assignment was awarded 2 Legions of Merit. Holds numerous other awards. Released from active duty, Mar. 4, 1946.

LIEUTENANT GENERAL ROY STANLEY GEIGER, USMC. Born Florida 1885. Stetson Univ., Class of 1907. Served 2 years as Enlisted Man; commissioned, 1909. In World War I, commanded a Marine Air Squadron, won Navy Cross. Served as Director, Marine Aviation, 1931-5. Directed all aviation in early days at Guadalcanal, 1942; awarded second Navy Cross. Had overall command of Marine and Army troops in Bougainville, Guam and Peleliu Operations; won 2 DSM's. Appointed to present rank, 1945, while in command of the Third Amphibious Corps on Okinawa. Temporarily commanded Tenth Army when Gen. Buckner was killed in action; first Marine ever to head an Army. In addition to 2 Navy Crosses, DSM's; holds numerous other Decorations.

FLEET ADMIRAL WILLIAM FREDERICK HALSEY, JR., USN. Born New Jersey 1882. Annapolis Class of 1904. First command, USS DuPont, 1909. Commanded USS Flusser, 1912; Jarvis, 1913. Awarded Navy Cross, 1918, for services as Comdr., USS's Benham and Shaw. Commanded USS Saratoga, 1935-7. As Rear Admiral, commanded Carrier Divisions 2 and 1, 1938-9. Designated Comdr., Aircraft, Battle Force, 1940. Awarded DSM, 1942, as Comdr., Marshall Raiding Force. Appointed Comdr., South Pacific Force, Oct. 1942. Awarded Army DSM, second Navy DSM for services, 1942-4. Assumed command famous Third Fleet, 1944; won third, fourth Navy DSM's for services, 1944-5. Holds numerous foreign Decorations. On Dec. 11, 1945, achieved highest rank, Fleet Admiral.

ADMIRAL HENRY KENT HEWITT, USN. Born New Jersey 1887. Annapolis Class of 1907. Advanced in rank to Admiral, 1945. Awarded Navy Cross as Comdr., DD Cummings, 1918. Served as Gunnery Officer, USS Pennsylvania, 1921-3; Aide to the Commander-in-Chief, Battle Fleet, 1927. Assumed command of USS Indianapolis, 1936; Cruisers, Atlantic Fleet, 1941. In 1942, led naval forces in North African Operation, won Navy, Army DSM's. Commanded Eighth Fleet in Sicily Invasion, 1943. Awarded Gold Star to DSM. Designated Comdr., Western Task Force, for Southern France Invasion, 1944; won Oak Leaf Cluster to DSM. Appointed Comdr., Naval Forces in Europe, 1945; Comdr., Twelfth Fleet, 1946. Has numerous foreign decorations.

ADMIRAL JONAS HOWARD INGRAM, USN. Born Indiana 1886. Annapolis Class of 1907. Progressed to Admiral, 1944. Won Medal of Honor, 1914, as Turret Officer aboard the USS Arkansas. Awarded Navy Cross for services aboard the USS New York as Aide to the Comdr., Division 9, Atlantic Fleet, 1918. First command, the USS Stoddert, 1924. Directed athletics at Naval Academy 1926-30. From 1932 to 1935, served as Public Relations Officer, Navy Dep't. Commanded DD Squadron 6, 1935-7; USS Tennessee, 1940; Cruiser Division 2, 1941. In 1942, designated Comdr., South Atlantic Force, Atlantic Fleet. Awarded 2 DSM's for services. As Admiral, became Commander-in-Chief, Atlantic Fleet, 1944. Has been decorated by Brazil and Belgium.

FRANK KNOX

FLEET ADMIRAL ERNEST JOSEPH KING, USN. Born Ohio 1878. Annapolis Class of 1901. As Lt. Comdr. assigned first command, DD Terry, 1914. Awarded Navy Cross, 1916, for service as Assistant Chief of Staff to the Commander-in-Chief, Atlantic Fleet. Promoted to Comdr., 1917; Capt., 1922. Commanded Submarine Base, New London, 1923-6; USS Lexington, 1930-2. Served as Chief, Bureau of Aeronautics, 1933-6. Promoted Rear Admiral, 1939. In Feb. 1941, with rank of Admiral, became Commander-in-Chief, Atlantic Fleet. Appointed Commander-in-Chief, U.S. Fleet, Dec. 1941, and Chief of Naval Operations, 1942. On Dec. 20, 1944, achieved newly established highest rank, Fleet Admiral. Awarded 3 DSM's, numerous other decorations, American and foreign.

ADMIRAL THOMAS CASSIN KINKAID, USN. Born New Hampshire 1888. Annapolis Class of 1908. Progressed to Admiral, 1945. Served aboard USS Arizona, 1918-20. First command, USS Sherwood, 1924.

Served as Executive Officer, USS Colorado, 1933-4. Commanded USS Indianapolis, 1937-8. Assigned as Naval Attache, Rome, 1938-41. Commanded Cruiser Division 6, 1941; Cruisers, Pacific Fleet, 1942. Awarded 2 DSM's for services in Coral Sea and Solomon Islands Battles, 1942. Won third DSM while Comdr., North Pacific Force, Pacific Fleet, during Attu and Kiska Operations. As Comdr., Seventh Fleet, supported Leyte Operation, 1944; awarded fourth DSM. Holds numerous other Decorations. Designated Comdr., Eastern Sea Frontier, 1945.

ADMIRAL ALAN GOODRICH KIRK, USN. Retired. Born Pennsylvania 1888. Annapolis Class of 1909. Progressed to Admiral, 1946. First command, USS Schenck, 1931-2. Served as Executive Officer, USS West Virginia, 1932-3. Commanded USS Milwaukee, 1936-7. Assigned, Naval Attache, London, 1939-41. As Comdr., Amphibious Force, Atlantic Fleet, 1943, awarded Legion of Merit for services in Sicily Invasion. While Comdr., U.S. Naval Task Forces, 1944, won Army DSM for executing naval phases, Normandy Invasion. Served as Gen. Eisenhower's Naval Comdr.; exercised overall command, Naval Contingents, Rhine Crossing, 1945. Retired, 1946, and appointed Ambassador to Belgium and Luxemburg. Holds Decorations from Great Britain and France.

COMMODORE DUDLEY WRIGHT KNOX, USN. Retired. Born Washington 1877. Annapolis Class of 1896. Progressed to Commodore, 1945. Served consecutively as Fleet Ordnance Officer with Pacific, Atlantic Fleets, 1910-2. As Aide to Comdr., U.S. Naval Forces, European Waters; won Navy Cross. Served on Faculty, Naval War College, 1919-20. Commanded USS's Brooklyn and Charleston, 1920-1. Placed on Retired List, 1921, continued on active duty as Chief of Historical Section, Naval Records' Office. During World War II, assigned additional duty as Deputy Director, Naval History. Holds Decorations from Great Britain and Italy. Wrote "The Eclipse of American Sea Power"; "The Naval Genius of George Washington", and "History of the U.S. Navy."

COLONEL FRANK KNOX, FORMER SECRETARY OF THE NAVY, Deceased. Born Massachusetts 1874. Alumnus, Alma Coll., Mich., 1898. Enlisted as Pvt., 1st Reg., U.S. Volunteer Cavalry, 1898; served in Cuba with "Rough Riders." City Ed., Grand Rapids Herald, 1899; Circulation Mgr., 1900. Vice-Chair'm, Theo. Roosevelt's Campaign Comm., 1912. Published Manchester (N.H.) Leader, 1912; Union-Leader, 1913. Commissioned Capt., Cav., 1917. Mustered out Lt. Col.; held Reserve Commission; retired Colonel. Cand., New Hampshire's Governorship, 1924. General Mgr., Hearst Newspapers, 1931, Repub. Cand., for Vice-Pres., 1936. Appointed Sec't of U. S. Navy, 1940; supervised Navy's expansion to mightiest in world history. Died Apr. 28, 1944.

REAR ADMIRAL MILTON ED-WARD MILES, USN. Born Arizona 1900. Annapolis Class of 1922. Progressed to Rear Admiral, 1945. Served in Asiatic Fleet, 1922-27. Attached to USS *Saratoga*, 1930-2. In 1934, joined USS *Wickes* as Executive Officer; 1936-9, assigned as Material Officer, Destroyer Squadron 5. First command, USS *John D. Edwards*, 1939. From 1939 to 1942, Recorder, Interior Control Board, Navy Dep't. Since May 4, 1942, has served as Comdr., U. S. Naval Group, China, and Deputy Director, Sino-American Cooperative Organization—"Saco." Latter contributed vitally to the smashing blows of the Pacific Fleet against Japanese-held Islands and Navy. Awarded Navy Expeditionary and China Service Medals, numerous others.

ADMIRAL MARC ANDREW MITSCHER, USN. Born Wisconsin 1887. Annapolis Class of 1910. Progressed to Admiral, 1946. First command, Naval Air Station, Rockaway, L. I., 1918. Awarded Navy Cross, 1919, for services as pilot on first Navy trans-Atlantic Flight. Commanded USS *Wright*, 1937; USS *Hornet*, 1941-2. Awarded DSM for services as Comdr., Air, Solomons, 1943. While Comdr., Carrier Force, Central Pacific Force, won second DSM for services at Truk and Saipan, 1944. Commanded a Carrier Task Force, and the famous "Task Force 58" throughout Pacific, 1944-5. In those commands, awarded 2 additional Navy Crosses, third DSM, and Legion of Merit. Has been decorated by Portugal. Designated Comdr., Eighth Fleet, Atlantic Fleet, Dec. 1945.

FLEET ADMIRAL CHESTER WILLIAM NIMITZ, USN. Born Texas 1885. Annapolis Class of 1905. First Command, USS *Panay*, 1907. Commanded Atlantic Submarine Flotilla, 1912-13; USS *Chicago*, 1920-3. Promoted to Capt., 1927. Commanded USS's *Rigel*, 1931; *Augusta*, 1933. Attained flag rank, 1938. As Admiral, commanded Pacific Fleet, 1941; awarded DSM, and DSM by Congress, for services. In 1943, designated Commander-in-Chief, Pacific Fleet and Pacific Ocean Areas. On Dec. 19, 1944, achieved highest rank, Fleet Admiral. Signed for U. S. when Japan formally surrendered aboard USS *Missouri*, Sept. 2, 1945. Awarded third DSM on Nimitz Day in Wash'n, Oct. 5, 1945. Designated Chief of Naval Operations, Nov. 1945.

CAPTAIN JEAN TILFORD PALMER, WOMEN'S RESERVE, USNR. Born Nebraska 1903. Bryn Mawr Class of 1924. In 1931, became Business Manager, Association of Junior Leagues of America, Inc. Commissioned 1942; assigned as Exec. Ass't in Dir. of Women's Reserve Office. As Ass't to the Dir., Enlisted Personnel, Women, Bur. of Naval Personnel, 1943-5 was awarded Ltr. of Commendation. Promoted to Lt. Comdr., Nov. 1943. Assigned, Ass't Dir., Women's Reserve, Nov. 1945; promoted to Comdr. On Feb. 2, 1946, became Dir., Women's Reserve, with rank of Capt. Serves as Special Ass't to the Chief of Naval Personnel. One of first two Waves to go overseas, Oct. 1944. Made survey of billets prior to assignment of Waves to permanent duty, Hawaii.

MAJOR GENERAL HARRY SCHMIDT, USMC. Born Nebraska 1886. Commissioned 1909. Progressed to present rank, 1942. Served as Operations Officer, Second Brigade, in Guam, 1911, Philippines, 1912; and Nicaragua, 1928-9. Had sea duty aboard USS's *Oklahoma*, *Montana*, 1916; *Tennessee*, 1920. Served as Ass't Chief of Staff to the Commanding General, Dep't of Pacific, 1927. Executive Officer, Paymaster Dep't Wash'n, 1932. Appointed Ass't to Marine Commandant, 1942. Commanded Fourth Marine Division in Saipan Operation, and the Fifth Amphibious Corps during the Tinian Island Invasion, 1944. Participated in Iwo Jima Operation, and occupation of Kyushu, Japan, 1945. Awarded Navy Cross, 1928; DSM 1944, holds numerous other Decorations.

LIEUTENANT GENERAL HOLLAND McTYEIRE SMITH, USMC. Born Alabama 1882. Alumnus Alabama Univ. Commissioned 1905. Won Croix de Guerre with palm in World War I. Served in Office of Naval Operations, 1921-3; first Marine member of Joint Army-Navy Planning Comm. Appointed Chief of Staff, First Marine Brigade, 1925. Served as Force Marine Officer to Comdr., Battle Force, 1931-3. Commanded Marine Barracks, Wash'n, 1933-5; Fifth Amphibious Corps, 1942. As Commanding Gen., Fleet Marine Force, Pacific, was overall Comdr., of the Gilberts, Marshalls and Iwo Jima Campaigns, 1944-5. Awarded DSM for training amphibious units, second DSM for execution of Gilberts and Marshalls Campaigns; third, for Marianas. Holds numerous other Decorations.

MAJOR GENERAL JULIAN CONSTABLE SMITH, USMC. Born Maryland 1885. Alumnus, Delaware Univ., 1907. Commissioned 1909. Progressed to present rank, 1942. Served in Nicaragua, Cuba, Panama,

Mexico and Haiti. Awarded Navy Cross for services as Comdr., Central Area, Nicaragua, 1930-3. Assigned, Ass't Naval Attache, London, 1941. Commanded Fleet Marine Force Training Sch., N. C. 1942. As Commanding General, Second Marine Division, 1943-4, won DSM for his part in Tarawa Invasion. Later led Forces into Palau Islands. Holds numerous awards plus Order of Military Merit from Dominican Republic. Formerly commanded the Pacific Dep't, with Hq., in San Francisco; currently assigned as Commanding General, Parris Island, S. C.

ADMIRAL RAYMOND AMES SPRUANCE, USN. Born Maryland 1886. Annapolis Class of 1907. Progressed to Admiral, 1944. First command, USS *Bainbridge*, 1913. Served as Ass't Chief of Staff to Comdr., Naval Forces, Europe, 1924-6; Executive Officer, USS *Mississippi*, 1929-31. Commanded latter, 1938-40; Caribbean Frontier, and Cruiser Division 5, 1941. As Junior Task Force Comdr., at Midway, 1942, awarded DSM for services. Designated Comdr., Central Pacific Force, 1943. For services at Gilberts, Marshalls and Carolines, 1943-4, awarded 2 additional DSM's. Designated Comdr., Fifth Fleet, 1944. For services in 1945, won Navy Cross. In Dec. 1945, assigned as Pres., Naval War College. Holds several foreign Decorations.

CAPTAIN DOROTHY C. STRATTON, DIRECTOR, WOMEN'S RESERVE, USCGR. Born Missouri 1889. Holds 5 college degrees. Joined Faculty, Purdue Univ., 1933, as Dean of Women. Appointed full Professor of Psychology, 1940. Entered service, 1942. Holds distinction of serving in three women's divisions of armed forces. First, a Wac; secondly, a Wave; was named Director of Spars on Nov. 24, 1942, with rank of Lt. Comdr., the first woman officer in history of the Coast Guard. Progressed to Captain, Feb. 1944. Coined Spar's title from USCG's motto: "Semper Paratus," and translation: "Always Ready." Under her leadership, organization expanded to 1000 officers; 10,000 enlisted women. Retired, Jan. 16, 1946; awarded Legion of Merit for services.

COLONEL RUTH CHENEY STREETER, former Director, Marine Corps Women's Reserve. Born Massachusetts 1895. President Bryn Mawr Class of 1918. Prior to service, was active in health and welfare work in New Jersey. Acted as Chairman, Citizens' Comm. for Army and Navy, Inc., at Ft. Dix, 1941. Received pilot's license, 1942. Joint donor, with mother, of Cheney Award, given annually to an Army Air Corps' member for valor. Entered as Director, Women's Reserve, Feb. 13, 1943, with distinction of being first woman major in Corps' history. Progressed to present rank, Feb. 1, 1944. Under her leadership, Women's Reserve grew to an approximate strength of 19,000. Retired, Dec. 7, 1945, and awarded Legion of Merit for services.

ADMIRAL RICHMOND KELLY TURNER, USN. Born Oregon 1885. Annapolis Class of 1908. Progressed to Admiral, 1945. First command, USS *Stewart*, 1913. Commanded Aircraft Squadrons, Asiatic Fleet, 1928. Served as Executive Officer, USS *Saratoga*, 1933-4. As Rear Admiral, 1941, became Assistant Chief of Staff to the Commander-in-Chief, U. S. Fleet. In 1942, appointed Comdr., Amphibious Force, South Pacific Force. Led amphibious operations on Guadalcanal, 1942; New Georgia and Gilberts, 1943. Commanded Joint Expeditionary Forces against Marshalls and Marianas, 1944; Iwo Jima, 1945. Awarded Navy

Cross, DSM, 1942; 3 additional DSM's 1943-5. In 1945, assigned duty on Military Staff Committee, Security Council, UNO.

GENERAL ALEXANDER ARCHER VANDEGRIFT, USMC. Born Virginia 1887. Attended Virginia Univ., 1906-8. Commissioned 1909. Progressed to General, 1945; first Marine Officer on active duty appointed to four-star rank. Served with U. S. Occupation Force, Vera Cruz, 1914; Haiti, 1919-23. Commanded Marines at Peiping, 1935-7. Duty at Hq., USMC, Wash'n, 1937-41. Joined Fleet Marine Force, New River, N. C., 1941. Led Forces at Guadalcanal, 1942; won Navy Cross. Promoted to Lt. Gen., 1943; designated Commanding Gen., First Marine Amphibious Corps. Led Marines into Bougainville, 1943; awarded Medal of Honor for services in South Pacific. Appointed Commandant, USMC., Jan. 1, 1944.

Holds numerous awards, plus 3 Decorations from Haiti.

ADMIRAL RUSSELL R. WAESCHE, USCG., Retired. Born Maryland 1886. Coast Guard Academy Class of 1906. First command, the *Arcata*, 1911. Commanded the *Snohomish* and *Bothwell*, 1920-4; the *Beale*, 1924-6. In 1932, served as Liaison Officer, War Plans Division, Chief of Naval Operations' Office; later became Aide to Commandant, Coast Guard. Appointed Commandant, Coast Guard, with rank of Rear Admiral, 1936. Reappointed for second four-year term, 1940. Promoted to Vice Admiral, 1942. Reappointed, third term, 1944. Promoted to full Admiral, 1945. Retired, 1946. Awarded DSM. Under wartime conditions, presided over greatest personnel expansion in Coast Guard history. Service increased to 170,000 officers and men.

INDEX